SNATCHING
DEFEAT
FROM THE JAWS
OF VICTORY

20th Century
Military Blunders

DAVID WRAGG

SUTTON PUBLISHING

First published in the United Kingdom in 2000 by
Sutton Publishing Limited
Phoenix Mill · Thrupp · Stroud · Gloucestershire GL5 2BU

A catalogue record for this book is available from the British
Library

ISBN 0 7509 2474 8

Typeset in 10/14pt Photina.
Typesetting and origination by
Sutton Publishing Limited.
Printed and bound in England by
J.H. Haynes & Co. Ltd, Sparkford.

CONTENTS

CONTENTS

LIST OF PLATES

The plates are found between pp. 150 and 151.

INTRODUCTION

Going to war is no easy task. It is not an activity to be embarked upon lightly. The politicians, with whom the decision rests, should first decide what would be the outcome of a failure to fight. That has to be the question. Some wars are worth fighting, and sometimes there is little choice in the matter. Others simply reflect the vainglorious ambitions of politicians. This is one reason why dictatorships are so prone to war; while war can be a means of ignoring domestic problems.

Suggesting that professional military leaders also make mistakes is easy to do with the benefit of hindsight – which strangely always comes with clear 20/20 vision. After all, one would hope that no one can attain the most senior ranks in the armed forces without both considerable experience and ability, added to which must be qualities of insight and leadership, intelligence and, hopefully, common sense.

Today, it is tempting to fall into the habit of the management consultant, and try to categorize the mistakes made by military commanders and their political masters. This itself would be a mistake. It is not that there are not categories into which some, but not all, of the errors can be placed, but that circumstances change, and often it takes more than one blunder for disaster to strike. For example, it is too easy to blame the generals on the Western Front in the First World War for simply trying to fight the war along the same lines as the last one. The 'last war' for the British Army was the Boer War, the lessons of which were the importance of mobility and camouflage. Trench warfare, machine guns and barbed wire had all been encountered earlier, as had aerial observation. Complacency was the greater problem, especially at Gallipoli, where advantages were frittered away. Rigid adherence to doing things by the book could be another category, again at Gallipoli, where, after the Suvla Bay landings, Lieutenant-General Stopford refused to order his troops to advance until after an artillery barrage, even when there were no targets for the guns.

A persistent theme in many wars has been that of underestimating the enemy. Early in the century, the Russians made this mistake with the Japanese, and the error was repeated many years later in the defence of Malaya and Singapore. Later still, this, coupled with complacency, made the clash in Korea inevitable. At Gallipoli, there were missed, and mishandled, opportunities. The same could be said about the Axis failure to invade Malta, the crossroads of the Mediterranean.

Bad timing can also be a problem. The Argentine seizure of the Falklands might have worked if they had waited another year or two for defence cuts to cripple the Royal Navy. The German invasion of the Soviet Union was badly timed, starting too late to achieve its objectives before winter came, but it was also a case of underestimating the enemy, of poor preparation, and of the failure to concentrate forces. Poor timing and coordination, and a simple inability to think through the problems, also accounted for the fiasco at the Bay of Pigs, and the inability to follow up a success explains many failures. This was why the attack on Pearl Harbor failed to achieve its objectives and why, in the end, the German blitz of British cities also failed.

None of this detracts from the outstanding successes, achieved by courage, brilliance and persistence. The Royal Navy achieved a more lasting success at Taranto with 21 elderly biplanes than the Japanese managed with 353 modern aircraft at Pearl Harbor. Who could really have expected a task force with just 20 Sea Harriers to retake the Falklands, with the Argentine forces entrenched and within reach of their own shore-based aircraft? Could anyone really have expected the United States Navy to bounce back so quickly after Pearl Harbor, so that within six months it had the Japanese on the defensive?

In choosing what to put into a book such as this, and what to leave out, certain criteria have had to be applied, otherwise it would be unfair to accuse those entrusted with the fate of armies, navies and air forces, and of nations, of incompetence. The argument is that wars are lost as much by the blunders of one of the participants as they are lost by the successes of the other side. It would be unfair to criticize the airborne assault at Arnhem. This is because the bridge was taken, and held for seventy-two hours instead of the forty-eight originally planned. During the Falklands campaign, the commander later admitted to a mistake in not providing additional troops and light armour in the battle for Goose Green, but such mistakes are easily made and can only be assessed with the benefit of hindsight. In this book, blame is attributed to politicians and commanders when they have failed to make reasonable preparations, take adequate precautions, and have allowed opportunities to slip past them.

One

COLLISION COURSE, THE FAR EAST: BATTLE OF TSUSHIMA, 1905

Russian and Japanese ambitions in the Far East put both nations on a collision course.

On 27 May 1905, one of the great naval battles of history started. Today, Tsushima is less well known than, say, Trafalgar, a hundred years earlier, probably because the protagonists were Japan and Russia, fighting far away. It has also been eclipsed by battles with more relevance, such as Midway and Leyte Gulf. Yet, this was that relative rarity, a truly decisive battle at sea, bringing to an end a war that had been hard fought at sea and on land.

The dawn of the twentieth century had found Russia and Japan on a collision course, as both countries sought to strengthen their position on the Asian mainland. Both nations saw China, at the time weak and divided, as a potential colony. In the regional rivalry between these two nations lay the origins of one of the forgotten wars of the twentieth century, the Russo-Japanese War of 1904–5: the first major conflict of the new century.

In one sense, the Russo-Japanese War was also a throwback to the previous century, in that both countries were anxious to create empires for themselves, having missed the opportunity for empire building enjoyed by the western European nations during the eighteenth and nineteenth centuries. Russian and Japanese ambitions were not as extensive as those of the European powers.

1

Japan was emerging from centuries of isolation. The country had rejected western ideas and technology at first, only coming to take an interest in what the west had to offer in the second half of the nineteenth century. Japan saw China as a territory that had to be controlled, largely for political and commercial advantage, but also because in the distant past the Chinese emperors had posed a threat to Japan. To us today, the term kamikaze refers to Japanese suicide pilots during the Second World War. Yet it means 'Divine Wind', and was coined for the storm which had sprung up just in time to save Japan from invasion by the forces of the emperor Kublai Khan in 1274.

Russia had similar ambitions for China. As the nineteenth century closed, Russia had come to take its territory bordering the Pacific more seriously, and at last was able to do so, following the construction of the Trans-Siberian Railway. A parallel course for the final part of the Trans-Siberian was routed through China. British and American concessions in China had their counterpart in a concession granted to Russia in Port Arthur. Such concessions stopped short of granting colonies to the European powers, as at Hong Kong, but enabled the Europeans to have a monopoly on trade at major Chinese ports. To the Japanese, the Russian concession at Port Arthur was a threat. Port Arthur had tremendous regional strategic significance, allowing control of the Yellow Sea, without which successful land warfare in either Korea or Manchuria would be impossible.

All the evidence suggests that the Russians seriously underestimated their Japanese opponents. Alarm bells should have started ringing when Japan suspended diplomatic relations early in 1904, but the Russians were remarkably complacent. The mood changed abruptly when Japan mounted a surprise attack on Russian forces on 8 February 1904 and – as at Pearl Harbor almost forty years later – without declaring war.

At the outset, the respective fleets in the area were well matched. Russia had 7 battleships, 4 cruisers and 6 light cruisers, as well as 27 destroyers, which made up the grandly titled First Pacific Squadron, even though it was the only Pacific squadron. Against this Japan had 6 battleships, 6 cruisers, 12 light cruisers and 19 destroyers. In reserve were 4 elderly Japanese armoured ships, while Russia had a number of older vessels in the Baltic – too far away to be of any immediate use. Both countries were expecting additions to their navies, Japan having ordered two cruisers, bought second hand from Argentina; Russia was completing new battleships, but these were also in the Baltic, as Siberia, Russia's 'wild east' lacked heavy industry, and was a sparsely populated agricultural area.

Woefully inadequate Russian preparation was apparent when, on the night of 8/9 February, ten Japanese destroyers attacked the Russian First Pacific Squadron as it lay in the outer roads of Port Arthur. This surprise attack saw the battleships *Tsesarevich*, *Retvizan* and the cruiser *Pallada* torpedoed. The two battleships were seriously damaged and out of action for some months. Such an attack would have had any navy worth its salt at sea, ready for battle, but not this one. Daylight found the Russian ships as sitting targets, still at anchor. Shortly afterwards, Admiral Togo appeared with a more substantial force to fight a short action. Little further damage was inflicted on the Russians, but the action enabled the Japanese to land an expeditionary force at Inchon in Korea, where a Russian cruiser and gunboat were so badly damaged that they had to be scuttled. Japan finally declared war on 10 February.

The Russians were to be unfortunate, as well as incompetent. They were to lose two naval commanders in succession, as Vice-Admiral Makarov and then his successor, Vice-Admiral Vitgeft, were killed in action. Makarov, described as 'energetic', was lost when two battleships were sunk in a Japanese minefield. The Russians were then effectively blockaded in Port Arthur until 10 August, when they attempted to break out, and engaged the Japanese in open combat at the Battle of the Yellow Sea. As the Japanese opened fire, they killed the new Russian commander, Vice-Admiral Vitgeft. Leaderless once again, it took just one further hit on the Russian flagship to persuade the Russians to return to Port Arthur.

The Japanese had also suffered setbacks, failing twice to sink block ships in the approaches to Port Arthur, and early in the war they also lost two battleships in a minefield. After their defeat at the Battle of the Yellow Sea, the Russians briefly attempted to fight a trade war with armoured cruisers, leaving their heavier units bottled up in Port Arthur. Just four days later, after a battle between cruisers in the Battle of the Japanese Sea, which cost the Russians one of the three armoured cruisers engaged in the battle, even attacks on Japanese merchant shipping were abandoned as too costly. Faced with this dismal performance, the Russians decided to create a Second Pacific Squadron under Vice-Admiral Rozhestvensky. The new squadron with modern ships had been working up in the Baltic since the start of the war. While the arrival of this fleet was awaited, the remains of the First Pacific Squadron sat in Port Arthur. Gradually, their crews were absorbed into the land battle as the Japanese besieged the port.

The decision to send a second squadron to the Baltic was badly flawed – it was too late. The idea was that Russia would hold on to Port Arthur, and that the second squadron would reinforce the first, taking the battle to the Japanese. Yet, even while the decision was being made, it seemed unrealistic to expect Port Arthur to be held for long. Distance and the lack of adequate support facilities at Vladivostok in Siberia were only part of the problem. Russia's naval logistics were hopeless. Unlike the western European colonial powers, Russia did not have any naval bases between the Baltic and Port Arthur. It did not even have a fleet train, the supply ships or auxiliaries needed to support such a venture. Vladivostok was Russian territory and secure, but was at the end of a long, almost entirely single-track, railway line, while the Japanese dominated the sea route.

Russia had few allies, as world opinion sided with Japan. Even British opinion was against her. Only France could be counted as an ally but, after centuries of mutual antagonism and mistrust,

France was by this time more anxious to develop the growing entente with her age-old rival, Great Britain, than to take action in support of Russia. The reason for this French interest in an alliance with the British was simple: it was to counter any future German aggression.

In times of stress, the Royal Navy could always count on volunteers or conscripts from the fishing fleets and the merchant marine, but the Russians lacked these sources of ready reserves. Russia was attempting to present itself as a maritime nation without being one. Her best sailors had been with the ill-fated First Pacific Squadron. The best of those assembled for the Second Pacific Squadron were those taken from the Black Sea Fleet, augmented by engineers taken up from the merchant fleet, although many of these were soon found to be unfamiliar with the water tube boilers of the newer battleships. There were, of course, many raw recruits, but there were also those who had been previously rejected as being unfit or unintelligent, those who had criminal records, and, of course, those marked as having revolutionary tendencies. There were also reservists, unhappy at being called up, and unfamiliar with the newer equipment being introduced to service. Readiness and training was so poor that the guard of honour at the burial of the victims of a typhus epidemic aboard one of the new cruisers did not know how to load their rifles for the salute. The epidemic had been caused by poor water distillation – an ill omen for a vessel that would have to voyage through the tropics. Leadership was in short supply. The best officers had also been at Port Arthur. Many of those left were unsuitable. They included drunkards, bullies and harsh disciplinarians. There were those with a distorted order of priorities, including some that refused to allow gunnery practice because it made the decks of their ships dirty! Too few had any understanding of the way in which naval warfare had developed, or how to make the best use of their new equipment.

Given this state of affairs, it is not surprising that the Russians had difficulty in finding a commander. A succession of the best men refused to accept the command, many believing that the campaign had already been lost. Eventually, the buck passed to an officer who had served with distinction in the Russo-Turkish War, Vice-Admiral Rozhestvensky. Opinions of Rozhestvensky vary. He is reputed to have had a short and extremely violent temper, and was capable of throwing his binoculars at anyone, regardless of rank, who displeased him. Whether or not he was incompetent, or simply frightened those around him so that they believed that he would make a good fighting admiral, is not clear. He did seem to appreciate the enormity of his task, for it is hard to disagree with his view that, 'It was at a previous stage that another course ought to have been taken. Attack should have been met with attack. . . . Sacrifice the fleet if need be, but at the same time deliver a fatal blow to Japanese naval power.'[1] This gung-ho attitude suggested that he might have been the right man to command the First Pacific Squadron – we shall never know. We do know that he did not believe that his mission would succeed. As regards his own responsibilities, the lack of optimism among those around him meant that he was also paranoid, and this was to have a bearing on the time taken to deploy his squadron. The operation could still have been aborted, but international politics intervened. The German Kaiser was anxious to negotiate an advantageous trade agreement with Russia, and the Hamburg-Amerika Line was encouraged to provide eight ships on charter to supply the squadron, mainly with coal. These German merchant ships allowed the operation to go ahead.

Rozhestvensky believed that his ships were too large to pass through the Suez Canal, and opted to steam around Africa, fatally delaying the relief of Port Arthur. The only advantage of the much longer Cape route was that isolated French anchorages could be used as far as Madagascar, after which the fleet would have to replenish at sea because of the huge ocean distances involved on the first part of that passage across the Indian Ocean. This would be followed by a passage through

South-east Asia, where the best anchorages were in British colonies and closed to the Russians.

To Rozhestvensky's dismay, it was decided to provide a Third Pacific Squadron, using elderly ships from the training squadrons and a number of armoured coastal vessels, not really suited to offensive operations on the open sea, but instead designed for a defensive role in relatively shallow and sheltered waters. The crews assembled were either too old, insufficiently fit, or of even more doubtful character than those scraped together for the Second Pacific Squadron. Vice-Admiral Nebogatov was given command of this makeshift fleet. This force of, at best, the second rate, was expected to catch up with the main force by using the Suez Canal.

After waiting for the new battleship *Orel* to complete her fitting out and undertake repairs for damage done by a reservist who had put metal shavings into her propeller shaft, the first squadron set sail from Libau in October 1904. On the face of it, the squadron was impressive. It could even be said that the term 'squadron' was an inadequate description for what would now be called a task force, even having its own repair ship and a hospital ship. Behind the scenes, it was far from impressive. The four new battleships had not completed their sea trials, and so each had a naval architect on board to deal with any problems that might arise. There had been no time for each ship to work up with its new crew, an essential preliminary even in peacetime naval operations.

Rozhestvensky's paranoia took over. The new weapon feared most was the torpedo – so much so that the 'torpedo-boat destroyer' had evolved in the main navies as the predecessor of the larger destroyer. Torpedoes were feared as much as an Exocet missile would be almost eighty years later during the Falklands Campaign. Alarmed by false stories from an unscrupulous intelligence agent that there would be Japanese torpedo boats active in the North Sea, Rozhestvensky warned his commanders to be on the lookout. Quite how the relatively small torpedo boats, with a very limited range, were to voyage from Japan and take up positions in the North Sea was a minor detail that seemed to have escaped the Russians.

With its officers drunk, the repair ship sailed some fifty miles behind the main force as it made its way down the North Sea. During the night this ship fired some 300 rounds at various commercial ships, with its commander under the impression that they were Japanese torpedo boats. The main force was signalled that the repair ship was under attack, and prepared for battle. The appearance of one of their own cruisers, *Aurora*, on the horizon brought down upon her the full might of the guns of the fleet – fortunately, their aim was none too good, but a number of shells did land on the ship, killing at least one member of her crew.

Also unlucky to be at sea that night were some Hull trawlers, fishing on the Dogger Bank, the area of shallow water in the North Sea which has traditionally provided a good fishing ground. The trawlers were using rockets to signal to each other, and were immediately taken to be hostile Japanese torpedo boats. They, too, suffered the squadron's firepower, and several fishermen were killed. This was an act of war, and only the fear of ruining the growing entente with France prevented an actual war between Russian and Britain.

The squadron called at Vigo in Spain to take on supplies of coal, and then docked for more at Tangier, shadowed by a British cruiser squadron. On leaving Tangier, the anchor of one of the ships fouled the international telephone line between Africa and Europe, which she cut to save time, severing telephone and telegraphic communications between the two continents for four days.

Rozhestvensky's paranoia continued to manifest itself. His ships had to be prepared for battle at all times, so coal had to be taken on board every four or five days. This meant stopping, and transferring coal from the transports to the warships – a process which was prolonged even further once the decision was taken to use small boats rather than transfer direct from the colliers, after one collier had fouled a warship's secondary armament with its coal-handling equipment. To store as much coal as possible aboard each ship, it was even stored in the living spaces. The quantities of coal required were enormous; one captain estimated that his ship consumed twice her own weight of coal on the outward voyage.

The already slow progress to battle was made even slower by a prolonged sojourn at Madagascar, where the fleet stayed for two and a half months waiting for orders from Russia. As they waited, Port Arthur fell to the Japanese. The time at Madagascar was not put to good use: much-needed gunnery exercises had to be abandoned because practice shells and half charges had been sent direct to Vladivostok. In any navy, this prolonged period without practice, and without ships of the same command exercising together, would have been a cause for concern, even in peacetime. In the squadron, standards were especially bad. The crew lacked basic instruction. In gunnery, they inflicted more damage on their own ships than on the trailed targets. They couldn't manoeuvre together as a fleet without colliding. Someone had overlooked the fact that it takes time to become proficient in ship handling, and in any case, watch-keeping officers need practice to adjust to new ships. The time spent in Madagascar undermined still further the already low efficiency of men and ships. The heat took its toll on the men in ships designed for the colder climate of the Baltic. It also took its toll on the ships, as inactivity allowed marine vegetation to take a hold on the hulls. Eventually, they sailed from Madagascar, with the supply ships towing the destroyers to save on fuel and wear and tear on the engines. They steamed at just 5 knots. On a route devoid of anchorages, restocking with coal once again could only take place on the open sea, still using small boats.

By now, the world was watching the Russians. Everyone expected them to maintain secrecy by steaming south of Australia, avoiding the enclosed waters of the direct route through the Straits of Malacca, between the Malay Peninsula and Indonesia, to keep the Japanese guessing. Instead, Rozhestvensky decided on the shortest and most direct route. Far from maintaining secrecy, this entailed steaming at a stately eight knots, four abreast, off Singapore, which the ships took an hour to pass. The fleet then spent some time in Camranh Bay, in French Indo-China, while they waited for the Third Pacific Squadron. This upset the Japanese, who even hinted at war with France. The French were realistic enough to appreciate that a Franco-Japanese war would put French possessions in Indo-China at risk so, as a matter of form, a French cruiser would appear, and request that the Russians move on. A game of cat and mouse developed, with the Russians putting to sea for a few hours, and then returning once the French cruiser had gone. Three weeks into their four-week stay in French Indo-China, Nebogatov's elderly fleet finally arrived. This even included an old ironclad, a forerunner of the battleship, the *Imperator Nikolai I,* and an old rigged cruiser. The officers of the Second Pacific Squadron sneered at the coastal defence whips, which had done well to get so far, describing them as 'flat irons'.

Even after leaving Indo-China on the final, fateful, leg of their journey, there were still two more recoaling operations, making a total of thirty-two since leaving Russia.

Given the highly visible route taken, it would have been difficult to retain any element of surprise, but as it was, the Russians effectively managed to broadcast their arrival to the Japanese. Togo had placed a series of armed merchant cruisers on picket duty a hundred miles or so south of the Tsushima Straits, simply to provide early warning of the Russians arriving. The first ship the waiting Japanese saw in the darkness was the hospital ship, which in accordance with international convention was brightly lit, painted white and had a red cross on her side. Had she been kept a hundred miles or so astern, at least some element of surprise could have been maintained. A Japanese cruiser squadron was now able to keep track of the Russians, shadowing the fleet and relaying information to Togo.

With the remaining ships blockaded in port, Russia's commanders at Port Arthur had not attempted a further breakout. Instead, they tried to make the best of a bad job by using the guns of the ships to support Russian ground forces, with the ships' companies absorbed into the land battle.

Early in December, the Japanese made major advances ashore and were able to fire at will on the Russian ships at Port Arthur, sinking two battleships, leaving a third aground, while a fourth was so badly damaged that she had to be scuttled. A fifth battleship, *Sevastopol*, was moved from the inner harbour to the outer roads, and engaged in actions against Japanese torpedo boats for several days, but had to be scuttled before Port Arthur fell on 2 January 1905.

The Japanese had just four battleships, *Mikasa*, *Asahi*, *Fuji* and *Shikishima*, the four veterans of the Battle of the Yellow Sea. In itself, this was an advantage, in that the ships were well tried and proven and, even more important, so were their crews. The Russians had managed to assemble a force of no less than seven battleships, many of them new, with crews that had trained, but never fought, together. Of the seven, five were modern, the *Osliabia*, and the new *Orel*, *Kniaz Suvorov*, *Borodino* and *Imperator Alexander III*, while there were two older ships, the *Navarin* and *Sissoi Veliky*. There was also the old ironclad *Imperator Nikolai I*, as flagship for Nebogatov's squadron, plus the armoured cruiser, *Admiral Nakhimov*, and five cruisers, three of which were new. There was a flotilla of destroyers, and an armed steam yacht for the use of Admiral Alexeev, the commander at Vladivostok.

The disparity in battleships was more than reversed by the presence of eight Japanese cruisers, and two armoured cruisers, the *Nishin* and the *Kasuga*, with the Russian fleet also having two vessels of this type as well as the three armoured coastal defence ships. The importance of the battle to both sides was underscored by the desperation that required the presence of old armoured cruisers in both fleets. The Japanese outnumbered the Russians in destroyers, at twenty-one to nine. Operating close to home, the Japanese could also deploy many light forces, such as torpedo and gunboats. The Russian auxiliaries, so necessary to the deployment so far from secure ports, now became a disadvantage, needing protection.

This was the last major sea battle to be fought without the benefit of aerial reconnaissance, leaving the opposing fleets to use reconnaissance vessels, and in this way the Japanese spotted the approaching Russians early on the morning of 27 May 1905. Expecting battle, the Russian admiral, Rozhestvensky, formed a line ahead at 0500 hr. The disadvantage of having auxiliaries so close to the fleet manifested itself later at 1340 hr, when the Japanese fleet appeared and the auxiliaries had to be detached to a safe distance with a cruiser escort.

Admiral Togo moved the Japanese fleet north-west of the Russians. Half an hour later, both sides opened fire at a distance of 4 miles, with the Japanese concentrating on the leading Russian ships. At 1430 hr, the Russian battleship *Osliabia* was hit, veering out of the line of battle and capsizing thirty minutes later. As the battle continued, the Japanese ships, being faster than their opponents, forced the Russian line to turn to the south-east. Then at 1500 hr the Russian flagship, *Kniaz Suvorov*, was hit and set on fire. A Russian destroyer took Vice-Admiral Rozhestvensky off, badly wounded, along with key members of his staff, leaving the crippled vessel to be sunk by Japanese destroyers using torpedoes at 1930 hr. Command then passed to the *Imperator Alexander III*. The Russian fleet turned back, but Togo gave chase, overhauled them and once again forced them to turn south. In worsening weather, at 1600 hr the two main fleets lost sight of each other in fog and smoke, leaving the cruiser forces to fight an inconclusive gun battle in high seas, which meant that accuracy was poor. While the Russian cruisers were hampered by the need to look after the supply ships, they gave a far better account of themselves than the battleships. The Russians also used their armoured coastal defence ships to hold off the Japanese, with Nebogatov's unlikely force managing good gunnery, putting several Japanese cruisers out of action, despite the shallow draught of his vessels, which meant that they rolled considerably.

Two hours later, with Rozhestvensky unconscious, Rear Admiral Nebogatov assumed command of the Russian fleet. He immediately got the fleet to regroup and set course northwards again, attempting to withdraw to the safety of Vladivostok, only to be rediscovered by the Japanese yet again, and the battle resumed at 1820 hr. The Russian fleet received heavy hits. At 1900 hr the *Imperator Alexander III* sank, having been forced out of line, and as her signaller sent the 'In Distress' signal, she suddenly rolled over and submerged completely, taking her entire crew with her. She was followed half an hour later by *Borodino*, which rolled over and capsized, before exploding, leaving just one survivor. After inflicting heavy losses on the Russians, Togo withdrew his heavy units, leaving the Russians to the tender mercies of his destroyers and torpedo boats.

Togo's withdrawal gave the Japanese battleships and cruisers time to recover from the day's fighting while maintaining the pressure on the Russians. In turn, the Russians mounted a strong resistance to the Japanese, who suffered some losses between 2030 hr and midnight. Nevertheless, several torpedoes hit their targets, with *Navarin* sinking the next day at 0200 hr, followed by the armoured cruiser *Admiral Nakhimov* at 0500 hr, and then the battleship *Sissoi-Veliki*. Having lost their numerical advantage in battleships, the main elements of the Russian fleet attempted to continue their progress north. A number of ships, including the *Aurora* and two other cruisers, turned back and headed towards the neutral Philippines, to be interned by the United States for the remainder of the war.

Nebogatov took the battleships *Imperator Nikolai I* and *Orel*, two coastal armoured ships, *Admiral Seniavin* and *Admiral Apraksin*, and two cruisers, northwards, but at 1030 hr he was discovered once again by the Japanese and surrendered. One cruiser attempted to escape, but ran aground. The commander of another coastal armoured ship, *Admiral Ushakov*, refused to surrender, and went down fighting, while the armoured cruiser *Dimitry Donskoi* also continued to fight throughout the day, surviving to be scuttled by her own crew at 0700 hr on the morning of 29 May. Meanwhile, a destroyer carrying the badly wounded Rozhestvensky was found and his staff officers persuaded the vessel's commander to surrender, so that Rozhestvensky become a prisoner of war.

Out of the entire Russian fleet, just one cruiser and two destroyers managed to reach Vladivostok, with the Russians having lost their battleships, only two of which survived to be surrendered. Four of the eight auxiliaries that had made the whole adventure possible were sunk. In terms of manpower, the Russians lost 5,000 men dead, 500 wounded. Another 6,000 Russians became prisoners of war – but only after they had broken into their ships' vodka stores and consumed the contents, doubtless starting captivity with a massive hangover. Against this, the total Japanese casualties were 600 dead and wounded, with the loss of three torpedo boats while two cruisers were badly damaged. The damage to three of the battleships needed dockyard attention.

Tsushima was the last in a series of humiliating defeats for the Russians, leaving Japan as victor in the war. At the Treaty of Portsmouth, Japan took Port Arthur and South Sakhalin from the Russians. This left Japan with a significant foothold on the Asian mainland, and control of Korea. This was to be the starting point for renewed Japanese expansion during the 1930s, which ultimately resulted in the international crisis that led to the Japanese attack on Pearl Harbor and the entry of the United States into the Second World War.

NOTES

1. J.N. Westwood, *Illustrated History of the Russo-Japanese War* (London, Sidgwick & Jackson, 1973).

Two

TRAGEDY OF LOST OPPORTUNITIES: GALLIPOLI, 1915–16

The master stroke, which would break the deadlock on the Western Front and relieve the pressure on Russia, the ally of Britain and France.

British and Australian troops landed in Turkey, at Gallipoli, on the morning of 25 April 1915, while French troops landed nearby on the Turkish mainland, overlooking the Dardanelles, the stretch of water giving access to Constantinople. This was the start of a military campaign that has remained controversial to this day. Indecision, complacency and a failure to take the enemy seriously all played their part, alongside incredible stupidity.

Gallipoli is the narrow peninsula stretching south from European Turkey, or Thrace, dividing the Aegean Sea from the Dardanelles and the only approach to the Sea of Marmara on which lies Istanbul, although during the First World War this was known as Constantinople, then the Turkish capital. Beyond Constantinople lay the Bosporus, and then the Black Sea and allied territory in Tsarist Russia. The reasons for taking the war to the eastern Mediterranean were sound. Although neutral at first, Turkey was closely allied with Germany, even before entering the war. Turkish forces posed a threat to Russia and to British forces in the Middle East, and most particularly to the Suez Canal.

Traditionally, Britain and Turkey had been, if not allies, at least good friends. A combination of circumstances during the early years of the twentieth century put Turkey in what may be described as the German camp. The change was partly due to poor British diplomacy, but it also reflected British and French disgust at the Turkish treatment of minorities. Britain had refused to provide loans for the Turkish government, and both Britain and France refused to accept Turkish officer cadets at their military academies. An Anglo-Russian agreement of 1907 only served to make matters worse, confirming suspicions planted in Turkish minds by German diplomats, since Turkey and Tsarist Russia had a long history of enmity. Government was in the hands of a clique of ministers who really were the original 'young Turks', and the Germans made much of them. If British relations with Turkey suffered from poor British diplomacy, the Germans showed exceptional diplomatic skill at this crucial period. Developing relations between Germany and Turkey eventually resulted in a substantial force of several hundred German military advisers being sent to Turkey in 1913, led by General Liman von Sanders. This was followed early in 1914 by a courtesy visit to Constantinople by Germany's new battlecruiser *Goeben*, even though visits by foreign warships while Turkey was at peace had been banned by the 1856 Treaty of Paris and the 1871 Treaty of London.

News on 3 August 1914 that the Turks were laying mines in the Dardanelles caused Britain to cancel the order for two major warships being built in Britain for the Turkish Navy, transferring them to the Royal Navy on completion. Britain's declaration of war on Germany the following day brought the *Goeben* and her escort cruiser *Breslau* back to Turkey, chased by the Royal Navy. Although still neutral, Turkey gave these ships sanctuary, allowing the Germans to turn this new state of affairs to their advantage, arranging for the two ships to be 'sold' to Turkey, becoming the *Sultan Selim* and *Medilli* respectively, while retaining their German crews. As the relationship deteriorated, Britain continued to treat Turkey with caution, and it was not until 31 October that war was declared on Turkey. This was despite earlier provocative action by the Turks, whose army had been responsible for raids on British forces in Egypt, and a fleet attack on the Russian ports of Odessa and Sebastopol, any of which could have justified an earlier declaration.

Early in the war, on 20 August, Britain had even rejected the offer of the Greek armed forces, for fear of damaging relations with Turkey. The Greeks had a plan to use 90,000 troops to take the Gallipoli Peninsula, and give the Allies control of the Dardanelles. Such action so early could have achieved many of the ambitions held for the Gallipoli campaign, for at this time Turkish defences were out of date, with many gaps, and insufficient trained troops to man them all. The Turkish fleet, including its new German additions, could have been squeezed between the British Mediterranean Fleet and the Russian Black Sea Fleet, and Turkey's two munitions factories, on the Bosporus near Constantinople, could have been blown to pieces by naval gunfire.

Decisive action so soon could have eased the pressure on both Egypt and Russia, and might even have made conditions on the Russian front with Germany easier. Whether or not it might have staved off the Russian Revolution is difficult to say, although it remains a tempting possibility.

Inaction until the Allies were ready to tackle Turkey might just have been excused. What happened next could not be. Strategically and tactically, the British managed to produce what amounted to a succession of serious blunders, alerting the Turks and their German allies.

Once war was declared on Turkey, Winston Churchill, First Lord of the Admiralty, ordered ships of the Mediterranean Fleet to bombard the lower Dardanelles forts, causing serious damage to their outdated defences, which suffered from poorly sited and badly served guns. This was the first serious blunder. Admiral Limpus in Malta had objected, arguing that an army should be landed instead. The bombardment did succeed in neutralizing the forts, but it also alerted the Germans and Turks to both British intentions and Turkish deficiencies.

Demolition of a railway line by a shore party from a British cruiser, to which no Turkish resistance was offered, also convinced the British that Turkey did not present a serious threat. This notion should have been cast aside in December, when 100,000 Turkish troops invaded the Caucasus, and at first made rapid progress against the Russians in severe winter weather. If this had any effect on British opinion at all, complacency was doubtless restored when the invasion of Russian territory fizzled out. A major Russian victory at Sarikamish on 29 December, with the Turks fighting at an altitude of 10,000 ft in a blizzard, left just 18,000 Turkish soldiers still fit enough to fight on their return home. Yet again, the British were convinced of Turkish weakness.

Perhaps the one decisive and convincing British action at this early stage was that of the British submarine, *B11*, which sneaked past the minefields and entered the Sea of Marmara on 13 December. The battlecruiser *Messudieh* was sunk, and the submarine's commander, Lieutenant Holbrook, was awarded the Victoria Cross. Had this been part of a sustained campaign, it could have done much to undermine Turkish resistance, but as an isolated incident, all it achieved was to further alert the Turks to the Allied threat.

Gallipoli was controversial even before the expedition started. The British War Council was in favour of the campaign. Its members believed that Germany could be hurt most by an attack on her allies, and of these Turkey was both the most obvious, and the one likely to yield the maximum benefit. The hard-pressed Russians shared this view. An attack on Turkey would relieve the pressure on Russian forces in the Caucasus. This fitted in with the First Sea Lord, Admiral of the Fleet Lord Fisher's idea for a combined operation. The Army objected. Field Marshal Sir John French, commanding British forces on the Western Front, was in favour only if it remained a naval operation. French was, throughout the campaign, determined to keep the best generals in France, and not to weaken the British effort there, which had entered a stalemate, with the opposing forces trapped in trench warfare.

If the Army view seems short-sighted, even Fisher wanted to keep the best for his own plans. He saw the Dardanelles operation as using elderly warships, while the best, including the three new shallow-draught battle cruisers *Furious*, *Glorious* and *Courageous*, were to be reserved for planned landings in the Baltic, as close to Berlin as possible. Armoured, shallow-draught, landing craft were also being prepared for the Baltic adventure, but were denied the Dardanelles force.

So here was a mission that was plausible in outline, promising much, not least being the breaking of the stalemate in the war resulting from the failings on the Western Front. Yet, hardly anyone with influence over events showed any sense of realism, still less any determination and wholehearted commitment. When Field Marshal Lord Kitchener, the Secretary of State for War, received in his office an intelligence officer with experience of both the Turkish Army and the Dardanelles, he enquired whether a purely naval attack would work. When he was told it must fail, Kitchener sent him away. Meanwhile, the Germans and Turks strengthened the defences.

Gallipoli was conceived as a masterstroke that would simultaneously break the deadlock on the Western Front, and ease the pressure on Russian forces on the Eastern Front. The British even expected success at Gallipoli to draw Turkish forces away from positions that threatened the British presence in the Middle East, and end any German or Turkish threat to Egypt and to the Suez Canal. It would also hasten the departure of Turkish forces from those parts of the Arab world that were still part of the Ottoman Empire.

Given these high hopes, it might have been expected that preparation would have been thorough, and the resources allocated at least adequate, with the best leadership possible. But the preparation was flawed, the initial landings and subsequent attacks were bungled, and even the relief operation at Suvla was

19

an almost unbelievable failure to seize the initiative, which could have won the campaign. As for leadership, there was none. There was no excuse for the poor preparation. A considerable British diplomatic presence in the area before the war meant that the landing sites at Gallipoli had been visited and were well known to at least one senior British Army officer, Lieutenant-Colonel Charles Cunliffe Owen, who had been attached to the British embassy. In the preparations, he was not consulted, even though he was back in England and working at the War Office, and available to the small planning group. When he eventually did take part in the campaign, it was at battlefield level rather than staff level, where his advice could still have made a difference.

Many blame the then First Lord of the Admiralty, Winston Churchill, for the failings at Gallipoli, but the decisive failings lay further down the line, with the generals themselves. The worst that can be said of the politicians is that they allowed the wrong men to go to Turkey, and then left them there, where they did more damage to the Allied war effort than to that of the Turks, or to Turkey's allies and sponsors, the Germans. In theory, the idea was sound. The problem lay in convincing both the Admiralty and the War Office of its importance. The Commander-in-Chief of the British Army, Sir John French, regarded the whole matter as no more than a 'sideshow', doubtless influenced by the Minister for War, Lord Kitchener. The Admiralty sent their oldest and least efficient battleships, with the one exception of the new HMS *Queen Elizabeth*. Both the Royal Navy and the British Army displayed the utmost contempt for the Turks as a nation and for the Turkish Army. Their contempt was to be misplaced.

At sixty-two years of age, General Sir Ian Hamilton was near to retirement and serving in the British Isles. Rather than transfer a fighting general, Hamilton was chosen, with the implied promise that if all went well, he could retire as a field marshal – the British equivalent of a five-star general. Hamilton was cultured and charming, an author, and had been left behind in Britain because many, including Sir John French, didn't like him. Hamilton was given Major-General Walter Braithwaite as Chief of Staff. Braithwaite was in many ways the opposite of his new master, frequently abrasive and with a knack of upsetting those around him. He was not without good ideas, however. At their first meeting with Kitchener, he suggested that the invasion force should have better air power than the enemy, perhaps a squadron of the latest aircraft, with experienced pilots and observers. Kitchener turned on him and barked, 'Not one!'

Neither man had known what was on offer when they were called to the meeting. Neither knew the area, or the disposition of the enemy. As Hamilton was to write later, 'My knowledge of the Dardanelles was nil, of the Turk nil, of the strength of my own forces, next to nil.' Reference material was out of date by some ten years, the maps were worse, being designed for tourists and wildly inaccurate. Hamilton had little idea of the topography, less about sea conditions and the weather. Kitchener even assured Hamilton that the Turkish defences could be brought to a state of collapse with a single British submarine in the Sea of Marmara, even saying that: 'Supposing one submarine pops up opposite the town of Gallipoli and waves a Union Jack three times, the whole Turkish garrison on the peninsula will take to their heels and make a bee line for Bulair.'[1] Bulair was the town at the neck of the peninsula. Hamilton knew so little that he didn't know the sinking of a major Turkish warship by a British submarine had already failed to bring about a collapse of Turkish resistance. Worse was to come – it was not until after the first troops had landed that anyone realized that they were not facing gently sloping terrain, but instead a land of steep gradients, interspersed with deep ravines cut by many watercourses.

The French were to provide a division of 18,000 men. Command was given to General Albert d'Amade. His war record was hardly distinguished: he had been relieved of his command in France after losing his nerve and ordering an unnecessary withdrawal. Despite this, the French wanted him to be in overall command of the land forces. Like his British counterparts, he was almost completely ignorant of the situation facing him. Nevertheless, a weakness for self-promotion led him to give a newspaper in Egypt an interview, in which he managed to reveal the full extent of Allied aspirations.

The expeditionary force set off without adequate artillery or any hand grenades at all, but with motor vehicles and armoured cars, both of which would be unsuitable on the inhospitable terrain and, worse, would take up the limited level space on the invasion beaches. It was left to the force's officers to visit Egypt to find mules and stores, while the Royal Navy turned the port of Mudros, on the Greek island of Lemnos (the recovery of which was a Turkish war aim), into a harbour to provide a forward base. Egypt had to be scoured for the necessary supplies, while jetties and pontoons also had to be assembled. The effort did not compare with the Mulberry Harbour assembled for the Normandy landings, but neither did the resources made available or the commitment of those in the UK, France or even among the British forces in Egypt. Throughout the campaign, those endeavouring to achieve success were to struggle against the odds. General Sir John Maxwell, the British Commander-in-Chief in Egypt, was another of Hamilton's enemies and only provided support grudgingly when ordered to do so by Kitchener.

Hamilton's own team cannot be completely absolved from any blame at this early stage. For all their hard work, they failed completely to appreciate the great value of the support arms and the needs of those commanding them. The specialists were left behind in Egypt rather than becoming part of Hamilton's headquarters staff. Those left so far behind included such key figures in any campaign as the Quartermaster-General, the Director of Medical Services and the Adjutant-General. It was not until later in the campaign, when it had become bogged down, that an efficient supply operation was created on Lemnos with an experienced general in command. Casualty rates during the initial landings were expected to be high, yet just two small hospital ships were provided, and when he finally managed to reach Lemnos, the Director of Medical Services had to order more ships.

Floating piers for use in the landings, designed by an enterprising Army officer, were supposed to be delivered to the beaches by the Royal Navy, who considered this important task beneath them. The job was subcontracted to merchant shipping, who abandoned seven of the eight piers in the Mediterranean, and left the eighth on Lemnos. Hamilton, meanwhile, had assembled 75,000 men, many of them Australians and New Zealanders who were to prove to be among his best troops.

The commanders of the expeditionary force had a choice of landing sites, with the most likely being:

1. Asiatic Turkey, near Besika Bay, which had the advantage of being easy, with few commanding heights from which the Turks could direct their fire. The German General von Sanders saw this as one of the most vulnerable spots.
2. The Gulf of Saros, near Bulair, where Gallipoli joined the mainland of Thrace, and the peninsular was just three and a half miles wide. Here the terrain was easiest and offered the prospect of cutting off the rest of the peninsula, but at a cost of having to defend the landings from attack on two sides.
3. Gaba Tepe, which was the next best choice on the peninsula itself; it was just six miles wide and the terrain was relatively easy, with a low valley that could be protected if high ground on either side was also taken, giving a good defensive position.
4. Cape Helles at the tip of the peninsula, which was at least within easy range of the guns of the fleet, and meant that fighting would take place on one front.
5. Suvla Bay, which offered a good beach, with manageable heights nearby. There was a large salt lake behind it, but this was dry in summer.

To some extent, Hamilton's options were more limited than this list suggests. He ruled out Suvla Bay because, when he saw it, the salt lake was flooded after the winter rains, and the available intelligence material was too poor to indicate that in summer it would not be an obstacle. Kitchener ruled out for him a landing in Asiatic Turkey, or Anatolia. In the end, Hamilton chose options 3 and 4, Gaba Tepe and Cape Helles, with a feint attack by the Royal Naval Division at Bulair, while the French made two feint attacks on the Asiatic coast. British troops would land at Cape Helles. The Australians and New Zealanders, whose numbers included many that had not completed their training, were to land at Gaba Tepe. These plans were modified shortly before the start of the assault with the addition of two additional beaches: code-named Y, on the Aegean coast; and S, at Morto Bay at the entrance to the Dardanelles.

Meanwhile, the Turks had provided an army specifically for the defence of the Dardanelles, under the command of General von Sanders. The experienced and energetic von Sanders needed just eight days to get his forces into position: the British allowed him four weeks, with the result that he had 84,000 men in six divisions, against just 14,000 Allied troops at the time of the Royal Navy's initial hit-and-run gunnery raids. The extra time had been put to good use, improving communications through repairing and improving the road network. Convinced that the British attack would come in the Gulf of Saros, von Sanders made his headquarters at the neck of the peninsula, but on the side overlooking the Dardanelles.

Landings started on the morning of 25 April 1915, with 1,500 Australian troops who disembarked at 0130 hr, from the battleships into small boats, which were towed by small steam pinnaces towards the beach. First light came at 0405 hr, and the pinnaces cast off their tows at 0425 hr, leaving the boats to be rowed towards the shore by sailors. It was at this moment that the first fire came from the defenders. Initially badly aimed, it became increasingly accurate as the light improved and the boats closed on the coast. Even so, most of the first wave reached the beaches safely, but those who were wounded in the boats had to remain in them during subsequent trips between the destroyers bringing the next wave of men and the beaches.

Once ashore, the Australians soon discovered that they had been landed too far north, and as they attempted to leave the beaches and advance inland, they were faced with steep cliffs rather than the low and gently rising sand hills at the correct landing place. This mistake meant that the 8,000 men of the initial landing were unable to achieve their objective of overrunning Turkish outposts and taking a ridge dominating their positions before the Turks had time to respond. Meanwhile, at Cape Helles, just a thousand Turkish troops watched the landings by the British troops. At two of the five beaches – the two added at the last minute, code-named Y and S – men went safely ashore without encountering opposition. The same could not be said at the remaining three beaches. At the one known as X, opposition occurred once the men had advanced half-a-mile inland, but this at least left the beach safe for the main body to follow. Troops landing at W beach were far less fortunate. As the naval bombardment ceased, the surviving Turks overlooking the beach held their fire as they watched the British troops being rowed towards barbed wire, much of it out of sight under the water. However, as the boats grounded they opened fire on the men of the Lancashire Fusiliers; their commander, Brigadier Hare, found a safer landing for as many of his men as possible. Then started a magnificent fight, as they advanced slowly on to higher ground to outflank the Turks, forcing them to withdraw. At this stage, a vital point, known as Hill 138, was open to the advance, but Hare had been wounded and his replacement was shot dead after a few minutes. Effectively leaderless for the moment, the men concentrated on helping their wounded and missed the opportunity to take the hill. More than half the 950 men landed at W beach were casualties.

Elsewhere, at V Beach, an old merchant ship, the *River Clyde*, had been converted with doors cut in the sides of the hull so

25

that a large number of troops could land quickly and run across a 'bridge' of lighters. The lighters were towed into place by a tug, and almost immediately began to break away in the strong currents, only being held together by the prompt action of Commander Unwin and Able Seaman Williams, who dived into the water and held the lashings secure. As the first of 2,000 men of the Munster Fusiliers and the Hampshire Regiment ran through the *River Clyde*'s doors, they were immediately cut down by a well-planned and well-aimed burst of Turkish fire. About half the men were caught on the pontoon bridge, with half remaining inside the ship, whose machine guns mounted in the bows were used to stop the Turks from advancing onto the beaches. Meanwhile, men of the Royal Dublin Fusiliers had been caught in the same defensive fire while attempting to land in open boats.

Despite hearing the firing, the officer in charge of the landings, Major-General Hunter Weston on board the command ship *Euryalus*, failed to take any action. At 0830 hr, the order was given for the main force to land in the face of the fire, led by Brigadier Napier, who ignored the warnings from the officers trapped aboard the *River Clyde* – within minutes Napier and his staff were dead. Help did not come until Hamilton, aboard the new battleship HMS *Queen Elizabeth*, ordered heavy supporting fire, but while this moved the Turks from their firing positions, they were soon back once it stopped. Hamilton wanted to divert the troops from V beach to Y beach, but Hunter Weston rejected this as interfering with the planned arrangements.

At Gaba Tepe, where the nearby beach had been given the name Anzac Cove by the invaders (for Australian and New Zealand Army Corps), Turkish prisoners reported that they had just two regiments south of this location. Despite this valuable information being passed on to Hamilton at 1240 hr, and again at 1700 and 2230 hr, no action was taken – officially because the information was not believed; it was later found out to be accurate, but too late. A similar missed opportunity occurred at

Y beach, where the troops had advanced a short distance inland, and waited in vain for fresh orders from Hunter Weston. By evening, Turkish reinforcements had arrived and the two sides had dug trenches and settled into a stalemate, the inevitable outcome of not making the most of the initial advance, which in Hamilton's view, could have 'cut off the enemy troops on the toe of the peninsula'.[2]

By evening, the Australians and New Zealanders on their narrow beach at Anzac Cove were facing determined and repeated counter-attacks by large Turkish forces, whose positions were favoured by the terrain. In the brutal hand-to-hand fighting which followed, seven battalions were severely mauled. Evacuation was considered, but rejected out of hand by the Royal Navy as administratively impossible. Those ashore were told to hang on, and were supposed to be comforted by the news that the submarine *AE2*, had passed through the Dardanelles to sink an enemy ship. The following morning saw prospects of an early victory much diminished. Far from folding, the Turkish defenders had managed to bring the invaders to a halt. Hunter Weston was warned that the situation on Y Beach was desperate, but although this was directly under his command, and he had six battalions of French troops ready to deploy, he simply passed the matter up to Hamilton, claiming to have no reserves to spare. Hamilton was seriously worried but to him military etiquette and supporting a subordinate commander were more important.

In the confusion and absence of clear orders, when the British troops finally started a withdrawal at Y Beach, Hamilton assumed that this was on Hunter Weston's orders, as did Colonel Matthews, the commander, who had received no orders from Hunter Weston for thirty hours. At this point, fresh troops, with clear orders and a resolute commander, could have taken the southern end of the peninsula, but instead, the Turks realized that an evacuation had taken place by mid-afternoon and reclaimed the beach. Ashore on Anatolia, an even greater farce was being played out. The heroic

General Albert d'Amade was behaving true to form and wanted to withdraw his troops, even though they had inflicted 1,700 Turkish casualties against 500 of their own, and taken 500 prisoners. The French had defeated the defenders and had secured the area. The French Navy gave Hamilton the true state of affairs, and permission to withdraw was rescinded, but too late as the evacuation was already well under way.

By the afternoon, British troops had secured the position at Cape Helles, but were by now suffering from a chaotic supply position that prevented them from making further progress. The situation was even worse at Anzac Cove, where again the position had stabilized, but within the extremely confined beachhead, the men were at the mercy of Turkish small-arms and mortar fire.

From here on, the situation deteriorated into a crude resemblance of the trench warfare of the Western Front, but with three differences. One was the lack of water, the second the proximity of the opposing front lines, which highlighted the third: the lack of grenades; these were so needed that home-made bombs were improvised out of tins. At such close quarters, the hand grenade was the weapon of choice. As on the Western Front, attempts to break the deadlock were costly, wasteful and bungled. There is evidence that Hamilton was concerned about this; Hunter Weston, though, in telling a brigade commander whose newly arrived troops had suffered grievous losses that, 'he was glad to have blooded the pups', showed a callous disregard for the welfare of his own men.

There was much wrong with Hamilton, who failed to impress himself on his subordinate commanders, and who with his naval counterparts neglected to develop true inter-service cooperation. Yet, by the standards of some of his subordinate commanders, Hamilton shone in comparison. One problem was that it was not until very much later that the British adopted a policy that encouraged Commanders-in-Chief to remove incompetent subordinate commanders.

The whole operation could have been a striking success of Allied arms, with a relatively easy and bloodless victory putting the Central Powers on the defensive. Instead, within days the whole affair degenerated into trench warfare reminiscent of that on the Western Front, except that the summers were hotter and drier, and the winters were colder. When air support was provided, under the command of none other than the courageous and colourful Commander Charles Rumney Samson of the Royal Naval Air Service, their reconnaissance reports were ignored or not passed on. The RNAS were restricted to one-hundred 100-lb bombs per month – a supply that they could happily have used within a single day.

Hamilton called for a further assault to break the deadlock, and asked for a young and vigorous general, one with a strong constitution who could stand the extreme climatic conditions and the stresses of the command. He was sent Lieutenant-General Sir Frederick Stopford, aged sixty-one and in such poor health that he sometimes could not leave his bed. No less important, Stopford, Kitchener's choice, had not held a significant command throughout his long career.

The idea was that 22,000 men would be landed at Suvla Bay, where only a token Turkish opposition was expected. A rapid advance inland would follow to occupy a semicircular range of hills, from where the Suvla Bay troops could join the Anzacs and make a surprise attack on a major Turkish strongpoint, a hill at Sari Bair. Ideally, the combined force could then cut across the peninsula and enable the Royal Navy to take control of the Dardanelles. Surprise was essential, speed at least as much so if the objectives were to be gained before the Turks, aided by superb German commanders in the field, were not to be able to react and redeploy their forces.

The landing at Suvla Bay went ahead on 7 August 1915. Just 1,500 Turkish troops stood between the Suvla Bay force and their objectives, a fact soon verified by junior officers on the ground, yet Stopford regarded the landing itself as a great achievement, and decided that the men should rest for a day before advancing inland. Going by the manuals, he also demanded an artillery barrage before they could seize their objectives, despite the lack of any suitable targets. Not hearing from Stopford, but aware from aerial reconnaissance that there were no Turks in the hills, Hamilton sent two senior officers to find out what was going on. They discovered what has been described as 'August Bank Holiday in England' with soldiers bathing in the peaceful bay. Stopford himself was resting, happy with the progress made, and blissfully unaware that the sort of military opportunity commanders can only dream about was slipping through his hands. Even as the two officers urged him to make progress, news arrived of a major Turkish advance, but without artillery support, Stopford, supported by his two almost equally inactive divisional commanders, would not order an advance. Hamilton himself arrived to receive the same complacent response. Later, Major-General Hammersley went ashore to order an advance. This military genius ordered the troops who had occupied Scimitar Hill, one of the initial key objectives, to return to the beaches, where they were ordered to form up before advancing a short distance inland to prepare trenches. While this was going on the, by now unoccupied, Scimitar Hill was taken, unopposed, by Turkish forces. When Stopford finally went ashore the next day, 800 Turkish troops were allowed to hold up 6,000 British troops. In one sector a junior officer complained that they were not allowed to advance against three Turkish soldiers, whom he described as 'one little man with a white beard, one man in a blue coat and one boy in shirt sleeves'.[3]

If Stopford was awful, so too were many of his senior officers. Hammersley was a good example. He had been rejected for active service and was recovering from a nervous breakdown. When Hammersley first encountered fire after what amounted to an unopposed landing at Suvla Bay, it is reported that he lay down on the floor of his tent with his hands over his head. After nine days, Stopford was sacked, but the damage was done. The British assault on the major strongpoint of Oglue Tepe, unoccupied at the time of the Suvla Bay landing, resulted in 8,000 casualties, and cost the Allies any chance of making a success of the Gallipoli campaign.

There could only be one outcome from this chaotic mismanagement – withdrawal. The decision to evacuate the forces from Gallipoli was taken on 10 December 1915, by which time 134,000 British and Empire troops had been committed to the peninsula. The remaining French troops left two days later. British and Empire troops, however, had to wait a little longer, but despite high winds and rough seas, all but 40,000 troops were evacuated at the beginning of the New Year, and these, divided almost equally with 20,000 men each at Anzac Cove and Suvla Bay, were taken off on the night of 8/9 January 1916.

Gallipoli has become a byword for a badly judged campaign. Usually, Churchill is seen as the main culprit, while Kitchener seems to have been treated far more kindly by history. Yet, while Churchill could have done much to ensure that the Royal Navy placed better ships at the disposal of the Army, the real fault was Kitchener's, for he alone decided to send two unsuitable officers, Hamilton and Stopford. It seems clear that he wanted them out of the way. On a campaign in which good generals could have made an impact on the outcome of the war, failures were sent. They in turn appointed failures and neglected to countermand them when senseless commands were issued. In this case, putting the two men in question out of the way could only have meant retirement, despite – or perhaps because of – the demands of war.

NOTES

1. John Laffin, *Damn the Dardannelles! The Story of Gallipoli* (London, Osprey, 1980).
2. Ibid.
3. Ibid.

Three

STALEMATE: THE WESTERN FRONT, 1914–18

The Western Front in the First World War has become synonymous with bad leadership and military incompetence.

On the first day of the Battle of the Somme, 1 July 1916, the British Army sent 120,000 men against the German front line, promising them that the barbed wire had been destroyed by the artillery barrage. It hadn't. The reasons for the survival of the barbed wire were appallingly simple. The massive call-up of men of fighting age, and the often extreme social pressure on fit men to enlist, had so affected the munitions factories that temporary workers had to be recruited. This in turn had led to a reduction in quality that ensured that one-third of the massive 1.5 million shells fired in the run-up to the Battle of the Somme failed to explode. Instead of firing high-explosive shells which would have cut the barbed wire, shrapnel shells had been used instead. The shrapnel shells were intended for use against infantry in the open, exploding above ground to pepper the victims with shot. They had little or no impact on barbed wire. Blissfully unaware of this, the British were so confident that officers told their men that it would be like going for a walk. They were told that the barrage would have killed the Germans, and many of the officers advanced armed with nothing more offensive than a swagger stick or umbrella; one officer in the East Surrey Regiment even kicked a football towards the German lines. Persuaded that all would be well, it is not surprising that the troops advanced without wire cutters.

A creeping barrage as the troops advanced would have forced the Germans to keep their heads down. But not only was there no creeping barrage, it was decided that the artillery barrage would end ten minutes before the attack started, with that of the field artillery ending two minutes before. This gave the Germans plenty of warning that an attack was coming.

The Germans, of course, had not been killed in the artillery barrage. Instead of remaining in their trenches, they had taken refuge in deep shelters. As they saw the advancing British troops walking towards them, they opened fire with their machine guns, cutting through the ranks of men completely exposed and with no cover whatsoever. Behind, in the trenches, fresh waves of troops were being sent 'over the top' to take their place in the carnage. The cost of this incompetence was that almost half the troops became casualties, with 21,000 killed and another 36,470 wounded. Some battalions were almost wiped out. Most of these casualties occurred within the first thirty minutes of the attack.

The blame for much of this rests fairly and squarely on a senior British officer, Major-General Aylmer Hunter Weston. The decision to end the barrage prematurely was entirely his. Known as 'Hunter Bunter' to his troops because his considerable waistline reminded them of the fictional schoolboy anti-hero, Billy Bunter, historians have been less kind to Hunter Weston. To them, this man was the 'Butcher of Hellas', after his mistakes during the Gallipoli campaign, already mentioned. He once remarked, 'Casualties? What do I care for casualties?' He was bloodthirsty and also insensitive.

It was not a case of technology overtaking experience. Trench warfare had already been seen in the American Civil War half a century earlier, along with early types of machine gun. Both sides knew the problems created by barbed wire, especially while attempting to cross it under fire. Even the aeroplane had been used in the Balkan Wars between the Italians and the Turks, while observation balloons had been used as early as 1794.

Genuinely new weapons in the First World War were the tank, and the willingness to use gas against the enemy.

Ignorance of developments in any profession is unacceptable, and in few cases more so than in the profession of arms. There was incompetence, and an inability to see the soldiers both as human beings and as irreplaceable military assets. In conflict, a commander cannot be spared the awful inevitability that many of those he has ordered into action will not return, but will be killed, crippled or taken prisoner. This is one of the hardships of command, but to send so many to almost certain destruction, and then to keep on repeating the mistake, has to be regarded as both inexcusable and unforgivable.

The British Army did no better with its equipment. At the start of the war, machine guns had been issued on the basis of just two per battalion. It was not until David Lloyd George became Minister of Munitions in 1915 that this figure was raised to sixteen per battalion. At this stage, the main manufacturer, Vickers, could not meet demand. Before the war, the company had been told to arrange production on the expectation of orders for just eleven machine guns a year for the British Army. The production line was only kept open on the basis of export orders, mainly for Tsarist Russia.

During the first winter of war, the British suffered from a shell famine so acute that artillery pieces were limited to just ten shells a day. This curbed offensive activity, and contributed to the heavy losses among the professional soldiers who were the backbone of the British Army in the beginning. The blame for this rested not with the generals, but with the politicians and civil servants.

When given the tank, the British Army had what could have been a war-winning innovation. The Germans couldn't match it, and it marked a way out of the trenches and the stalemate of the Western Front. Three times, tanks were tried and the generals failed to make the most of the opportunities suddenly opened up before them, at Flers on the Somme in 1916, at

Cambrai the following year, and at Amiens in 1918. The tank was the great innovation of land warfare during the First World War. (They gained this rather odd name by accident, because for security reasons the shipping documents for the short crossing to France listed them as 'water tanks'.) Security was so tight that the first the British commander in France, the then General Sir Douglas Haig (later Field Marshal Lord Haig), knew of them was in December 1915, but his subordinate commanders were not sure how to use them to best effect. At this time, Haig was under pressure from the French commander, Joffre, to resume action on the Somme, but he knew that his forces would not be ready until September 1916. Haig's own preference was for an attack across Flanders, to seize those Belgian channel ports being used as naval bases by the enemy. As for the tanks, Rawlinson, Haig's deputy, wrote to the King's assistant private secretary that: 'We are puzzling our heads as how best to make use of them and have not yet come to a decision. They are not going to take the British Army straight to Berlin as some people imagine, but if properly used and skilfully handled by the detachments who work them they may be very useful in taking trenches and strong points. Some people are rather too optimistic as to what these weapons will accomplish.'[1]

Guarded optimism over the prospects for the tank seemed reasonable. Rawlinson was giving a fair assessment of the first batch of tanks that arrived in France in early September 1916, and suffered from teething troubles and the poor reliability of many motor vehicles of the day. The tanks were officially part of the Heavy Section, Machine Gun Corps, and were taken by rail to Bray-sur-Somme. Altogether forty-nine tanks were available for operations with the Fourth Army, and of these, thirty-two were sent into action on 15 September. The initial results were not promising. Canadian troops, supported by tanks, which were to spearhead an attack on a sugar factory near Courcelette, found that the tanks were too slow to keep pace with the infantry. Worse, many of the tanks broke down. The commander of a

British division even wanted his tanks to pass through a wood, overruling objections that the ground was unsuitable.

Nevertheless, when twelve tanks headed for Flers, operating as the largest single concentration of tanks on the Somme, they created panic among the German troops, allowing the town to be taken. Famously, an RFC pilot reported: 'A tank is walking up the High Street of Flers with the British Army cheering behind it.'

As the war progressed, the fortunes of the tank fluctuated. At Messines, the British commander, later to become Field Marshal Viscount Plumer of Messines, had 300 aircraft and 72 Mk IV tanks, and although the latter were a big improvement on the original tanks, the terrain was unsuitable for their use.

General Sir Hubert Gough, the commander of the British Fifth Army, was also given command of the Second Army, so that he could break through at Flanders on 31 July. The initial attack would be to seize a ridge north of Ypres, and a plateau to the east of the town, followed up by a swing north-east to take the Roulers–Thourout railway a week later. The theory was fine, but war is not won by theory alone. The massive artillery barrage that preceded the attack fired 4.5 million rounds and destroyed the drainage system that was so vital to the delicate environment of the low-lying Flanders fields. Woodland was also destroyed. The result was a landscape that was difficult and dangerous to the infantry, many of whom were to drown in the Flanders mud, and impassable for tanks. The initial assault began at 0350 hr on 1 July, and initial good progress was soon stopped as the summer weather broke in the afternoon, turning the battlefield into a quagmire. Half the tanks were soon out of action, and the British suffered 30,000 casualties for an advance of less than two miles.

Second Lieutenant Gerry Brooks was in his tank *Fay*, one of four attempting to make progress over this impassable terrain on 2 August, and recorded:

The fun began when the tape we were following led through some very swampy ground. It was so wet we found it hard to swing. The four of us got rather bunched and the *Foam* received a couple of direct hits and Harris her commander and two more of the crew were wounded. Harris was in great pain having his left arm nearly blown off from the elbow and also armour plate and rivets in his leg. . . . We passed a good many dead who had fallen on July 31. Soon we came up to our infantry who were hiding in shell holes with very heavy machine gun fire. This splattered against our armour and some came through in a fine spray so that we were all soon bleeding from small cuts.[2]

The tank was soon bogged down after this, and abandoned by her crew, one of whom was killed in the process. The rest, including Brooks, managed to escape, despite being surrounded by counter-attacking Germans.

The big tank battle of the war was at Cambrai in 1917. In northern France, Cambrai was a tempting target for the British Third Army, as an important link in the German communications chain. German defences at Cambrai were based on two canals, Napoleon's St Quentin Canal and, to the west of Cambrai, the new Canal du Nord, not yet filled with water. In between the two canals lay a large wooded hill, Bourlon Wood. The ground was firm, ideal for tanks, and Brigadier-General Hugh Elles, commander of the Tank Corps, was anxious to show what his unit could do, as was his opposite number in the artillery, Brigadier-General Tudor, who had done much to improve marking of artillery targets. These two officers were among the more imaginative and enlightened. Unfortunately, though, someone had the bright idea that the tanks could cooperate with cavalry. The war had been a frustrating one for the cavalry, whose role by this time was to exploit the gap created by the infantry and then pursue the enemy. Regrettably there had been no breakthroughs by the infantry lasting long enough for this to happen, and the terrain was often unsuitable. The tanks were to provide the gap so desired by the cavalry, and no less than five cavalry divisions were assigned to this role.

For the first time, Cambrai showed tank warfare on a grand scale, with 378 battle tanks, 54 supply tanks, which pulled sledges loaded with supplies and equipment, another 32 tanks fitted with grapnels for dragging clear barbed wire, ready for a cavalry charge, while 2 more carried bridging equipment. There were also 5 wireless tanks for communications. No less than 216 of the battle tanks were to cross the St Quentin Canal, while 108 tanks would take Bourlon Wood. There would be supporting fire from 1,000 guns, and extensive air cover.

The attack got off to a good start, at 0620 hr on 20 November, quickly breaking through the first two stages of the four-stage German front lines. In one section of the front, ground troops and tanks became separated in difficult ground. Worse was to follow. The German commander, Lieutenant-General von Watter, had a brother who had encountered tanks on the Somme and had passed on advice on how they might be dealt with. As a result, the German artillery had been trained in moving their guns out of their positions so that they could aim level fire at tanks, so the British tanks ran into this intense artillery fire. Within minutes, twenty-eight tanks were lost. Meanwhile, to the south-east, British forces had reached the St Quentin Canal, where at Masnieres, the tank *Flying Fox* had crashed through the bridge, making it unusable for those following.

The initial results were good, despite these difficulties, with a four-mile advance into heavily defended enemy territory. Yet, as so often happened, the operation ran out of steam after the first couple of days. Cavalry were unable to exploit the gap created by the tanks because of the difficult terrain, made worse by barbed wire, and because mounted operations could not be conducted in the face of heavy machine-gun fire. As for the tanks, almost half the 378 battle tanks were soon out of action, with 65 destroyed, and another 114 ditched in unsuitable terrain or suffering mechanical failure. A lengthy battle for Bourlon Wood developed, and then, on 30 November, the Germans mounted a successful counter-attack. By 5 December, the British had lost most of their hard-won gains.

However, one should not see this inability to convert a tactical victory into a strategic success as being a purely British phenomenon. Just as the Germans also lost large numbers of troops on hopeless frontal attacks, they also mounted assaults that soon lost their way. A massive German advance in 1918 quickly ran out of steam, as supply lines became stretched, troops lost artillery cover in their advance, and as casualties mounted, but also through a breakdown in discipline. German troops began looting and gorging themselves on captured food, all washed down by large quantities of wine and cognac. The Allied response saw the Germans forced back, with newly arrived American assistance, into Belgium. The Channel ports of Ostend and Antwerp, so long desired by the British, were taken. While it is true that the German line never actually broke, giving Hitler cause to claim that German troops had never been defeated in the war, the fact was that the Germans were losing ground and the Allies were taking it, in Haig's glorious final hundred days of the war. At home, thanks to a successful British naval blockade, Germany was on her knees, with millions suffering from starvation.

The tank was a timely arrival on the Western Front, and after the inevitable initial failures could have been put to more effective use. A covering artillery barrage might have helped to counter the German anti-tank fire, although a creeping barrage could have been as dangerous to the tank crews as to the Germans as gunners adjusted to the pace of the tank. Given the imagination that led to such things as supply tanks and even bridging tanks at such an early stage, it is a shame that some form of armoured personnel carrier had still to be invented. This type of vehicle would have helped the infantry to keep pace with the armour and protect them from small-arms fire and shrapnel.

Manpower shortages were a growing problem on both sides as the war progressed, as shown by the difficulties in munitions production, and it is hard to believe that large numbers of men were still kept in mounted units, waiting for an opportunity that never came, and would never come. Trench warfare, barbed wire and machine-gun fire, as well as high-explosive shells and the risk of shrapnel, all told against the use of mounted cavalry. Yet the generals ignored the evidence of their own eyes and retained their cavalry units. The effort expended in moving fodder and providing drinking water for the horses should have been sufficient to force a review of their effectiveness, for once this was taken into account, they would be seen to be not simply a wasting asset, but a liability.

NOTES

1. Richard Holmes, *The Western Front* (London, BBC Books, 1999).
2. Liddell Archive, University of Leeds.

Four

WHEN THE ROYAL NAVY LOST THE PLOT: THE CONVOY WAR, 1917

As the First World War dragged on, the Germans resorted to unrestricted submarine warfare in an attempt to deny the British the food, fuel and munitions essential to survival.

At the outbreak of the First World War, the Royal Navy was the world's largest; the result of a policy that the British fleet should equal the total strength of the next two largest in the world. Neither the United States nor Tsarist Russia could match the might of the British fleet, which was augmented further by ships from the colonies, although these were few in number and included nothing larger than a cruiser. Far larger than the German Navy, the First World War Royal Navy has sometimes been portrayed as being technically backward. The truth was far more complicated.

The British had been among the first to introduce the steam turbine to warships, increasing speed and reducing the space needed for the engines. More importantly, steam turbines needed less height inside the hull than the old steam piston engines, which allowed better armour protection over the engine rooms. The Royal Navy had led the way in the all big-gun warship with HMS *Dreadnought*. It had also adopted the submarine, but initially without enthusiasm, at least at senior level. The same could be said about the aeroplane, again adopted with mixed feelings, although the Royal Navy had the first seaplane carriers.

Where the Germans did score is that during the immediate pre-war period, they had been able to increase output of modern ships more quickly than the British.

Despite being the world's largest, the Royal Navy saw just four major operations during the First World War years, at the Falkland Islands, off the Dogger Bank, at Jutland and in support of the Army at Gallipoli. The first two were clear successes, but hardly the major fleet action for which the two combatant navies were thirsting. This came at Jutland: the battle was indecisive, for the Royal Navy suffered the heavier losses, but German High Seas Fleet never again ventured into the open seas. Gallipoli, as already seen, was a military disaster. During the entire war, there was nothing as conclusive as Lepanto, Trafalgar or Tsushima, or the major sea battles in the Pacific and Mediterranean of the Second World War.

The First World War was the first in which the submarine became a force to be reckoned with, with the potential to be a decisive weapon. The danger of the submarine had been recognized even before the outbreak of war in 1914. Seafarers knew the threat posed by the submarine, and also by the contact mine, first used in the Crimean War.

At first, the Germans played by the so-called prize rules. This meant that merchant vessels were not attacked without prior warning, allowing time for their crews, and any passengers, to take to the ships' lifeboats, leaving the submarine or U-boat to either capture the merchantman, or sink it by gunfire or torpedoes. This chivalrous attitude didn't last for long. By the start of 1915, an unrestricted U-boat campaign was initiated within British territorial waters, on the grounds that it was a counter to the Royal Navy's blockade of German ports, including the Baltic approaches. This campaign ended in September, because U-boat losses in British coastal waters were too high for the results, with about one U-boat lost for every twenty merchant ships sunk. The ships were often small coastal vessels, which meant that the exercise was not cost-effective from the German perspective. International opprobrium had followed the sinking of the liner *Lusitania* in May 1915, and the many Americans among the casualties meant that this helped to bring the United States into the war.

The U-boat campaign did not stop, but for the rest of 1915 and throughout 1916, once again U-boat commanders were under orders to apply the prize rules. The best that could be achieved in this way was a loss of some 300,000 tons of Allied shipping per month. This was not enough to hamper the Allied war effort. As the stalemate in France continued, and the number of operational U-boats rose to more than a hundred, pressure for an unrestricted campaign increased, since with the United States now in the war, and troops being sent to Europe, international goodwill no longer mattered.

By February 1917, there were twenty-three U-boats based in Flanders, comfortably close to the English Channel supply routes for the British armies in France. It was calculated that monthly losses of 600,000 tons of merchant shipping would cripple the British war effort, and hamper that of the French. The impact was dramatic. Merchant shipping losses rose sharply to 520,000 tons in March 1917, and 860,000 tons in April. U-boats sunk 250 ships in February, 330 in March and 430 in April, and all for the loss of 4 U-boats in February, 5 the following month, and just 3 in April. The chance of Britain being starved to death was suddenly very real, as the supplies were cut by one-fifth, and because of the priority given to supporting the armed forces fighting in France and the Middle East, the full impact of the losses fell on the civilian population.

Especially during the early years, the submarine was the weapon to be feared because anti-submarine warfare was in its infancy. U-boat losses were usually the result of bad luck. Surface vessels had primitive hydrophone listening devices, and sometimes submarines, especially when operating at shallow depths, could be spotted by aircraft or airships. There were no sonar devices, and depth charges were not invented until 1915.

German strategy was twofold. They sought to reduce the size of the British merchant fleet, with losses outstripping shipbuilding. They also wished to frighten neutral vessels from carrying essential supplies to the United Kingdom, and although neutral vessels did stop voyaging to British ports at first, financial incentives soon brought them back. Yet, initially, the British Admiralty resisted suggestions that it should instigate a convoy system. There was nothing new about the concept of the convoy; it had been invented by the Romans and much later by the Spanish to protect shipping from pirates in the Mediterranean and the Caribbean respectively. Protection of merchant shipping was a prime reason for the existence of the Royal Navy, for as well as having the world's largest navy, Britain also had the world's largest merchant fleet.

Of course, there were reasons for not instigating a convoy system, such as the pressures on the fleet caused by blockading the German and Turkish fleets. The Admiralty also maintained that putting merchant shipping into convoys would only encourage the U-boats to concentrate on the convoys rather than having to seek out individual merchant ships. Convoys, by their very nature, would also have to proceed at the speed of the slowest vessel. These arguments were true up to a point. Seeking a submarine in the open sea was akin to searching for the proverbial needle in a haystack. If submarines were drawn to convoys, then at least their likely position would be known and countermeasures could be taken. The problem of proceeding at the speed of the slowest could be eased to some extent by having faster and slower convoys.

Convoys did have disadvantages. Supplies were likely to be held up as ships waited for a convoy to form and, at the receiving end, ports were likely to be working at peak pressure as a convoy arrived but were idle in between. Warehousing was also placed under pressure as convoys arrived. Some argued that U-boats looking for solitary merchant vessels had a succession of targets, as opposed to a single chance against a convoy.

A counter-argument was that if a U-boat managed to evade the escorts and get among a convoy, it did have a large number of targets to choose from, and might have many successes before being caught by escort vessels.

In May 1917, a convoy system was finally introduced, by which time a total of 120 U-boats were operational. Losses continued until the second half of the year, when U-boat losses reached 46, while new construction provided 42. The tide had started to turn. Other measures helped. A new and much improved form of mine laid at the southern end of the North Sea meant that U-boats at their forward bases in Belgium could no longer slip through the Straits of Dover, but instead had to take the lengthy route around the north of Scotland.

During 1918, 1,133 allied merchant vessels were sunk, a big reduction with just 134 of these sailing in convoy and the remainder being individual sailings. In May, 36 convoys crossed the patrol line maintained by 8 U-boats off Ireland, but only 5 convoys were attacked and just 3 merchant ships were lost.

In the end, the combined effort of the convoy system and the blockade of German ports, plus the British commander in France, Field Marshal Haig's, successful final hundred days of war, brought about German surrender. It might not have been so. The German forces in France were being reinforced by the collapse of the Russian armies on the Eastern Front, and the Germany Navy was planning to increase submarine production to new heights in 1919 and 1920.

Five

HANDING RUSSIA TO THE BOLSHEVIKS: ALLIED INTERVENTION IN RUSSIA, 1918–20

Aimed originally at keeping Russia in the First World War, to maintain the Eastern Front, Allied intervention remained after the Armistice to assist the White Russians.

Russia's revolution was in two stages, in March and November 1917, with unrest and upheaval in between, while the country continued to try to fight a war with its arch-rival, Germany. Russia had entered the twentieth century as one of the most unsettled of the great powers. Long before the Bolshevik Revolution, it had been in a state of unrest, with the earliest uprisings starting in 1905. It has been claimed that Germany needed the unifying force of the First World War, but it can also be claimed that Russia finally fell apart under the strains of war. Dates can be confusing since Russia was at this stage using the Old Style calendar, so events taken to have occurred in November by western standards actually took place in October using Russian dating, hence the 'October Revolution'.

The first stage, in March, saw the abdication of the Tsar, and the establishment of a provisional government. The Provisional government assured the Allies of its continued support for the war against Germany and Austro-Hungary, the Central Powers, but the assurances were worthless, as it soon emerged that the Provisional government was not in full control. Power was being shared with the Soviet of Soldiers' and Workmen's Deputies at the then capital, Petrograd – the so-called Petrograd Soviet, or Council. The Soviet was in control of such key areas of the economy as the central bank and treasury, post offices and railway stations.

Throughout the spring, Russia's military effectiveness melted away along with the winter snow, and by late July, Russian forces on the Eastern Front were in full retreat. This didn't stop Kerensky, the unpopular Minister for War, from becoming Prime Minister. Kornilov, commander of the Russian Eighth Army, and one of the few successful commanders, became Commander-in-Chief. Almost immediately he started to plan a military *coup d'etat*, hoping for the support of the many Russians who were beginning to have second thoughts about the revolution. Neither was to hold his post for long. Kerensky sacked Kornilov, losing the support of liberal members of the Provisional government. Then, on 12 September, the Petrograd Soviet embraced what was in effect a full Communist programme, including the creation of a republic, and Kerensky himself was soon replaced. While this was going on, the Germans were advancing through the Baltic provinces, reaching Riga in September.

The second stage, the actual Bolshevik Revolution, started on 7 November, although to the Russians, using their Old Style calendar, this date was 25 October – 'Red October'. Early in the morning of 8 November, at 0100 hr, Red Guards imprisoned ministers of the Provisional Government. Kerensky, away from Petrograd, raised a force of Cossacks, which reached the outskirts the following day, and might have taken the capital if the force had included a small body of infantry. Four days later, a brief skirmish with the Red Guards forced the Cossacks back, while Kerensky fled from Russia by way of Murmansk. By 15 November, Provisional government forces in Moscow had also collapsed, leaving the Bolsheviks free to seize power.

Ten days later, elections were held for a Constituent Assembly, with the Bolsheviks taking just 25 per cent of votes, against almost 60 per cent for the more moderate Social Revolutionaries, and 13 per cent for liberals and conservatives. The main rivals to the Bolsheviks, the Mensheviks, had almost disappeared. Lenin assumed leadership of the revolution and delayed the Constituent Assembly from meeting until 18 January 1918, when it was broken up by the Red Guards. It never met again. Earlier, on 20 November, Kornilov's successor, General Dukhonin, had been ordered to negotiate an armistice with the Central Powers. In the absence of a central government he refused and was immediately sacked, being replaced by an ensign, Krilenko, who succeeded in negotiating an armistice on 28 November. The appointment of such a junior officer was not lost on the remaining senior officers, who followed their men in deserting.

It took until March 1918 for Russia's participation in the First World War to finally end, with the Treaty of Brest-Litovsk, which was highly controversial in Russia. It gave Germany the countries of Poland and Lithuania, as well as the western part of Latvia. The Bolsheviks had tried to delay signing the treaty, but this led the Germans to launch a fresh onslaught in late February, occupying Romania and the Ukraine, and securing access to the Black Sea. Germany had gained the granary of Russia, and Romanian coal and oil, denying these resources to Russia. It meant starvation for many Russians.

Germany was now free of the problems of the Eastern Front, and at last able to move men and equipment to the Western Front, where the Allied armies were now being joined by the Americans.

For those living in smaller countries, it is difficult to fully comprehend the size of Russia. Distances are huge. The famous Trans-Siberian Railway is 5,500 miles, or 8,800 km, in length. Siberia alone, which occupies much of Asian Russia, is 5,200 million square miles in area, compared with the 95,000 square miles of the United Kingdom. Russia at this time was even bigger than during the Soviet era, for it included many territories that subsequently became independent states.

It was not surprising that attitudes differed between communities throughout this vast country. In the north, on both sides of the Baltic, Poles, Finns and the people of the Baltic provinces all saw the chaos brought about by the German advance and the revolution as an opportunity to seize their independence. In the south, the situation was confused in the Caucasus, especially among the nationalistic Mensheviks of Georgia. In the Ukraine and in the Cossack states, independence from Moscow was declared.

While the term 'Bolshevik' means 'majority', it is estimated that the number of Bolsheviks in the whole of Russia, a nation of 175 million people at the time, amounted to no more than 250,000. Poor communications, the vast distances involved and the comparatively backward state of much of the country meant that it took more than a month for news of the coup to spread. The tide started to flow strongly against the Bolsheviks. Kaledin, the Ataman, or leader, of the Don Cossacks became the main hope for the aristocrats, senior officers and businessmen, with an influx of middle- and upper-class refugees. These included Kornilov and many other generals, who were to find Alexeiev, Kornilov's predecessor as Commander-in-Chief, hard at work establishing the Volunteer Army. A similar train of events was taking place in the Ukraine, where there already existed an organized nationalist government, the Rada. Bolsheviks in the Ukraine were disarmed and a People's, as opposed to a Soviet, Republic proclaimed.

In Finland, independence was declared and accepted at first by the Bolsheviks, to give themselves a breathing space, before bringing down the provisional Finnish government on 26 January 1918, through a general strike and action by Red Guards. War broke out between Red Guards and anti-Bolshevik forces until the landing of German forces on 3 April 1918 swung the conflict in favour of the anti-Bolsheviks.

Russia was in a worse state than ever. Without fuel and raw materials, industry ground to a halt. Without work, the mass of the population lacked the means to buy food, even if they could find any. Food was available in far-off Siberia, but lacking fuel, the railways could not move it. The Russian Orthodox Church denounced the Bolsheviks, and riots broke out across the country.

These developments encouraged the Allies to consider intervention. The interventionist powers included the United Kingdom, France, Canada, the United States and Japan, with a number of Australians and Italians. In the middle of Siberia, there was also, by accident of history, a substantial Czechoslovak force. In principle, these countries intervened to keep Russia in the war after the Treaty of Brest-Litovsk ended the war between Germany and the new Bolshevik government, but there were other reasons. Britain and France were seeking to maintain the Eastern Front, which occupied fifty-eight German and Austro-Hungarian divisions, stopping Germany from transferring forces to the hard-pressed Western Front. Japan sought to intensify its hold on Manchuria, and even absorb parts of Siberia, as part of the policy of expansion that had earlier resulted in the Russo-Japanese War. The United States was wary of Japanese ambitions. Although they also wanted to ease the pressure on the Western Front, many Americans were inclined to favour the revolution at first, before the true nature of the Bolsheviks was understood. The Canadians were there largely at the instigation of the British, because of their geographical proximity to Siberia.

The forces deployed were small, and widely scattered, but they were there to support the White Russians and their allies, and on a number of occasions these 'White' forces came close to toppling the revolution. Interventionist forces and the White Russians and other anti-Bolsheviks usually defeated far larger Red forces, benefited from anti-Bolshevik uprisings and enjoyed popular support.

Despite holding much promise, counter-revolution was bedevilled by divisions and a lack of clear aims among both the interventionist powers and the counter-revolutionaries. Inside Russia, the various Cossack groups opposed the revolution, despite rivalries between the Don Cossacks and the Kuban Cossacks. Siberian peasants were opposed to the revolution. Conditions in much of Siberia were different from those in European Russia, with farmers often owning their land. Although undoubtedly harsh in the northern areas, in climate and topography, the southern areas of Siberia were similar to the west of Canada.

Greater flexibility on the part of the White Russians would have helped their cause, but for them the aim was a single Russia, 'united and undivided'. The Finns, the Poles, the Ukrainians and the Estonians, the Latvians and the Lithuanians of the Baltic provinces all wanted independence. The Cossacks wanted autonomy at least. These natural allies were often denied the White Russians. This situation saw some curious local alliances once British forces arrived. For example, at an early stage, they found themselves fighting alongside the Finnish Bolsheviks against German occupation. This didn't last long.

Britain and France agreed to apportion themselves 'spheres of influence', with Britain being responsible for the Cossack territories, Armenia, the Caucasus and territory east of the Caspian Sea, to which northern Russia was later added, while France took responsibility for Bessarabia, the Ukraine and the Crimea. The problem was that most of these territories were not easily accessible.

By early 1918, the British War Cabinet was clear about its aims, that the Allies should provide the nucleus of a force around which the opponents of the Bolsheviks could muster, supported by economic and military assistance from the Allies. Intervention would be through the north and south of Russia, and through the Far East. The northern operation would take the major ports at Archangel and Murmansk. In the south, access would be through Persia to the Caucasus, to protect British interests in India, amid reports that the Germans were providing 300,000 rifles to hostile Persian and Afghan tribes. The decisive operation would be in the Far East, with the main force provided by Japan.

Under Major-General L.C. Dunsterville a British mission to the Caucasus was authorized in January 1918, with 150 officers and 300 NCOs, who were to organize, train and lead native troops. This operation became known as 'Dunsterforce'. The situation in the Caucasus was chaotic. The Trans-Caucasian government that seized independence after the Bolshevik Revolution was quickly replaced by a Federated Trans-Caucasus Republic, which denounced the Treaty of Brest-Litovsk. Dunsterforce was never able to act as the catalyst for a sustained counter-revolution in the Caucasus, although it did manage to deny the region's oil to Germany and Turkey at a critical period in the war.

Allied operations in northern Russia were to be longer lasting, taking control of the ports of Murmansk and Petsamo, known to the Russians as Petchanga. The Germans had an army of 55,000 men in Finland, supporting a 50,000 strong Finnish army, the 'White Finns', whose aim was independence. Initially, a small force of 150 Royal Marines landed at Murmansk in March 1918, followed by another 370 in May, joining local forces hostile to the Germans, and occupying the town. On 3 June, the British War Council sanctioned an expeditionary force to take control of a substantial area, including Archangel, 370 miles south-east of Murmansk. This was to help organize anti-Bolshevik forces, both of which reached Murmansk in late June. It was not until the end of July that a force of 100 Royal Marines with French and Polish infantry landed at Archangel, aided by a local uprising against the Reds. Landings at Petsamo followed later.

Eventually, there were almost 7,000 British and Canadian troops at Murmansk out of a total of 14,475 troops, of which 4,440 were Russian, while at Archangel, there were 6,300 British and Canadian troops out of a total of 16,000, including almost 3,000 Russians. There was also a small Royal Navy force, which had previously been engaged in protecting convoys to Russia from German submarine attack. The irony of the situation was that, while the armistice negotiations with the Germans dragged on, at one stage the Russian Bolsheviks told their local commanders in Murmansk to collaborate with the British against the Germans. At Archangel, the Bolsheviks were always the enemy.

Elsewhere, the White Russian Volunteer Army was firmly established by April 1918, and positioned on the border between the Don and Kuban Cossack territories. The field commander, General Denikin, was aware that the Don Cossack territory had been cleared of Bolshevik elements with German assistance. A new Ataman of the Don Cossacks, Krasnov, wanted an alliance with the Volunteer Army, to take the major centre of Tsaritsin (which later became Stalingrad), on the River Volga. The White leader, Alexeiev, agreed, seeing the Volga as the pivotal theatre for the war, with a substantial Czechoslovak force already in existence and fighting the Bolsheviks. The Czechs were eventually to take over most of the Trans-Siberian Railway from the Volga.

At this time, the combined Cossack, Czech and Volunteer Army force could have swept aside the ill-organized and untrained Red forces placed between the Volga and Moscow. Instead, Denikin wanted to seize the Kuban, the region between the Sea of Azov, the Black Sea and the Caucasus, to provide a secure base for the Volunteer Army. This army had just 9,000 troops and 21 artillery pieces, against 80,000 Red troops. Despite being outnumbered, in a short campaign between 25 June and 16 August, the Volunteer Army inflicted a series of defeats on the Red forces, gaining strength as they advanced, as more volunteers – objectors to the Bolsheviks and their methods – swelled their ranks. At this stage, it seemed as if the Volunteer Army, now reinforced by the Kuban Cossacks, would be unstoppable, but for its own internal divisions. The Volunteers wanted the restoration of Russia 'great, united, undivided', while the Cossacks wanted to create a federation of autonomous provinces including the Kuban, the Don, much of the Caucasus and the Terek. Once they had expelled the Bolsheviks from these areas, they wanted to stop fighting.

Both sides ignored the implications. Soviet forces would not allow the existence of an autonomous federation, and without natural boundaries the Cossacks would once again be at the mercy of the Communists. They had everything to gain by supporting the Whites. At the same time, the Whites could not triumph without the support of the Cossack forces. It didn't matter whether they wanted a united Russia rather than a federation, or even a smaller Russia surrounded by newly independent states. Without compromise they were likely to have nothing.

At first, all went well. Apart from a temporary reverse, at Stavropol on 21 September, Denikin continued to gain territory, even though by now he was fielding 40,000 troops against 150,000 Red Guards. By late October, the Whites held the territory from the Caucasus Mountains to the Caspian Sea. At this critical stage, early military success was marred by sheer bad luck. Alexeiev, the White leader and a brilliant strategist, had been invited to Siberia, with the opportunity of uniting all White forces in a coordinated campaign which the Bolsheviks would have found difficult to resist. He died suddenly on 8 October. Denikin took his place, but lacked his late leader's skill in finance and politics. After this, the White forces would never again be coordinated. They were to be drawn into too many different operations, gaining tactical victories at the cost of strategic success, giving their enemies much trouble yet failing to inflict the crippling blows essential to ultimate victory.

Failure to make the best use of the Czechs was just part of this weakness. The Czech forces had been in Russia before the outbreak of hostilities in 1914. Officially they were Austrian citizens resident in Russia, but a thousand of them had renounced Austro-Hungary and volunteered to join the Imperial Russian Army. Rejected at first by the Russians, who had ethnic minorities in their own empire, the mood changed once Russia decided to fight for the freedom of the smaller Slav nations within the Austro-Hungarian Empire. The initial force was split into small units to infiltrate the front line and encourage their fellow countrymen to desert, with such success that on one occasion 7,000 men changed sides. Nevertheless, Russian concerns over the loyalties of their new recruits, whose families suffered reprisals, meant that they were put to work on farms and in factories alongside Czech prisoners of war.

After the March revolution in 1917, objections to the formation of a large Czech corps disappeared. Eventually, the Czechs totalled 50,000 men, with the status of an Allied army. The value of the Czech forces can be judged by the fact that, by August 1918, they had reached Kazan, just 500 miles from Moscow. With the capture of the town, the Czechs and troops loyal to former members of the Constituent Assembly also gained the gold reserve of the former Imperial government. Much of this gold was passed to Admiral Kolchak, who had emerged as White leader in Siberia, and used it to purchase arms from abroad.

The Allies, stalled in their invasion through southern Russia, realized that the best means of supplying the White Russians was through the Trans-Siberian Railway, even though the distance from Vladivostok, Siberia's main port, to the Urals was 3,500 miles, and the Eastern Front had settled a thousand miles further west.

Instructions given to the American commanders in Russia were vague and contradictory, and the commanders in Siberia and the Baltic States interpreted them differently. General Graves in Siberia did little other than occupy Vladivostok. The Americans were already suspicious of Japanese motives, believing that Japan saw intervention as an excuse to hasten that country's growing stranglehold on China, and perhaps even seize part of Siberia itself.

The British and French could only spare a token force, little more than 1,000 men between them, while by November there were 72,400 Japanese troops under the command of General Kikuzo Otani, effectively in command of all Allied forces in the region. Meanwhile, a 5,000-strong Canadian Expeditionary Force had arrived. This force was supposed to advance to the Urals and establish a defence line west of Omsk, between Ekaterinburg and Cheliabinsk. British, French and Italian troops moved in October, but the bulk of the Allied force, now some 100,000 men, remained in Eastern Siberia, amid rivalry between American and Japanese commanders. The Americans opposed attempts by the Japanese to move substantial forces west. Worse still, the Trans-Siberian Railway increasingly became a pawn in this game of chess. Food supplies started to become scarce and what food there was became expensive, causing unrest behind the front line.

In Siberia a civilian government, the so-called Directory, had been formed, consisting of five prominent Russian politicians, as an interim measure until a new all-Russian Constituent Assembly could be convened. This moved to Omsk in October. It had been the Directory which had earlier invited Alexeiev to take command of its forces. After Alexeiev's death, Admiral Kolchak became the Directory's Minister for War. The Directory itself soon became embroiled in disagreements.

The British General Know reported in November 1918 that:

The Allies have never agreed. American forces . . . crowd the barracks in the Far East.

The Japanese have landed 70,000, but owing to lack of American pressure, they refuse to go beyond Irkutsk. In relation to the policy of Great Britain, France and Italy, America may be said to be neutral, while Japan is actively hostile.

The Japanese do all in their power to weaken Russia by subsidising every freebooter in the Far East and so enable them to defy the central government [the Directory] which the Allies wish to strengthen. They irritate the local population beyond endurance and among the Allies they make nothing but enemies. Their opposition to the American railway scheme has indefinitely postponed the provision of economic assistance and so immeasurably increased the difficulties of the much tried Russian Government . . .

Owing to the failure of the Americans to understand the situation and owing to the purely selfish policy of the Japanese, Allied assistance to the Russians and Czecho-Slovaks has so far been reduced to a few British sailors, one British garrison battalion, one French battalion, and a battery and a couple of Italian batteries. . . . There are also Rumanian, Polish and Serb units in formation.

Yet the present situation, though difficult, shows what magnificent results might have rewarded a sane and united policy. There can be no reasonable doubt that one Allied division or even a brigade, if pushed through to the Volga when the railway was opened in early September, would have reached Moscow before the winter, shattered Bolshevism and delivered the starving peasantry of northern Russia. . . .

Where we modestly hoped for a Russian contingent of 50,000, the Russians have raised and maintained for several weeks an army of upwards of 300,000. . . . The British Government has promised equipment for 100,000 and this is now en route. Equipment for another 100,000 will probably be sent. . . . The one thing wanting is tangible Allied force at the front. . . . The Czech Corps is tired and wants to go home. Its principal complaint is the failure of the Allies to send help to the Urals. . . .

The arrival of such a force would give new heart to the Russians and Czechs. The delay and hesitation in sending such a force is endangering the whole position. It has lost us the Volga Bridgeheads. The Russians now hold the enemy at the front, but more is required, for against a rabble like the Bolsheviks, to stand still is to confess weakness.

If we keep our promises we have a reasonable hope of reconquering European Russia in the spring. . . . If we fail to rise to the occasion, what will be the result? Bolshevism will once more overrun Russia and all Siberia. All those who trusted us will be massacred.[1]

The Armistice in November 1918 between the Allies and the Central Powers changed the situation. The British and French wanted to maintain order and support the White Russians. The Americans were non-interventionist. The Canadians wanted to go home, as did the Czechoslovaks, to realise their ambition of independence. The need to keep an Eastern Front had gone, but White and Red forces were locked in battle alongside their allies, including the Czechs. As Lord Balfour, the British Foreign Secretary, pointed out:

Recent events have created obligations which last beyond the occasions which gave them birth. The Czecho-Slovaks are our Allies and we must do what we can to help them. In the southeast corner of Russia in Europe, in territories adjacent to the White Sea and the Arctic Ocean, in Siberia, in Trans-Caucasia and Trans-Caspia, new anti-Bolshevik administrations have grown up under the shelter of Allied forces for whose existence His Majesty's Government are responsible and whom they must endeavour to support.[2]

The British saw themselves as remaining in control at Murmansk and Archangel, providing whatever help they could to Denikin, supplying military material to the Baltic States, taking the Baku–Batum railway and continuing to support the Czechs. But of course, the Czechs now wanted to extricate themselves from Siberia. In Canada, public opinion was moving against any commitment to Russia, with militant trade unionists presenting the Bolsheviks in a favourable light and the Whites as supporters of the *ancien régime.*

After the Armistice, the Directory was overthrown, and Admiral Kolchak became dictator. Kolchak had divided his forces into three armies, but he had no control over forces outside

Siberia. He had the Northern Army, based on Ekaterinburg, and in the centre was the Western Army, which was based on the forces raised by the Constituent Assembly, and in the south, appropriately enough, the Southern Army, consisting largely of Cossack units.

The Northern Army commenced a planned winter offensive on 18 December, and rapid progress was made, taking Perm on 24 December. No less than 30,000 prisoners of the Bolsheviks were released, and the liberators found 4,000 railway wagons stuffed with goods looted from shops, factories and homes. Having made such good progress in the face of the Russian winter, the Northern Army was soon halted, not by the Bolsheviks or the weather, but by the bad management of the railway by a protégé of the Japanese, Grigori Mikhailovich Semenov. Semenov was at best a local warlord, with an irregular army that had plundered and pillaged Siberia, often forcing many peasants into the arms of the Bolsheviks in desperation. The Japanese gave him control of the railway, and in so doing condemned the armies in the west and the communities in between to an acute shortage of the necessities of life – and war.

The Americans were not free of blame. The Japanese had the railway, or at least most of it. The Americans had the warehouses in Vladivostok packed with supplies – some estimates go as high as 750,000 tons – of war material, which had been provided by the Allies for the use of the Tsar's forces. There was even a submarine. General Graves refused to issue these supplies until peace had been restored.

A French attempt to coordinate events in Siberia – with a single commander, General Maurice Janin, taking command of all forces west of Baikal – floundered on Russian objections to a foreign commander, although the idea had British support. The Japanese intervened again, asking for territory, including the northern half of Sakhalin Island and part of Kamchatka, as well as control of the Chinese Eastern Railway, which was in effect a major branch and alternative route for the

Trans-Siberian Railway. In return, they would send a large army to western Siberia to crush the Bolsheviks in two months.

With the coming of spring, Kolchak was able to deploy his armies more widely. Logic should have dictated that his main thrust should have been southwards, en route for the Volga in order to link up with Denikin, and a step towards a single united White Russian front. Instead, the three armies, with just 100,000 men between them, advanced on three fronts, making a front line of more than 700 miles. The Southern Army was supposed to link up with Denikin, and the Northern with the forces coming south from Archangel. Rivalry broke out between the Northern and Western Armies for scarce supplies.

Even so, at first, the front advanced. By May, the Whites had a substantial chunk of European Russia. Further victories by Denikin's Volunteer Army, smashing no less than four Red armies in May, caused even Lenin to have doubts, telling the Revolutionary Military Council, 'if we don't conquer the Urals before winter . . . the destruction of the Revolution is inevitable'.[3]

Nevertheless, Canadian resistance to the involvement in Russia saw withdrawal start on 21 April 1919. This put the British in a difficult position, since their small force in Siberia depended on Canadian logistics. The Canadians refused to leave even a token logistics unit behind, forcing the British to withdraw as well. The symbolism of the loss of his staunchest ally was the first step towards the collapse of Kolchak's initiatives. Meanwhile, in the north, the British had decided that continued occupation of the White Sea ports could only be justified for as long as the prospect remained of the forces there being able to link up with a drive by Allied forces from the east. Victory could not come from the north alone, it could only contribute to a White victory by, for example, catching Red forces in a pincer movement. During the first winter after peace in the rest of Europe, British commanders in northern Russia concentrated on securing their positions, while also helping anti-Soviet movements to resist Bolshevik pressure. This second consideration also meant that a push south was called for, to secure an area with a larger population, from which recruits could be obtained.

Nevertheless, Allied efforts were marred by sheer stupidity. Attacking in temperatures 20 degrees below freezing, Allied forces in the north attempted to advance south to take the town of Plesetskaya, with a flanking attack, on 30 December. They took Kodish, a short distance to the east of their objective, and might have taken Plesetskaya but for two unrelated but disastrous episodes by two of the commanders involved. Firstly, the British commander of a machine-gun company neglected to order his men to attack Russian forces retreating from Kodish, because he had 'succumbed to the festivities of the season'.[4] Secondly, the Russian Archangel Regiment failed to appear, because its commanding officer thought the day unpropitious for an assault. Having taken a gamble by attacking in poor weather, the opportunity to catch enemy troops in full retreat had been missed.

A further attempt to advance south in February was far more successful. Despite temperatures 40 degrees below freezing, the Allies took three small towns on 18 February.

Plans for a spring offensive were made but complicated by an uprising by the Karelians, who demanded separation from Russia and incorporation within Finland. Again, the problem lay with the White desire for a single united Russia. The Finns, who had stalled in a late April advance against the Bolsheviks, wanted Allied assistance, but this ran up against north Russian objections. Nevertheless, the tide of Finnish nationalism could not be stopped and by the end of July, Red forces had been forced out of much of what was to become Finnish territory.

In the south, meanwhile, Denikin advanced on too wide a front in the euphoria of a succession of victories during the summer of 1919. At one stage, he controlled the Don country, much of the eastern Ukraine with the Donetz Basin, and the region north of the Sea of Azov. The timing was wrong. Had Denikin been a month or two earlier, or Kolchak's forces a month or two later, a link between the two could have been established, but by June 1919 Kolchak's forces were in retreat. Although the Whites continued to enjoy victories throughout July and August, even getting to within 250 miles of Moscow by October, increasingly their operations degenerated into a series of large-scale raids rather than a strategic advance. The Ukraine proved to be a costly diversion, and it would have made better military sense for it to have been bypassed, with White guerrilla activity to tie down Red forces.

During the autumn of 1919, a White force raised in the Baltic had advanced towards Petrograd, the former Imperial capital, again holding the tantalizing possibility of a pan-Russian White front stretching from the Baltic to the Black Sea. Originally created in Estonia, this force was known as the White Russian North-Western Force. This ran into the difficulty that the Estonian support was half-hearted, yet again because of the White Russian insistence on a single united Russia.

Ideally, any attack on Petrograd needed to be coordinated with a move by Denikin against Moscow, the capital following the revolution. Yudenitch, the commander, wanted to invade while the Bolsheviks were still in disarray. He also feared that if his army remained inactive, desertions might reduce its strength – it had already fallen to 20,000 from a peak of 25,000. Yudenitch hoped for support from the other Baltic States, but this was lost among a series of internal squabbles.

At the outset, Yudenitch's campaign proved successful when he moved forward at the beginning of October. His troops were better trained, better motivated and better led than those of the Bolsheviks, whose resistance crumbled at the sight of his four British tanks. Yudenitch planned to move along the route of the railway line to Petrograd, while forces would be deployed to cut the other lines radiating out from the city, making the movement of reinforcements difficult. Unfortunately, as they neared the old capital, a force sent to cut the main Moscow–Petrograd railway line failed to achieve its objective because its commander was so confident that Petrograd would fall, that he wanted to be among the first victorious troops to enter the city. This was to prove fatal, as troops were hastily sent from Moscow to Petrograd.

On 20 October, the North-Western Force was at the outskirts of Petrograd, fully expecting to enter the city the next day. It was as close as they would get. On 21 October, Red forces counter-attacked, and the intense fighting continued for two days. By the evening of 23 October, the exhausted White troops were forced back. Although Yudenitch was able to hold out at Gatchina, launching raids against the Red forces and hoping in vain for an uprising in Petrograd, on 3 November Red forces diverted from the south drove him back into Estonia. By this time, the Estonian authorities had concluded a truce with the Bolsheviks, leaving the White Russians with the alternatives of capture by the Soviets or internment. They chose the latter.

Despite efforts by Winston Churchill, by this time Secretary of State for War, a concerted Allied policy in support of the White forces could not be agreed. Churchill was confident that substantial numbers of volunteers could be assembled, and war materials, with so much left over from the war years, could be provided in greater quantities.

Matters had started to go desperately wrong in Siberia. Kolchak had done extremely well, despite attempting to fight on three fronts. The Northern Army was between Perm and Viatka, the Western Army was just 500 miles from Moscow, and the Southern Army was just 30 miles from the Volga. Yet, these successes held the key to Kolchak's impending defeat. Supplies were scarce, and the supply lines, far from satisfactory even at the outset of the campaign, were now stretched to breaking point. Manpower and equipment were both spread extremely thinly. Attempts to recruit extra men from the newly occupied steppe country showed poor results, with insufficient instructors and equipment, so that the partially trained troops tended to desert once setbacks were encountered. By this time, too, the energetic and far-sighted intervention of Trotsky, no mean strategist himself, meant that better-quality forces were being fielded by the Bolsheviks.

The first big defeat for Kolchak's White Russians came during April 1919. A strong Red army struck at the Western Army, whose front was spread over a hundred miles, quickly making a breakthrough. This was bad enough, but a Ukrainian regiment then mutinied, killed its officers and deserted to the Bolsheviks. A wedge was driven between the White Armies. The Northern Army, which could have done something to help, continued to pursue an advance of its own. By 9 June, the Western Army had been driven back to Ufa, from where the three armies had started their offensive. Red forces now began an attempt to cut off the Northern Army, or at least press for its withdrawal, while also sending strong forces south to prevent the Southern Army linking up with Denikin's Volunteer Army, and drive a way through to Turkestan to join an isolated Red force. The Northern Army was soon in full retreat. At this stage, the situation might still have been saved, had reserves been amassed at Omsk. Perm fell on 3 July, followed by Ekaterinburg on 14 July. From this time onwards, the White forces were in retreat.

In January 1920, a new government was formed at Irkutsk, many of whom were strongly opposed to Kolchak, who was left to make his escape with the Imperial treasure. He joined a retreating Czech regiment on a train decorated with the flags of the Allies, but the new administration at Irkutsk demanded that the French commander, General Janin, hand Kolchak over to them. The train was surrounded, Kolchak was seized and imprisoned, while the regime at Irkutsk also gained the Imperial treasure of gold bullion worth 650 million roubles, or £65 million (US $325 million) at the then exchange rate, and a similar amount in valuables and securities. These sums, by coincidence, were about equal to the value of British and French supplies for the White armies during 1919 – when Britain had delivered £100 million of goods and munitions, and France between £30 and £40 million.

Within a few days, a Soviet Military Revolutionary Committee took over at Irkutsk. On 7 February, before dawn, Kolchak was murdered by a firing squad, working in the light of a truck's headlamps, and his body pushed through an ice hole into a river.

The White Russians had made serious mistakes, advancing on too wide a front, and failing to give priority to a link-up between Kolchak's forces and those of Denikin. The insistence on a single united Russia was another error, for surely it would have been better to save part of the nation than to lose all of it? The quest for autonomy and even independence by some of the less-well-situated states was also a misjudgement – Poland and Finland had the chance of independence, as did the small Baltic States, but for the Cossack territories, without defensible natural borders, it was an unworkable dream. It was not until the North-Western Force failed to take Petrograd that recognition was given by Kolchak to the desire of the Baltic States for independence, while Finland had to wait until May 1919.

The interventionist powers must also take some of the blame. They did not try to influence their White Russian allies, and instead of organizing themselves into a force around which anti-Bolshevik elements of all kinds could have mustered, they resorted to their own rivalries and political objectives.

During the early summer of 1918, support for the anti-Bolshevik cause was almost universal throughout Siberia, and the action of the Czechs was widely supported, yet failure still came. Meddling by the Allies which prevented the Whites from having full access to the mountain of supplies at Vladivostok, also impeded them from making full use of the Trans-Siberian Railway, essential for the civil population as well as for the military. Japan in particular stands accused of fermenting unrest that did so much to undermine the White Russian cause.

Had Kolchak adopted Lenin's sense of expediency, and been prepared to reverse any concessions later, having secured his political objectives in the meantime, the course of history might have been changed. Kolchak, like Denikin, was not prepared to concede anything that would affect his dream of a single Russia. This policy has been enduring regardless of who controls Russia, and the possibility exists that whatever the outcome of the Russian Civil War, the country could still have had a troubled twentieth century. Russia could also have been a difficult neighbour, regardless of the form of government chosen. After all, the Tsar did not always enjoy the support, still less the affection, of the other European powers.

NOTES

1. E.M. Halliday, *The Ignorant Armies* (London, 1961).
2. John Swettenham, *Allied Intervention in Russia 1918–1919, and the Part Played by Canada* (London, George Allen & Unwin, 1967).
3. Ibid.
4. Ibid.

Six

RESISTING THE BEAR: THE WINTER WAR, 1939–40

An attempt by the Soviet Union to regain the territory lost when Finland declared independence after the Bolshevik Revolution, taking Karelia with it.

On 14 October 1939, Finland was issued with a set of territorial demands by its much larger neighbour, the Soviet Union. Finland had gained its independence during the chaos of the Bolshevik Revolution, and was determined to maintain it. The Soviet demands were almost immediately rejected. The Soviet dictator, Joseph Stalin, scrapped a non-aggression pact with Finland on 28 October, and two days later started the invasion.

Finnish nationalism had been a force to be reckoned with long before the Russia Revolution. As with many of the ethnic minorities within Russia, the Finns had little in common with other European Russians. For a start, the language was different and, strangely, related to Magyar, the language of Hungary. Until the nineteenth century, Finnish territory had been the cause of rivalry between Russia and Sweden, before becoming part of Imperial Russia. The Russian Revolution gave the Finns the opportunity for which they had been waiting. Better still, the confusion and lack of effective organization in Russia which followed, including the Russian Civil War which lasted from 1918 to 1920, meant that the new regime had to accept the loss of Finland.

For many years after the revolution, the leaders of the emerging Soviet Union had far more interesting objectives at the outset, including annexation of the Ukraine, a country with rich natural resources including fertile farmlands. The Soviet Union suffered from internal troubles, with forced collectivization and then the Stalinist purges. Memories of the Allied intervention on the side of the White Russians were still fresh, so there can be little doubt that the Soviet leadership had been left with at least the suspicion that any attempt to invade Finland would result in British and American support for that country. This view was almost certainly correct, for despite massive defence cuts in the United Kingdom and growing support for isolationism in the United States, both countries feared the spread of Bolshevism.

The eruption of war in Europe in September 1939 changed this. The time was right, and Finland, with just 4 million people, appeared relatively small and vulnerable to Soviet military superiority.

The outbreak of the Second World War provided the opportunity the Soviet Union was waiting for. Britain and France had failed to provide any direct help for Poland, despite declaring war as a result of Germany's invasion of that country, so the Poles were left to resist German, and then Soviet, aggression alone. Once Poland was defeated and occupied, clearly neither Britain nor France could consider helping Finland, which had no strategic value to either country, when preoccupied with a war with Germany. The Germans, at this time officially 'allies' of the Soviet Union as the result of a non-aggression pact, controlled the most direct and important supply routes across the Baltic to Finland. It was also plain that the United States was not interested in foreign conflicts, and was even anxious to distance itself from foreign entanglements.

Despite Russian participation in the invasion of Poland, it was not until 14 December 1939, after the Russo-Finnish War started, that Russia was expelled from the League of Nations, the unsuccessful and toothless interwar predecessor of the United Nations. Poland had given the Russians the impression that blitzkrieg tactics would win the day. They had done so for

Germany in the invasion of Poland, which had allowed the Soviet Union to invade its agreed portion of that country, once Poland's heroic, but antiquated, armed forces had been crippled by the German onslaught. Soviet and German tactics had much in common: both believed in the concept of blitzkrieg, or lightning war, with the air forces given army support as their main function. Both armies believed in the tank and the paratrooper. It was the Russians who had been the leaders in developing the concept of airborne assault, even if it fell to the Germans to put this into practice a little later. But Finland was not Poland, and the time of year also meant that the meteorological conditions were not auspicious for attack.

Russian technology at the time was relatively primitive – the result both of the isolation of the country for the first twenty years after the revolution and the loss of many of the best and most inventive minds at the time of the revolution. Given the technology of the day, it would have been hard to find vehicles suitable for the arctic conditions encountered by Russian troops. But no one dared object, regardless of their rank, for the Stalinist purges had already seen the army lose upwards of half its officers, including many of the most experienced. Military questions were in any case subordinate to political ones, with each unit having a political commissar who could overrule its commanding officer. Troops were told that if they became prisoners of war, they would be imprisoned on being released, and that if they failed to achieve their objectives, their families would suffer. The cruelty of the regime was enough for these arguments to be convincing. In battle, many committed suicide rather than surrender.

The frozen Finnish tundra and forest was not the sun-baked Polish plain. Weapons and vehicles were unusable, including the tanks on which the Russians were to depend so heavily. The tanks skidded on the ice and motor vehicles became embedded in snowdrifts up to 10 ft deep. Beneath the snow in some areas, the ground was swampy during the day, and men who sank into this mess during the day were frozen in it by night as temperatures plummeted after dark. The transport system could not keep pace with the demand for food – so important in such freezing conditions. Soldiers immobilized by their wounds froze to death before they could be taken to a medical centre. However, if they could walk – as reported in the case of a wounded Finn, shot six times in the chest – they were able to make their way to receive medical help because, in the low temperatures, wounds bled so slowly.

The Russians had not taken even the most elementary preparations, despite the size of the Soviet armed forces and Russia's vast arctic regions. The troops sent into battle lacked adequate clothing, suitable tents, or even any tents at all in many cases. The transport system was not capable of sustaining combat, and no forward reserves of food, fuel or munitions had been established. The troops had not received any special training. None of this was surprising. The purges had left the Russians short of senior officers with practical experience, and even fewer risked taking an initiative.

The Russian Army deployed twenty divisions against Finland, a force of around 400,000 men. The infantry had to march the 200 miles from the railway at Murmansk, and lost a substantial part of its strength as men dropped out through frostbite. By contrast, the heavily outnumbered Finns had mobility, with good-quality skis and clothing.

The initial Russian assault on the Finnish Mannerheim Line was quickly checked, while further north, two incursions at Salla and Suomussalmi were repulsed. After the initial setbacks, the Russians renewed their assault in February, with an artillery barrage and advance at Summa in the south during February. Due to their overwhelming force, on 14 February 1940, Soviet forces overran Finland's forward positions. Despite fierce Finnish resistance, on 26 February the Finns lost the island fortress of Kolvisto, and were also forced to retreat from the port of Petsamo, north of the Arctic Circle. A second assault in the south, across the frozen Gulf of Finland, cutting off the town of Viipuri, led the Finnish government to put out peace feelers on 6 March.

Given the closed nature of Soviet society, and the desire to keep bad news away from anyone in authority, there have been no reliable statistics. A later Russian leader, Nikita Krushchev, estimated that a million Russian soldiers died in the campaign, against a known 25,000 Finns killed and 61 aircraft destroyed. He also claimed that Russia lost more than 1,000 aeroplanes, more than 2,000 tanks and vast quantities of supplies. Krushchev, of course, had every reason to exaggerate the losses in his campaign to discredit the Stalin regime, but there can be little doubt that this was a bloody campaign, with much waste. More recent and impartial estimates of Soviet losses suggest 200,000 men, some 700 aircraft and 1,600 tanks.

Throughout, the Finns fought a highly mobile war, with well-equipped and camouflaged troops. Yet neither side could be pleased with the outcome. The Soviet Union failed in its objective, but when peace came in this short war, on 13 March 1940, Finland had to cede the Karelia Isthmus and a major military base in the Hango Peninsula, as well as the town of Viipuri, to Russia.

Coming on top of the losses incurred through the Stalinist purges, these losses also placed the Soviet forces in poor condition to face the future threat from Germany. Indeed, the impression this gave of Soviet bungling and incompetence led Hitler to believe that Operation Barbarossa, the German invasion of the Soviet Union, could not fail. Stalin's paranoia and self-delusion nearly proved him right.

Meanwhile, Finland was drawn inevitably and not necessarily by choice into the Axis camp, depending on Germany for arms and equipment with which to counter any possible future Soviet onslaught. At first, the launch of Operation Barbarossa helped Finland, with the recovery of those areas ceded in the peace of March 1940. Finnish independence and the desire for neutrality reasserted itself when, in August 1941, the Germans asked the

Finnish General Mannerheim to advance beyond the recovered territory and cut off Leningrad, but he refused.

The Finnish desire not to be caught in the middle of a war between Nazi Germany and the Soviet Union was to be dashed. Once the Soviet counter-attack had gained sufficient momentum, in June 1944, and sufficient forces could be spared from the main onslaught against German forces, an offensive was launched against the Finns. Once again, Soviet forces took the Karelia Isthmus and Viipuri, but on this occasion they respected the 1940 border. Even so, the Finns rejected Soviet peace overtures until 4 September 1944, when it was clear that Germany was losing the war. A German attempt to land at Hogland was repulsed by Finnish troops. Nevertheless, postwar Finland was forced into neutrality and was unable to ally itself with the NATO countries or seek armed neutrality along the lines followed by Sweden.

Seven

NO PLANS FOR THE REAL WAR: THE FALL OF FRANCE, 1940

The German attack on France and the Low Countries in the spring of 1940 was brilliantly executed.

On the eve of the outbreak of war in 1939, the British had moved troops and aircraft to France. The British Expeditionary Force fielded by the British Army consisted of twelve divisions. Unlike the German Army, it was fully mechanized and all of its infantry could be moved quickly. Its equipment varied, the 25-pounder field gun was regarded as very good, while although the Matilda tank was difficult to knock out, it lacked a gun capable of engaging German forces at a worthwhile range.

The quickness of the British response to the threat to France was misleading. A far better idea of the readiness of the combatants at the outset of the Second World War can be gained from their respective descriptions of the first autumn and winter of the war. To the British, this was the period of the 'phoney war'; to the Germans, it was the 'sitting war'. There had been very little that was 'phoney' about the early months for many in the air forces and the navies, as bombers were shot down and ships were sunk. Conversely, once the Germans had occupied Poland, the opposing armies did just 'sit'. For the British and French forces this meant gathering behind the Maginot Line, constructed to protect France after the trauma of the First World

73

War. Unfortunately, the Maginot Line did not extend all the way from Switzerland to the English Channel. It stopped short, at the border with Belgium. While British and French war plans recognized the importance of providing support for Belgium, Belgium and the Netherlands were both neutral.

The British Army of the interwar years differed from those of continental Europe in that it was relatively small and based on long-service professionals, with a reserve, the Territorial Army. It has been regarded as being unable to expand quickly in a crisis, due to insufficiently strong and experienced reserve forces. Before the outbreak of war, conscription had been introduced alongside rapid expansion of the reserves. The British practice was to devolve considerable decision-making to the generals in the field.

By contrast, the French Army was on the continental pattern, that is with the majority of the troops being conscripts, other than in the colonial forces to which were allocated most of the regular personnel. Mobilization of its considerable reserve forces was necessary to bring the force up to its full strength. Despite the lessons of the First World War, the French made considerable use of horses, and even had horses in two out of the army's three cavalry divisions. Armour and artillery varied, with some equipment dating back to the First World War, and modern weapons, such as the 47-mm anti-tank gun, in short supply. The age and the variety of equipment in use, including no less than eight different types of tank, provided considerable logistics problems. This was topped by a cumbersome command structure, with limited power delegated to generals in the field.

Although the German Army was also a conscript force, it was built around a strong corps of regular professional officers and senior NCOs. It was a massive force, ready and waiting for the outbreak of war, with 2 million men in 106 divisions available in 1939, but, after the Polish campaign, it expanded by a further 50 per cent, with another 1 million men in 44 new divisions. The Nazi Party's Waffen SS provided another 3 divisions, while the Luftwaffe provided the paratroops, which amounted to another division at this time, although later a second paratroop division was added. Although viewed as the most efficient fighting machine of its day, with its 10 Panzer tank divisions and 4 motorized divisions, the German Army was heavily dependent on horses for transport and for the movement of artillery pieces.

In the air, the bulk of the Royal Air Force was kept in Britain, but an Advanced Air Striking Force (AASF) accompanied the BEF to France, with 456 aircraft, of which 261 were fighters, 135 light bombers and 60 reconnaissance aircraft. Even this was less impressive than the figures suggest, for many of the aircraft were obsolescent, with the impact of a few modern fighters and bombers diluted by a mass of elderly aircraft. Best of the fighters were Hawker Hurricanes, highly regarded by their pilots for their manoeuvrability, but without the speed and rate of climb or, on the early versions, the heavy cannon of their German counterparts. Most of the fighters were Gloster Gladiators, the RAF's last biplane fighters. Bombers included a few Vickers Wellingtons, the RAF's heaviest bombers at the time and aircraft which were both rugged and useful, but the remainder were Handley Page Hampden medium bombers and most were the Fairey Battle light bombers. The Fairey Battle had been an attempt to create a single-engined monoplane bomber with the performance of a fighter, but it failed on both counts as it was outclassed by the fighters of the day, and unable to deliver a worthwhile warload.

The French Armée de l'Air shared many of the equipment problems suffered by the French Army; it had some excellent new aircraft, such as the Bloch MB 151 and Morane-Saulnier MS 406 fighters, but too few. Many of the 400-plus French fighters were obsolete.

The Luftwaffe by contrast had the Messerschmitt Bf 109 fighter, which despite some weaknesses, was faster and more heavily armed than anything the RAF or Armée de l'Air could put into the air. It had overwhelming superiority in bomber aircraft, including the Junkers Ju 87 Stuka dive-bomber, and Dornier Do 17 and Heinkel He 111 medium bombers, whose crews were experienced in providing the strong tactical support required by ground commanders. Unlike its opponents, the Luftwaffe had modern aircraft in quantity, with 3,000 bombers ready for the Battle of France.

Belgium had no tanks in its army, and just four anti-tank guns. The equipment of its armed forces was poor, and the belief was that in an attack, British and French forces would come to the country's aid. While this was true, there was no system of joint command and there had been no joint exercises because Belgium was neutral. Belgium did not have a true equivalent to the Maginot Line, but its defence was also based on strongly defended fixed positions, including the forts covering the bridges at Eben Emael, overlooking the junction of the Albert Canal and the River Meuse. These modern forts were to be seen as major obstacles by the Germans.

The Netherlands also placed its faith in a policy of neutrality. Its forces were badly equipped and under strength, with the best forces deployed in the Netherlands East Indies.

In the Maginot Line, the French believed that they had an insurmountable permanent defence against any new German invasion. Built between 1930 and 1935, it consisted of a line of 'interdependent fortified regions'. The actual line consisted of three separate zones of defence. The first of these consisted of anti-tank obstacles, entanglements and pillboxes. The second zone consisted of larger concrete casemates and anti-tank ditches. Combined, these two provided a killing zone in which enemy forces could be delayed while heavy artillery fire was brought down upon them from the forts, the third zone, 5 miles behind the second zone. Built between 3 and 5 miles apart, the forts were constructed of concrete and the largest could accommodate 1,200 men. In preparation for a long siege, the occupants even had luxuries such as sun-lamp rooms, while the largest forts had electric railways to move munitions, and gun turrets that could be recessed out of sight. The line stretched from the Swiss frontier to the Ardennes region of Belgium. Consideration had been given to an extension along the Belgian frontier, but the additional cost and the impact this would have on relations between France and Belgium meant that the idea was quietly dropped.

Germany's early successes during the Second World War have often been presented as consecutive victories based on fighting just one major campaign at a time, but this is not completely true. While British and French forces were heavily preoccupied with the Norwegian campaign, which lasted until early June, the Germans struck westwards through the Netherlands and Belgium on 10 May 1940.

The Belgians had effectively buried their heads in the sand. They recognized the likelihood of an invasion by the Germans, but they maintained strict neutrality, even though the importance of British and French help was appreciated. They even held back on the deployment of forces to resist any German invasion until the attack developed. This inaction was incomprehensible, for it continued even after a German aircraft force-landed on Belgian territory on 7 January 1940, giving the Belgians a German plan for the invasion of their country. The Germans revised their plans as a result of this, but the Belgians ignored this early warning.

The Maginot Line, however, was seen as too big a fortification to be tackled head on, over most of its length, while the Belgian forts were also treated with respect. Unnecessary loss of life and waste of equipment at the outset of what was likely to be the most intensely contested campaign of the war so far was to be avoided. Such obstacles required an innovative solution, sometimes credited to Hitler himself. A force of seventy-eight specially trained engineers from the Seventh Airborne Division using ten DFS 230 gliders were to land on the roof of Fort Eben Emael and around it. They would use specially designed 'shaped' charges to blow holes in the roof and sides of the fort. This was to be part of a larger deployment of thirty-one gliders to seize the main crossings into Belgium.

At 0430 hr on 10 May, the force became airborne behind the towing Junkers Ju 52/3m transports. Dividing into their respective groups, a problem arose when the leader of the Eben Emael force was left behind in Germany after his glider's tow broke. The rest of his men continued, and by the time their leader caught up with them in a fresh glider at 0830 hr, their mission had been accomplished, keeping the 1,200 men inside the fort entombed for twenty-four hours while the Fourth Panzer Division crossed into Belgium and secured the position. The massive fortification was neutralized for the loss of just six German dead and another twenty wounded. Meanwhile, the remaining gliders and their occupants successfully secured the bridges at Velchrezelt and Vroenhoven, taking these intact; a last-minute plea by the defenders at Velchrezelt to destroy the bridge was refused by a disbelieving duty officer at headquarters. The bridge at Kanne was blown, after German gliders had been unable to land close enough to maintain the element of surprise; permission came from the luckless defenders of Eben Emael who had every reason to accept that an invasion was in full swing.

One cannot help but sympathize with the plight of the defenders. Few could have foreseen the speed of the German advance and the skill and coordination exercised by the invading Germans, who were never again going to display such brilliance in attack.

While the Belgians were struggling with the seizure of their bridges and forts by glider-landed troops, the Dutch were surprised by paratroops landing in a long carpet to seize the bridges at Moerdijk and Dordrecht, and over the Nieuw Maas at Rotterdam, as well as securing the airfield at Waalhaven. Despite heavy fighting at Waalhaven, 250 troop-carrying aircraft managed to land during the day. This was an audacious attempt to take control of a 30-mile stretch of the Netherlands along the route of the advancing Panzer armies. The paratroops had started landing at 0500 hr, with the main force augmented by others, seizing the airfields at Delft and The Hague, so that air-landed troops could be flown in force, ready to seize the Dutch Royal Family and the leaders of the main political parties.

Given the element of surprise, the Dutch did well to mount a stiff resistance, but this failed largely due to their reluctance to destroy the bridges, in the hope that if lost these could be recaptured. It was to no avail. The Luftwaffe paratroops managed to seize the bridge at Moerdijk and hold it for two days against strong Dutch counter-attacks until relieved by an advancing Panzer Division on 12 May.

Elsewhere, the Germans suffered heavy losses with, for example, eleven out of thirteen Junkers Ju 52/3m transports assigned to take Ypenburg shot down. The infantry division delegated to take The Hague suffered heavy losses after only 2,000 out of 7,000 troops were landed or dropped, causing the attempt to seize the Dutch capital to be cancelled. The division's troops were redirected to the battle for Rotterdam, and the Dutch government only surrendered after this important city and port was bombed.

The invasion of the Netherlands and Belgium diverted French troops from the developing Battle of France, as these hastened north to help defend the Netherlands. It also diverted attention from the German advance through the Ardennes, where the Panzer units in particular would have been vulnerable to a well-orchestrated aerial attack and well-planned anti-tank ground forces as they struggled through the narrow roads of the forests.

The invading Germans set themselves three objectives as they swept through Belgium and the Netherlands, ready to seize France, their prime objective. First, they wanted a rapid advance by the Panzer divisions to the coast, taking the mouth of the Somme beyond Abbeville. This would create a 'Panzer corridor'. The second objective was the destruction of the Franco-British force in Flanders, to the north of the corridor, while the third was to overwhelm what was left of the French Army to the south of the corridor.

Crossing the Meuse in strength on 14 May, the Panzers advanced quickly before hesitating on the Aisne for fear of a strong French counter-attack. Nevertheless, this was but a pause, and despite an attempt at a counter-attack by the French General Charles de Gaulle on 19 May, the Panzers reached their objective at the mouth of the Somme the next day. A counter-attack by British forces on 21 May at Arras delayed the consolidation of the German corridor. The British and French armies then attacked the German flanks in a series of unsuccessful operations between 22 May and 1 June, which were unable to stop the Germans increasing the pressure on the Channel ports held by the British, French and Belgian armies.

The use of air power by the defenders was limited. Increasingly, the best British fighter squadrons were repatriated, while bomber sorties were restricted. Part of the problem appeared to be an inability to understand the need to respond before the invaders could consolidate – it took two days before just six Fairey Battles were sent against the Vroenhoven and Veldwezelt bridges, primary routes for the invading German forces. This gave the Germans time to put substantial anti-aircraft defences in place and provide good fighter cover, so that four out of the six aircraft were shot down, and a fifth aircraft crashed on its return flight.

The French vetoed British plans for bombing raids on German industry and supply routes for fear of German reprisals against French targets. Given the forces available in France, and the tendency at the time to send bombers in small forces, easily vulnerable to anti-aircraft fire and fighters rather than in any attempt to overwhelm the defences, such attacks might have been of limited value, but no one even tried.

Convinced by the Luftwaffe's chief, Herman Goering, that air power could destroy the retreating BEF, Hitler stopped his Panzer divisions from making an all-out assault on the Channel ports after the surrender of Belgium on 28 May. Air power was ineffectual in dealing with groups of soldiers on the beaches, allowing most of the British Expeditionary Force and the French First Army to be evacuated through the port of Dunkirk between 26 May and 3 June.

By now, the French were badly overwhelmed, with 65 battered divisions, short of equipment and munitions, attempting to defend Paris against 120 German divisions. By 9 June, the Germans had reached the Seine below Paris, cutting the city off from the sea. Retreat started in earnest on 13 June, with Paris abandoned along with much of the Loire Valley, and the forces on the Maginot Line increasingly isolated. It was not until 14 June that the Maginot Line itself came under attack, being broken at Saarbrucken, and then at Colmar the following day. The new head of the French government, Marshal Petain, had little choice but to seek an armistice on 17 June, which was granted on 22 June, although it did not take effect until the 25th, when Italy, which had declared war on France on 10 June, also signed. The Italians had attempted to invade the south of France on 20 June but had been repulsed by a much smaller defending French force, the Army of the Alps.

The surrender of France was inevitable, given the poor planning and preparation and the inability to mount successful counter-attacks or air raids. A more mobile defence, and an early acceptance that the Netherlands could not be saved, could have staved off defeat. Better still, had Belgium been incorporated into the Anglo-French alliance, and its forces and planning integrated with theirs, that country would not have been overrun so quickly. As it was, the Germans destroyed four armies in a humiliating defeat, taking 1.9 million French troops prisoner, and more than 800,000 Belgians, while the French also lost 90,000 dead and another 200,000 wounded. British casualties were 68,000, Belgian 23,000 and Dutch 10,000.

By contrast, the Germans lost 27,000 troops – a blow to their families, but for what had been achieved, such losses were light.

It enabled the Germans to believe in their own invincibility and superiority, and to avoid the harsh realities of war. Victory in the Low Countries and France might have been inevitable, but had it been more costly, Germany might not have been able to strike east in Operation Barbarossa a year later. It would also have made German invasion of Yugoslavia and Greece more difficult.

Yet, the Allies were not the only ones to snatch defeat. Had Hitler allowed the Panzer divisions to drive straight into the Channel ports, capturing the BEF, the impact on British public opinion could have made continuation of the war less likely. As it was, despite Churchill's warnings about the evacuation being a defeat, the rescue of the BEF from the beaches at Dunkirk was seen as a morale booster and widely celebrated.

Eight

SQUARING UP TO THE INVADER: THE NORWEGIAN CAMPAIGN, 1940

Little could be done to stop the German invasion of Denmark, with no resistance the country was occupied within hours – but Norway was a different matter.

After a peaceful winter, consolidating the occupation of the German zone in Poland, invasion of Denmark and Norway was set by Hitler for 9 April 1940, a full month before the start of the massive onslaught in the west to occupy France and the Low Countries. Both countries had a long history of neutrality, but there the similarities ended. If anything was a warning to the Germans that they might one day overreach themselves, it was the invasion of Norway.

Some believe that Germany was prompted to invade Norway by the *Altmark* incident, in which the Royal Navy stopped the pocket battleship *Admiral Graf Spee*'s supply ship that had sought a route through Norwegian territorial waters to avoid a British naval blockade. Aware that the *Altmark* was carrying British prisoners, a British destroyer was ordered by the Admiralty to intercept her, with the release of some 300 British merchant seamen who had been taken prisoner by the pocket battleship while commerce raiding in the South Atlantic. Although the British allowed the *Altmark* to continue, after releasing the prisoners, the infringement of Norwegian neutrality provoked protests from the Norwegian government. Whether the

Norwegians also protested to Germany over the use of her territorial waters is not clear.

Regardless of the *Altmark* incident, Hitler needed to secure both countries to ensure the passage of German warships out of the Baltic, rather than depend on the Kiel Canal, vulnerable to mining by the RAF. The best route for Germany's iron ore from Sweden was into Norway by rail, then on to Germany using coastal shipping, because in winter the sea route from Sweden was interrupted when the Gulf of Bothnia froze. Finally, with an invasion of the Soviet Union in mind, Norway would also make it difficult for the Allies to send material via the North Cape to Russian ports.

While they were neighbours with much common history and culture, from the strategic point of view, Norway and Denmark were to prove very different. In Denmark's case, a series of pacifist governments had so reduced the nation's defences that it took just three small transports to sail into the harbour at Copenhagen, the capital, while the main force crossed the frontier, for Denmark to surrender. Norway was different. Given the country's size, and in particular its length, interspersed with mountains and deep sea fjords, a carefully coordinated plan was needed. Troops were landed from the sea at the major ports of Oslo, Kristiansand, Bergen, Trondheim and Narvik, and air-landed troops arrived at the airports at Oslo and Stavanger. For the most part, this operation went according to plan, but the loss of the troop transport *Bhicker* at Oslo, which carried the main headquarters staff, allowed the Norwegian government and the King to flee the city, and mobilize resistance.

In Great Britain and France there was considerable sympathy for the Norwegian position. The Norwegian Army had already started to mobilize, and this encouraged the two Allies to respond to Norway's plea for help by sending troops, assembling an initial expeditionary force of 13,000, supported by air and naval forces, including the dispatch of aircraft carriers. Carrier-borne aircraft were necessary because of the limited number of airfields available ashore, amid the harsh terrain, but the Royal Navy had no aircraft embarked on its carriers capable of matching German fighters.

From the outset, conduct of the Norwegian campaign was mixed. Apart from having agreed to Norway's request for help, Britain and France knew that keeping the country out of German hands would ensure that they had easy access to Swedish iron ore and ball bearings. At first it was hoped that Sweden would support Norway and assist the Allies, but it soon became apparent that Sweden intended to maintain her own strict neutrality. An attack by Sweden, with relatively strong armed forces, could have made all the difference.

The British and French agreed that the key to holding Norway would be the recapture of Trondheim, from which a counter-attack southwards could repel the invaders. Initially, Narvik was seen as being more easily taken and held. The difficulty was that both nations were short of trained personnel because of the deployment of forces in France in anticipation of a German attack. It was estimated that an army of at least 50,000 troops would be needed to liberate Norway.

At first, all went well. At sea, the Royal Navy soon established control. A destroyer action in Narvik fjord on 10 April saw two German destroyers and some merchantmen sunk, although afterwards two British destroyers were also lost. That same day, an air raid by Fleet Air Arm aircraft operating from the shore station at Hatston, on the mainland of Orkney, sank the cruiser *Konigsburg*, the first loss of a substantial operational warship to air power. Three days later, the veteran battleship HMS *Warspite* and nine destroyers sank the remaining eight German destroyers.

Aided by these successes, British and Free Polish forces were landed at Narvik on 12 April. These troops, under Major-General Mackesy, were expected to seize the town, using naval gunfire if necessary. It soon became clear that Mackesy had no intention of taking Narvik. At first, this was because he wished to wait for the snow to melt, and for his force to be joined by a half brigade of French Chasseurs Alpins, not appreciating that these troops were earmarked for other operations. Nothing the naval commander, Admiral Lord Cork, could say or do would make him change his mind. Later, Mackesy explained that he did not wish to cause civilian casualties through the use of heavy naval gunfire.

While the Germans were left to strengthen their defences at Narvik, British and French troops were also landed near Namsos, further south between Narvik and Trondheim, and at Andalsnes, 150 miles south of Trondheim. Troops from Namsos were to move south to Trondheim, a distance of 100 miles, while those at Andalsnes would move north. This ignored two important points. The troops at Namsos had 4 ft of snow, which hindered movement, and had no protection from German air attack. Their comrades at Andalsnes had a different problem. In theory they were to cut one of the two railway lines running north to Trondheim, but they could not devote all of their energies to mounting an offensive campaign as they had to fight off repeated German attacks from the south.

Inevitably, when a difficult operation starts getting bogged down, bad luck intervenes. A new British Army commander for the southernmost forces was taken seriously ill later on the day that he was appointed. A successor was found, but when he and his staff landed at Kirkwall in Orkney, en route to Norway, the plane crashed, killing two members of the crew and seriously injuring everyone else on board.

Meanwhile, the British War Cabinet and the Chiefs of Staff of the three armed services decided that the best way of taking Trondheim would be by an amphibious assault, supported by heavy naval fire from battleships and by carrier-borne aircraft. This was agreed on 17 April. The following day, the Chiefs of Staff changed their minds, telling the War Cabinet that the plan involved too many risks and would endanger too many major units of the Royal Navy. This change of mind angered Winston Churchill, later to become Britain's wartime Prime Minister, but at the time First Lord of the Admiralty, the role he had also performed in the First World War. Churchill attempted to instil a sense of urgency, pointing out that once the ice in the Gulf of Bothnia thawed, there was a real risk that the Germans would persuade, or even force, the Swedes to allow troop movements overland by rail. To Churchill's dismay, the Secretary of State for War, his opposite number with responsibility for the British Army, later pointed out that the revised plan, taking Trondheim in a pincer movement, posed almost as much risk as the amphibious assault which he favoured.

British and French troops then attempted to fight their way through to Trondheim, while Mackesy remained adamant about not taking Narvik. Advancing from the north, one British brigade managed to get to within 50 miles of Trondheim by 19 April, before the Germans counter-attacked two days later, forcing them back. This advance on Trondheim was soon back where it started, at Namsos, from where it was evacuated on the night of 3 May. South of Trondheim, British and Norwegian forces had joined up at Andalsnes, and eventually managed to advance as far as Lillehammer, in an attempt to take the railway. Heavy fighting again resulted in retreat. Typical of the attitude at the time was that of a senior commander, who was happy to withdraw, since if the British and French troops, including the Chasseurs Alpin, were finding it difficult to withdraw in the heavy snow, the Germans surely could not advance. He was wrong, and the Allied force was pushed back to Andalsnes, from where it was evacuated on the night of 1 May.

Throughout this period, both Namsos and Andalsnes were subjected to heavy bombing by the Luftwaffe, who did not share General Mackesy's misgivings over civilian casualties. Air cover was provided by fighters operating from British aircraft carriers, and by RAF Gloster Gladiators operating from a frozen lake at Lesjeshogen, 40 miles from Andalsnes. The Gladiators, the RAF's last biplane fighter, were no match for the Luftwaffe's Messerschmitts, while at this time the Fleet Air Arm did not have any high-performance fighters. A squadron of Hawker Hurricanes, based at an airfield ashore, proved too few and too late to make a difference.

Narvik by this time was surrounded by more than 20,000 British, French and Polish troops, facing a garrison of just 6,000 Germans. Eventually, the garrison was subjected to a three-hour pounding by heavy gunfire from the battleship HMS *Warspite* and three cruisers on 24 April, but this operation was wasted as the troops ashore failed to attack.

As the German invasion of France and the Low Countries started, the British and French decided on 24 May that the forces in Norway could be put to better use elsewhere. The irony of this was that to evacuate Narvik successfully, they finally had to take the town. This was done on 27 and 28 May, using two French Foreign Legion battalions and a battalion of Norwegian troops, all commanded by the French General Bethouart. Withdrawal started, and more than 24,000 British, French, Polish and Norwegian troops were taken off by 8 June, although this was too late to prevent the surrender of France.

Even the withdrawal had its problems. Having saved their high-performance Hurricanes by successfully landing these aboard the aircraft carrier HMS *Glorious*, many of the RAF personnel and the aircraft were to be lost as the ship was sunk, as can be seen in the next chapter.

The Norwegians continued fighting until 9 June, before finally surrendering. All that was gained was time for the King and the government to escape into exile. Winston Churchill blamed much of the failure of the Norwegian campaign on the commanders involved and them not having got their staff work correct at such an early stage of the war. The rapid advance of the Germans through France and the Low Countries meant that the evacuation at Dunkirk overlapped with that from Norway, and this, with the fall of France, undoubtedly played some part. Even so, Churchill was critical of Mackesy, and disappointed that

British forces could be defeated by German forces struggling over difficult terrain in conditions of snow and ice, when British forces were still able to land at any chosen point along the Norwegian coastline. He criticized the Chiefs of Staff for reversing his ambitious plan for the taking of Trondheim in an amphibious operation, and replacing it with a more difficult operation, over land under snow and ice, with almost as high a degree of risk.

Yet, the Royal Navy saw the campaign off to a splendid start with clear successes, showing that even if Germany had mastery of the air, it had still to use this to gain control of the seas. Had Mackesy followed his orders, Narvik could have been taken and secured as a base. While civilian casualties were to be avoided, especially at this early stage of the war, before attitudes had hardened, elsewhere in Norway, towns were being heavily bombed, with many civilian casualties. The irony is that Narvik eventually had to be taken, so that the Allied forces could be evacuated.

British and Polish forces could have remained at Narvik, and possibly been joined by some of their French comrades. Their presence would have been a thorn in the side of the Germans, keeping substantial numbers of troops tied down, along with Luftwaffe and naval units. Reinforced, they could have made headway south. The Norwegians were to prove themselves good resistance fighters, and with friendly forces in the north of their country, doubtless would have been encouraged still further.

Better still, what would have happened if the Trondheim amphibious landing had gone ahead? It seems that if there had been a mistake, it was to divide forces between Namsos and Andalsnes when these could have been more useful at Trondheim. After all, these landings were 100 and 150 miles respectively from the objective, which could only be reached by air – not an option for the Allies at this stage of the war, from the sea, or across difficult terrain in bad weather. Time wasn't on the side of the Allies. Waiting for the weather to improve not only meant the possibility of German reinforcements, perhaps coming by rail through Sweden, but also gave the Germans time to reinforce their positions.

A presence even at Narvik would have been invaluable once Hitler invaded the Soviet Union, making the work of the convoys easier. At Trondheim, it held the prospect of liberating Norway. Norwegian territory offered control of the sea routes to Russia by the North Cape, and prevented the Germans from taking the best route in and out of the Baltic. It meant access to Swedish iron ore, the closest source of imported ore to British factories. It would have meant not having to use a special unit of the British Overseas Airways Corporation (BOAC) for Mosquito flights carrying ball bearings from Sweden to the United Kingdom.

Reinforcement of British and French units in France was hardly a justification for withdrawal from Norway, for the Battle for France was lost before the withdrawal could be completed. A parallel can be drawn with the decision to reduce the British forces in North Africa in order to defend Greece, at a time when there was a real prospect of Italian defeat in North Africa. Greece was lost anyway, and the division of forces between two theatres gave the Germans time to mount a campaign of their own in North Africa and against the Maltese islands.

Meanwhile, the Germans were free to look for fresh conquests, their confidence in the success of their arms undiminished.

Nine

A BAD START FOR THE
AIRCRAFT CARRIER, 1939–42

*At the outbreak of war the Royal Navy was one of the world's
largest, and with a sizeable fleet of aircraft carriers.*

While the Royal Navy of 1939 no longer dominated the
world's navies in the same way as it had in 1914, when
Britain was the world's dominant sea power, it was still a
sizeable fleet, with many fine ships. An important part of this
fleet was the carrier force, the best of which compared with any
in the world. Having invented the aircraft carrier, and used it
operationally in August 1918 during the First World War, the
Royal Navy should have been able to press this advantage from
the outset of the Second World War. It possessed a carrier fleet
of seven ships, although two of them were small and slow, with
six ships of advanced design on order. Realizing that every ship
would be needed, the original intention that the first four of the
new ships would replace the most dated of the existing carriers
was abandoned before the outbreak of war, when the order for
new ships was increased to six.

Britain's preparation for an air war at sea suffered from a
fundamental flaw. This went beyond the belief in the supremacy
of the battleship and naval gunnery, shared with all of the other
combatant navies at the beginning of the war. It lay in the
decision, taken in 1918, to concentrate all British air power in a
single unified air service. The new Royal Air Force, short of
funds and aircraft, with at one stage just twelve operational
squadrons, decided to concentrate on developing strategic air

91

power. In many ways this was a wise use of limited resources, but unfortunately, it did mean that the needs of the Royal Navy were neglected, until the Fleet Air Arm was transferred back to the Royal Navy in 1937. Many have drawn attention to the fact that during the early years of the war, the Royal Navy had fine ships in service or on order, but poor aircraft.

The transfer found the Royal Navy with very few airmen of its own – those who had flown during the interwar years had been limited to flying seaplanes and amphibians from battleships and cruisers. The Royal Navy embarked on a crash programme of recruitment and training, since the RAF wanted those airmen and 'ground' personnel still on secondment to the Fleet Air Arm back as soon as possible. What has so often been overlooked is that the sidelining of naval aviation, to the RAF and to a few naval officers aboard major surface vessels, also meant that the Royal Navy lost the opportunity to develop a generation of senior officers who understood aviation. At the outset, air power was secondary, an extension of the guns of the fleet at best, and at worst, simply employed on a fleet spotting role.

Out of the seven aircraft carriers in service on the outbreak of war, no less than five were lost in the first three years. It is possible to regard the loss of the newest of these ships – HMS *Ark Royal*, off Gibraltar on 13 November 1941 – as due simply to the fortunes of war, but many naval officers blame poor damage control, pointing out that the ship remained afloat until the next day. The elderly HMS *Eagle* was sunk while on a Malta convoy on 11 August 1942, hit by four torpedoes. She went down in just eleven minutes, which suggests that even the best damage control could not have saved her. Of the other three ships, however, the losses were unnecessary, even though all three were lost in completely different ways.

A converted battlecruiser, HMS *Courageous* was the sister ship of HMS *Glorious*. Both ships differed considerably in appearance after conversion from the other battlecruiser of the same class, HMS *Furious*, the world's first aircraft carrier, which was converted in stages during and just after the First World War. A feature of the two ships was the relatively short flight deck, which didn't run the full length of the ship, because when first converted they had a separate take-off deck running to the bows from the hangar deck, although this had proved to be impractical. Both remained useful ships with a fair turn of speed.

Remembering the lessons of the First World War, the Admiralty was quick to institute a convoy system on the outbreak of the Second World War, but they made the mistake of sending *Courageous* on an anti-submarine sweep. This was as bad as looking for the proverbial needle in a haystack. A lesson of the earlier conflict had been that it was better to attract submarines to a target, such as a convoy, than to go looking for a submarine. Worse still, the carrier had an escort of just two destroyers, far below that recommended for such a large ship, although these were equipped with Asdic, an early form of sonar. *Courageous* met her fate little more than a fortnight after the war had started, on 17 September 1939. During the day, her Fairey Swordfish biplanes had swept the Western Approaches south-west of Ireland, looking for submarines. As night approached, the aircraft landed on and were struck down into the hangars. Charles Lamb was the pilot of the last aircraft to land, and he headed to the wardroom with his observer: 'I said to him: "What are you going to have?" but he had not time to answer because at that moment there were two explosions, a split second apart, the like of which I had never imagined possible. If the core of the earth exploded, and the universe split from pole to pole, it could have been no worse. Every light went out immediately and the deck reared upwards . . . in the sudden deathly silence which followed, I knew the ship had died.'[1] The German submarine *U-29* had fired a salvo of three torpedoes at the ship, two of which hit her, leaving the carrier to sink in twenty minutes, taking 500 men with her.

The Admiralty soon abandoned anti-submarine sweeps. This was at a time when the submarine war had still to intensify into the Battle of the Atlantic. As a carrier escorting a convoy, with a larger number of anti-submarine escorts, *Courageous* could have been an asset, a more potent forerunner of the escort carriers which were to do so much to overcome the German U-boat menace. She would have provided protection where it was needed, and to some extent been protected herself. As it was, she was little more than a sitting duck, a lucky break for a fortunate U-boat commander.

After conversion to an aircraft carrier, HMS *Glorious* had joined the fleet in 1930, two years after her sister ship HMS *Courageous*. She served with the Mediterranean Fleet for a considerable time. The idea for the Royal Navy's attack on the Italian fleet at Taranto has been credited to one of the carrier's senior officers at the time of the Abyssinian crisis, when the League of Nations had considered action against Italy.

British and French forces intervened after Germany invaded Norway and Denmark in April 1940. There was little they could do to help Denmark, which was overrun within hours, but Norway's inhospitable terrain and the gallant defence put up by the Norwegians gave the two allies time to dispatch forces to help that country. While the RAF did have squadrons based ashore, the shortage of suitable air bases and the topography of Norway – a long, thin country with many mountains penetrated by fjords – meant that the deployment of aircraft carriers and their aircraft was an attractive option.

As already mentioned, the Royal Navy had its successes during the Norwegian campaign, effectively taking control of the seas, but Germany's invasion of France and the Low Countries led to a withdrawal, and it was during this that HMS *Glorious* was lost. Although the British had invented radar and had been reasonably quick in fitting this to warships, as an indication of their priorities, the Admiralty had been slow to provide radar for the carrier fleet – even the new fast armoured carriers were without radar at first. Battleships and cruisers had priority for the new invention. This was a factor in the loss of *Glorious*.

The carrier's commanding officer, Captain D'Oyley-Hughes, in common with all of his contemporaries of senior rank, was not a naval aviator, and certainly did not appreciate the value of naval aviation. On one occasion, when asked what he would do if threatened by enemy surface vessels, he replied that he would steam towards them at top speed, with all guns blazing. It never occurred to him that his main means of attack and defence had to be his aircraft.

Two factors were to be crucial as the carrier withdrew from Norway to Scotland on 8 June. The first was that her fuel state was too low for safety's sake, and so she was proceeding at a leisurely pace. The second was that no reconnaissance missions were being flown, with her aircraft struck down into the hangars and their armament, torpedoes for the Swordfish, removed.

As with any aircraft carrier, the value lay not just in the ship, but in the aircraft she carried. In the case of *Glorious*, this was a more important factor than usual. On being ordered to evacuate their bases in Norway, RAF Gloster Gladiator and Hawker Hurricane pilots had been told to destroy their aircraft. Fully aware of the shortage of aircraft and the growing pressure on Britain's defences, they opted to try to land on one of the two aircraft carriers. Of these, *Glorious* was chosen over *Ark Royal*, which had the longer flight deck, because her lifts were larger and the aircraft would not need to have their wings removed before being struck down into the hangars. Despite the absence of arrester hooks on the Hurricanes, the RAF aircraft were successfully landed aboard the carrier, proving that high-performance aircraft could operate from carriers.

One of the RAF pilots was concerned at the lack of activity aboard the carrier, as she proceeded at a stately 17 knots towards the naval base at Scapa Flow on Orkney:

> . . . he was puzzled by the lack of activity. In contrast to his previous stay in the ship, when there had been anti-submarine patrols and CAPs (combat air patrols) flying almost around the

clock, the flight deck was silent and deserted. . . . One Swordfish and a section of three Sea Gladiators were at ten minutes' notice, but they were not ranged on the flight deck.

It seemed that risk of attack by surface ships had been completely discounted, but there were still other dangers . . . I said, 'Have we got a search up?' And whoever it was said, 'No, we're doing seventeen knots and that's too fast for any submarine to torpedo us.'[2]

Elsewhere on the ship, aircrew saw warheads being removed from the torpedoes on their aircraft, something that made them feel uncomfortable. And in clear visibility and without radar, there was not even a lookout in the crow's nest.

Many of the ship's company were below having tea at 1600 hr when the two German battlecruisers *Scharnhorst* and *Gneisenau*, among the few German warships to be fitted with radar, opened fire at 28,000 yd with their 11-in guns. The carrier's own weapons were outgunned. Frantic efforts were made to range the ship's five remaining Swordfish, although only one aircrew member, a telegraphist air gunner (TAG), climbed into his aircraft. He then climbed out again to look for his comrades, seconds before his aircraft was destroyed at 1615 hr, as the Germans scored their first hit. As the aircraft blew up, shells penetrated the flight deck and exploded among the Hurricanes and other aircraft in the hangar deck, detonating fuel and ammunition still in the aircraft. In an instant, the hangar deck was an inferno, with fires burning out of control. Above it, the flight deck was unusable, torn and splintered. Having found the range, the Germans now began a punishing assault on the carrier, as boilers, which had been shut down, were flashed up and speed increased to 27 knots. At 1700 hr, when a salvo destroyed the bridge, *Glorious* was a pillar of smoke and flame. The two escorting destroyers, *Ardent* and *Acasta*, made a desperate torpedo attack on the *Scharnhorst*, during which both were sunk, but not before *Acasta* had succeeded in damaging the battlecruiser, although this was unknown to the British at the time.

The end came for *Glorious* at 1800 hr. No one knows how many of her crew survived to abandon ship. Some estimate as many as 900 out of a ship's company and embarked aircrew of around 1,500, but of those who did get away, just thirty-nine survived the two days in the cold water, without food and drink, before they were rescued. Once again, the Royal Navy had left a major fleet unit exposed and undefended. Not all of the blame can be laid upon the Admiralty. Her commanding officer might not, in the circumstances, have been able to do much about her fuel state. British warships of the day were notoriously short on range, a legacy of a massive empire that could provide refuelling stations at convenient points. Nevertheless, he could have maintained aerial reconnaissance, and he could have kept torpedo aircraft ready to take off at short notice, keeping the Germans at a safe distance.

By the outbreak of the Second World War, HMS *Hermes* was obsolete. She was the world's first purpose-built aircraft carrier, and showed it. Her elegant lines could not disguise the fact that she was too small and too slow to operate an adequate number of aircraft with the right performance to make a difference in any fleet action. Her useful complement of aircraft was limited to no more than a dozen Swordfish. Even so, she could have made a valuable escort carrier, long before such ships were available to escort the Atlantic convoys. Had war not occurred, she would have been replaced by one of the new, fast, armoured carriers. Realizing the ship's limitations, the Admiralty sent her to the Indian Ocean against German surface raiders; almost as forlorn a task as the anti-submarine sweeps on which *Courageous* had been engaged. On one occasion *Hermes* took an Italian liner as a prize, becoming a commerce raider herself.

The Royal Navy had lost two heavy cruisers, *Dorsetshire* and *Cornwall*, on 5 April 1942, as they were caught without air cover following the withdrawal of the two new carriers, *Indomitable* and *Formidable*, to refuel. *Hermes* was not with this force, and would have been a liability, as she could not have kept up with them. Confusion over Japanese intentions meant that *Hermes* was ordered to sea when at Trincomalee in Ceylon (now Sri Lanka) on 8 April, to avoid being caught in harbour by Japanese air attack. She was spotted at sea by the Japanese early on 9 April, without aircraft and with just one escort, the Australian destroyer *Vampire*. In desperation, she was ordered back to Trincomalee and the protection of the harbour's defences.

At 1030 hr, the first of eighty Japanese aircraft, mainly dive-bombers, found *Hermes* and commenced their attack on her starboard side. The first bomb struck the ship at 1055 hr, and she sank at 1115 hr, along with her escort, within sight of the coast. Many of the bombs went straight through her plating to explode deep inside the ship.

The lack of awareness demonstrated by these losses reflected the Admiralty's failure to keep pace with developments in warfare. The best of the First World War naval aviators had either reached senior rank in the RAF or had retired. As a result, the Royal Navy lacked a generation of senior officers able to make good use of aviation at sea, the preserve not of the airmen who went to sea, but of the seamen who could fly.

Courageous was wasted on a fruitless operation that simply created a target for U-boat commanders. *Glorious* was sacrificed by the stupidity of her commanding officer. *Hermes*, like *Courageous*, was being deployed on a fruitless operation which took her into harm's way, while she could have been put to good use elsewhere, either on training or convoy escort duties as, for the most part, were two of the other early carriers, *Furious* and *Argus*.

NOTES

1. Charles Lamb, *War in a Stringbag* (London, Cassell, 1977).
2. John Winton, *Carrier Glorious* (London, Leo Cooper, 1986).

Ten

WHEN THE LUFTWAFFE GAVE UP: FAILURE OF THE BLITZ, 1940–1

The limited, but painful, experience of bombing during the First World War, allied to advances in aviation between the wars, led many to believe that the 'bomber will always get through'.

For many in the United Kingdom, the 'blitz' meant not the concerted and coordinated land and air campaigns which resulted in German submission of Poland, Denmark and Norway, France and the Low Countries, but the night bombing campaign of Britain which ran from August 1940 to May 1941. Many of these would have found it hard to accept that the 'blitz' was a failure as they saw the centres of British towns and cities flattened.

The night bombing blitz can be differentiated from other campaigns that followed, since the end of the blitz did not mean the end of German raids on British towns and cities. The height of the campaign ran from August to November 1940, and it was a distinct period of the war, with heavy raids attacking British cities in succession. London suffered most, with raids on 66 out of 67 consecutive nights. The campaign began with daylight raids, but was forced into a night campaign as losses inflicted by the RAF day fighters mounted. Later, these same factors dictated that the RAF's bombing campaign against Germany was also usually at night.

The start of the blitz was something to dread. During the 1930s, in the public mind, the bomber became one of the most feared weapons of war. This was based on experience of the limited bomber campaigns of the First World War. The famous British strategist, Basil Liddell Hart, had drawn attention many years earlier to the 857 Britons killed and 2,058 injured by German bombing raids during that conflict. He forecast 'nearly a quarter of a million casualties . . . might be anticipated in the first week of a new war'.[1] These fears grew as aircraft performance improved. The Spanish Civil War and the destruction caused by the bomber, notably at the Basque stronghold of Guernica, seemed to confirm many of the worst fears. As war spread across Europe, these fears strengthened, as the Germans devastated first Warsaw – among many other less-well-known Polish cities – and, in the advance westwards through the Low Countries, Rotterdam. The mighty Luftwaffe appeared invincible. Britain and France appeared powerless. German bombers got through at this stage because there was little on the continent of Europe to stop them. In any case, as mentioned earlier, the French were strongly opposed to air raids on German industrial and communications targets. For those at home in the British Isles, the early images of the Second World War were of Stuka dive-bombers screeching downwards onto their targets, or massed formations of Heinkel He 111s or Dornier Do 17s throbbing across the sky.

There were major differences in the strategic thinking around which the air forces of the main combatants operated throughout the Second World War. The Royal Air Force was a truly autonomous air force, and while support for the army was not overlooked, its thinking was strongly in favour of strategic operations. The bomber was regarded as a means of warfare in its own right, and so too was the fighter. The United States Army Air Force, while nominally still part of the United States Army, took a similar view. By contrast, the Luftwaffe, although again a truly autonomous air force, even to the extent that it controlled Germany's paratroops in much the same way as the major navies have their marines, operated in close support of the army. The equipment and doctrines of the Luftwaffe were centred on integrated operations with ground forces, with blitzkrieg, or 'lightning war', combining aerial bombardment, tanks and artillery. Germany went to war without heavy bombers, but with dive-bombers and medium bombers. Plans for heavy bombers had been scrapped during the late 1930s, partly in deference to doctrine, and partly because many more dive- and medium bombers could be built in the time and for the money available.

Erhard Milch, State Secretary for the German Air Ministry, later mentioned the RAF's strategy when addressing a meeting:

They have already in the years 1936/37 considered the development of four-engined bombers. The Englander planned right from the beginning to use these planes by night and not by day, because the speed and height of these planes were not suitable for daylight attacks in the face of our day-fighters' defence. . . . The attempt in our country to construct four-engined planes was started in 1934 . . . but on the basis of a tactical decision by the authorities in charge . . . was given up in favour of twin-engined planes . . . preferred because they could be constructed quicker and more easily.[2]

The Russians took the same view, although air force and army links were closer in Soviet Frontal Aviation.

With the successful evacuation of the British Expeditionary Force from Dunkirk, augmented by the remnants of French and other armies and air forces, the United Kingdom showed no sign of seeking an armistice after the fall of France in June 1940.

An invasion of Britain was expected, and the Germans did have a plan for this, code-named Operation Sea Lion. Many doubt whether Germany would have attempted such an assault for it would have been unlike anything attempted by the German armed forces at any stage of the war. It would have been bigger and far more difficult than the later costly invasion of Crete. The English coast closest to France and Belgium was protected by high cliffs, and on either side of these the distance to be crossed from France or Belgium increased rapidly. Then there was the difficulty of mounting an invasion in the face of resistance by the Royal Navy and Royal Air Force.

Yet, the Germans were keen to encourage belief in an invasion among the British. Invasion barges were assembled in many of the Belgian and French Channel ports, and although far less practical than the landing craft used by the Allies later on, the barges drew the RAF's bombers and delayed operations against Germany itself. Invasion or not, the Luftwaffe was given the task of destroying the Royal Air Force in a campaign that started on 10 June and lasted until the end of October 1940.

A preliminary to what became known later as the Battle of Britain consisted of German attacks on British coastal shipping and the Channel ports. This was to discourage any attempt at sending a fresh expeditionary force while the Germans consolidated their position in Europe, and was an effort to bring the RAF into decisive combat over the English Channel. The RAF refused to be lured into combat at the extreme operational radius of action for its fighters, which would have meant them fighting at a disadvantage against numerically superior German forces. Instead, on 10 August, the British stopped sending convoys through the Channel, diverting the traffic to the railways instead. The Luftwaffe was left with no alternative but to attack British airfields.

The RAF was not an equal match for the Luftwaffe, with about 700 fighters, many of them obsolescent, compared with 2,800 Luftwaffe aircraft. It was chronically short of pilots at this time, with many selected for pilot training still waiting to be called up as the training system struggled to cope, and Fleet Air Arm pilots having to be seconded to RAF fighter squadrons. By contrast, the Luftwaffe pilots were by this time highly experienced, some of them having fought in the Condor Legion, supporting the Nationalists in the Spanish Civil War. Most of the rest had seen action over Poland, and then over France and the Low Countries.

Operations against British airfields started in earnest on 5 August, intensifying until the 15th, when 1,500 aircraft were sent across the Channel. This level of activity was maintained for a further ten days, during which the Luftwaffe lost 602 aircraft compared to 260 for the RAF.

Although numerically inferior to the Luftwaffe, and with a lower level of operational experience among its pilots, the RAF had three big advantages that enabled it to survive. The first was the use of radar, the 'Chain Home' network, which allowed aircraft to be scrambled in time to meet the German threat, rather than being caught on the ground or wasting fuel and flying hours by maintaining heavy air patrols. The second was an excellent command and control system, which meant that squadrons were present in sufficient strength wherever they were needed. The third proved just how right the RAF had been earlier to avoid being drawn into combat over the English Channel on the Luftwaffe's terms; Luftwaffe fighters were at the limits of their range and could not remain engaged in combat on the British side of the Channel for long.

Luftwaffe weakness included fighter pilots too easily encouraged away from protecting the bombers, while bomber radios operated on a different frequency from those of the fighters, hindering communication.

The start of the blitz showed just what a formidable weapon the bomber could be, even though at first bomber tactics needed to be refined, with no attempt at short, concentrated attacks to overwhelm the defences. The first heavy daylight raid on London was on 7 September 1940, followed that night by the first night raid against the city, with 318 bombers deployed. This rapid follow-up of a day raid by a night raid made strategic sense, hindering repairs while the night bombers were able to use the fires for guidance. Yet, there was no intensive attack, as the first aircraft reached the target at 2010 hr and the last at 0430 hr. It was successful enough, though, and the raid caused many fires of which no less than 9 met the London Fire Brigade's description of a 'conflagration', a spreading fire which needed more than 100 pumps. There were another 19 major fires – those requiring more than 30 pumps – 40 serious fires and 1,000 smaller fires, with a total casualty rate of 430 killed and 1,600 injured. The following night, another 207 aircraft were deployed, so that by the morning of 9 September, there were 12 major conflagrations, as well as another 417 deaths and 747 seriously injured.

Even with the blitz on London at its height, the Luftwaffe still had the strength to visit other British cities. Many of the pilots never saw a British night fighter, and when 400 bombers were sent against London on the night of 15/16 October, they faced just 41 night fighters, many of which were obsolete Boulton Paul Defiants operating without radar.

As the war progressed, increasingly sophisticated equipment was introduced. An example of this was the technique known to the Germans as *Knickebein*, which enabled the Luftwaffe's bombers to find their target by flying along radio beams transmitted from ground stations in France. The RAF's countermeasures were another example, with 80 Wing of the RAF using a new invention to bend the beams, thereby sending the bombers off course. In turn, this led the Luftwaffe to introduce yet more sophisticated devices, including *X-Gerat* and *Y-Gerat*, which did more than simply point the way to the target, using additional beams to improve bomb-aiming.

Despite this overwhelming might, Britain's towns and cities recovered. In contrast to the situation later in the war in Germany and Japan, the inhabitants were never driven from British cities, while industrial production continued to rise. There were, however, shortages, production and communications were interrupted, and substantial areas were laid waste, often not being rebuilt until some years after the war ended, and, of course, there was a terrible cost in human life.

There were a number of factors at work. The first was the steady improvement in both the anti-aircraft defences and in night-fighter operations, such as when 178 fighters faced 339 bombers over Liverpool on the night of 12/13 March 1941. The second was the reduction in the scale and frequency of the raids as Luftwaffe units were transferred to the east, ready for the start of the invasion of the Soviet Union known as Operation Barbarossa. This gave the British the opportunity to repair the most serious damage, so that production and communications could be reinstated.

The third factor was the lack of repeat visits. Many British cities suffered a single major air raid. Some, such as Manchester and Birmingham, suffered several, but even Coventry, the important industrial centre in the English Midlands – and then, as now, a centre of the motor industry – with many of its factories converted to war work, was visited just once. That one raid, on the night of 14/15 November 1940, left 506 people dead and another 432 seriously injured, with production in many of its factories stopped, the city centre flattened and roads impassable. The 499 Luftwaffe bombers faced 119 night-fighter sorties – but of these just seven sighted bombers – and the only two bombers to be shot down were accounted for by anti-aircraft fire.

The impact of heavy bombing night after night would have been immense. As the Germans were to discover later, not only would repeated raids have prevented recovery, but also would have exacted a cruel toll on the ability of the survivors to manage.

The fourth factor was the absence of heavy bombers with a substantial warload and an effective range. The most distant British cities, such as Belfast, Glasgow, Clydebank and even Liverpool, suffered the fewest raids. All four of those mentioned were ports with major shipbuilding and repair facilities, while Belfast in particular was an emerging centre for aircraft production. On one raid on Liverpool, the Luftwaffe dropped

270 tons of high explosives and almost 2,000 incendiaries. This does not compare with the loads dropped by the RAF and the USAAF on Germany as the war progressed. The new Junkers Ju 88 was doing well to take four 550-lb and ten 110-lb bombs on the Liverpool raid. A single RAF Avro Lancaster carried four times as much and, even more important, would have been carrying at least 1,000-lb bombs, or 4,000-lb 'cookies' and even 8,000-lb 'double cookies'. Heavier bombs were far more effective and caused more lasting damage than the same weight in smaller bombs.

The aircraft and aircrew losses suffered by the Luftwaffe during the night blitzes were relatively light and sustainable in contrast to the losses suffered by the RAF during its early raids. The damage inflicted was substantial. Had the Luftwaffe's attentions not been diverted to the east, and had there been more repeated raids, the impact on the British war economy and on civilian morale would have been far greater and more lasting. Had the Luftwaffe had heavy bombers at this stage, the impact could have been devastating. When eventually the Germans did introduce a truly heavy bomber, these were too few in number and it was too late, added to which, the aircraft, the Heinkel He 177, was dangerously unreliable.

NOTES

1. Basil Liddell Hart, *The Defence of Britain* (London, Greenwood Press, 1980).
2. Address to meeting of Gauleiters, 6 October 1943.

Eleven

IGNORING THE LESSONS OF HISTORY: BARBAROSSA, 1941

After an unbroken series of successful operations, Hitler finally committed Germany to a 'second front', striking east through the Soviet zone of Poland and into the Soviet Union itself.

Germany's strike through the Soviet zone of Poland and into the Soviet Union itself started before daybreak on 22 June 1941. At first, all went well. Air attacks caught the Soviet armed forces by surprise, with the sixty-six airfields holding 70 per cent of Russia's air power in the west raided on the first morning. One Russian officer, Lieutenant-General Kopets, lost 600 aircraft without making any impact on the Germans, and committed suicide the next day. By the end of the first week, more than 2,000 Russian aircraft had been destroyed, and the Luftwaffe had complete aerial supremacy.

On the ground, the Panzer divisions raced ahead, operating at up to sixty miles in front of the advancing German infantry. This was where the weaknesses of the German Army now began to manifest itself. At one stage, there were seven large pockets of Russian resistance, but the more capable Russian commanders were able to fight their way out. The shortage of motorized infantry able to keep pace with the Panzer advance meant that opportunities were being lost. Brest-Litovsk was encircled on the first day, but it was a week before it could be taken. Paratroops could have been deployed to ease the situation, but the severe losses at Crete meant that this was not an option. Even so, the Red Army lost 164 divisions by mid-July, with the advancing

Axis forces capturing 2,256,000 Russian soldiers, 9,336 tanks and 16,179 artillery pieces.

At first, the operation seemed to confound the belief of the theorists; the first rule of war was never to march on Moscow. The Germans had already been forced to break the second rule – never to get involved in the Balkans – as they had to rescue their Italian allies from defeat in Yugoslavia and Greece. But confidence was high, because, for the Germans, the early years of the Second World War had been kind, with an unbroken run of victories, as success followed success, with few losses. The RAF had still to make itself felt in bombing raids on the Fatherland. The average German could feel well satisfied with the conduct of the war. For many, the loss of loved ones, shortages and the terror of not knowing whether each night would be their last were still to come.

To the man in the street, even if he was in uniform, the future looked good. Those with a strategic picture knew that in the longer term, the picture was far from rosy. Germany needed to secure its supplies of oil and other vital materials, and for too much of these it was heavily dependent upon the country's historic enemy and rival, Russia, by now an enlarged Communist Soviet Union and, following the decision to share Poland, effectively a next-door neighbour. The German–Soviet Pact of 1939 was a temporary truce, an expedient rather than a new and fruitful beginning. The two countries distrusted each other and the two leaders, who vied for the dubious distinction of being the more evil, hated each other.

National Socialism, the Nazi Party, had been a reaction to the Bolshevik Revolution in Russia. The paradox was that many comparisons could be drawn between the two ideologies. True, the Nazis did not murder wealthier members of society or send them to labour camps, and they did not confiscate German businesses, but they did believe in active political direction of the economy, the corporate state. They did not tolerate dissent. Both ideologies persecuted the Jews and many other minorities, although in the case of the Russians, much of this was the continuation of the traditional pogroms against the Jews that had been commonplace throughout much of eastern Europe.

Both leaders of Germany and Russia had much in common. Both were dedicated to continuing the traditional policies of their respective countries. Adolf Hitler followed Bismarck and the Kaiser in effectively wishing to establish a greater Germany, a *Mitteleuropa*. Stalin saw a greater Russia, a single nation united and undivided, incorporating territories such as the Ukraine and Georgia, as well as access to ice-free ports. Both were authoritarian in outlook. Neither could trust his lieutenants nor devolve power and responsibility. All too often, both interfered in operational matters, believing that they knew better than their generals.

So, to the man in the street, and to the common soldier, the invasion of the Soviet Union was to be another triumph of arms, a victory for the Fatherland, that would achieve *Lebensraum*, or living space, so frequently used as an excuse by Hitler in his expansion eastwards. As they advanced across Russia, soldiers were to identify areas in which they could settle after the war, including the Don Cossack country.

Senior commanders saw things rather differently, as did many of those in senior positions in government, commerce and the universities. Their main fear was that Nazi Germany, for the first time, would fight a war on two fronts – on the British Empire in the west, and on the Soviet Union in the east – and wondered whether this was one assault too many. They questioned whether the country had the manpower to cope with the demands of divided warfare, especially if the United States eventually entered the war, as it had done in the First World War.

Germany had gone to war with finite natural resources; having coal, for example, but little oil, while the Soviet Union had abundant natural resources, but was extremely inefficient at utilizing these. The Soviet Union often had difficulty in getting raw materials to the point of use. Germany was heavily dependent on her neighbours for many of the necessities of peace, which became all the more essential when engaged in total war.

The German armed forces had reached the zenith of their capability and confidence by the time the invasion of the Soviet Union was decided. By contrast, the Soviet armed forces had seen as much as half the officer corps purged before the war by the Soviet dictator Joseph Stalin. Just five of the eighty members of the Military Soviet in 1934 were still alive in 1938. No military district commander had survived the purges. Russian commanders at all levels shared their command with a political commissar, who could countermand their orders, report them for inefficiency, regardless of whether or not this was warranted, and generally have the opportunity to second-guess them. Not surprisingly, Russian commanders lacked confidence and experience. Much of their equipment was obsolescent, and industry was inefficient and even primitive. Out of a total of 18,000 aircraft in the USSR, only one-fifth could be regarded as modern.

For the most part, German military equipment was the match of anything any other country could put into operation at the time. Yet, not all was as efficient as it could be. There were four serious omissions in the German war machine. The first was the lack of a truly heavy bomber for the Luftwaffe. This was to be as big a drawback in Operation Barbarossa as during the blitz on British cities, because Stalin had repositioned most of the Soviet Union's heavy industry to the east of the Ural Mountains, out of reach of the Luftwaffe bombers.

The second omission was the absence of a truly modern and well-equipped air transport fleet. Whenever transport aircraft were needed, these were the obsolescent Junkers Ju 52/3m, or *Tante Ju*, the 'Iron Auntie', rather than newer types such as the Ju 252. Aircrew for the transport force were drawn from the instructors of the bomber training schools, rather than having dedicated transport pilots, so that bomber aircrew training ceased during major operations needing air transport, and was affected afterwards by the inevitable losses.

The third problem was that the German Army still depended on horses for most of its transport and much of its artillery limbers. The lack of an efficient motor transport fleet was to prove to be a major drawback in the vast expanses of the Soviet Union. It was made even worse by the fact that Russia's railways operated on a different track gauge from that used throughout most of western Europe, so that time had to be wasted in regauging the lines as the German forces advanced. There was a severe shortage of dual-gauge rolling stock, and as the lines of communication extended, the shortage of rolling stock became more acute.

Anyone who believes in German efficiency would be surprised by the fourth problem. The German armed forces were unprepared for the Russian winter, lacking the technology to ensure that aircraft and armoured vehicles could operate in severe cold. On its own, that could be dismissed as a failing of the technology then available. What was completely incomprehensible was the failure to provide adequate winter clothing for the men in either quantity or quality. It has been argued that this was due to overconfidence on the part of the Germans, who expected to have gained their objectives before the winter weather arrived, but conquering armies do not return home for the winter!

The stage was set for a disaster.

As a concept, the invasion of the Soviet Union dated from at least as early as August 1940, when General Marcks produced a plan that he felt would ensure the defeat of the Soviets in no more than seventeen weeks. It would take 146 divisions, almost the entire strength of the Germany Army at the time, although the Germans were counting on a substantial contribution from their allies: Italy, Finland, Hungary and Romania. Marcks envisaged a two-pronged assault, with the northern prong aimed at Moscow, the capital, and the southern at the resources of the Ukraine.

The eventual plan evolved from discussion and war games differed, with a three-pronged attack. There would still be a southern force aimed at the Ukraine. To the north, there would be two prongs, with one to encircle Leningrad (now St Petersburg) before eventually taking Moscow, while the other would simply concentrate on crippling communications into Moscow, the centre of the Russian railway system, effectively isolating the city until the Leningrad force was ready. These changes reflected Hitler's belief that Moscow was not the centre of power, while he also wished to avoid the mistake made by Napoleon by concentrating on Moscow. Of the 144 divisions, 19 would be Panzer divisions, with another 9 consisting of lines of communication troops. Out of 116 infantry divisions, just 14 would be motorized.

At this stage, circumstances and personalities intervened. The first unpredictable factor was the Italian failure to secure Yugoslavia and Greece. Instead of invading the Soviet Union in April, these operations deferred the start of the campaign until June. The second factor was Stalin's refusal to accept that an invasion was likely, despite warnings from diplomats, including many from other countries. It seems that Stalin wished to ignore the unpleasant facts, and even contemplated allowing some territory to be ceded to the Germans. A more robust and well-prepared Soviet defence at the start might have avoided later German defeats. At the last moment Stalin panicked and ordered his armies to disperse and be camouflaged, but the order was received too late for the divisional headquarters to pass it on to all units in time.

Starting the campaign in June had one advantage. The roads, many simply dirt tracks, were dry and easily passable. The land on either side was in a similar condition, so that movement was easy and the 'roads' were often as much as 100 yd wide. Against this, the campaign had lost two months when it started on 22 June, leaving the Germans fourteen weeks in which to achieve their goals, after which the weather would be unpredictable, at first wet, then cold, and then freezing with heavy snow.

Air power was already important to any campaign at this time. The Russians had some 9,000 aircraft in the west, the Luftwaffe had 1,945, of which 1,400 were ready for combat. The Luftwaffe force included 510 bombers, 290 dive-bombers, 440 fighters, 40 fighter-bombers and 120 long-range reconnaissance aircraft, divided among three air fleets. In addition, another 1,000 aircraft had been provided by Germany's allies, including Romania with more than 400, while Finland provided more than 300. Italy provided just 100.

On the ground, the Russians outnumbered the Germans and their allies.

Had Hitler decided to take Moscow and Leningrad all might have been well for the Germans, and they might even have forced Stalin to cede the Ukraine. Alternatively, had the Germans concentrated on the Ukraine, simply containing Soviet forces in the north, Germany could have achieved a major war objective, secured vital supplies, and, in doing so, also denied these to the Russians. The three-pronged attack was to prove to be another fatal weakness in the plan.

On 21 August, Hitler diverted most of the Panzer divisions of Army Group Centre to assist Army Group South in the Ukraine. This enabled Kiev to be taken with more than 600,000 Russian troops, but it delayed the advance on Moscow for some six weeks, until early October, when the Panzer divisions returned. The six-week break was put to good use by Moscow's defenders, while the excursion into the Ukraine used valuable fuel and munitions reserves, and took its toll on the tanks and other vehicles. One result was that it took Napoleon's Grand Army less time to reach Moscow than it took the Germans. The delay meant that the campaign had stretched into winter without achieving its key objectives. This might just have been manageable had German troops been equipped for winter operations, but the German forces were unprepared for the onset of winter. Temperatures dropped to between -30°C and -50°C for lengthy periods, occasionally falling further to -70°C. Snow and ice affected mobility, as tanks skidded and slipped, and aircraft engines froze, so that fires had to be lit under them to prepare aircraft for flight.

Also completely unforeseen was the way in which munitions were affected. The explosive impact of bombs and shells was muffled whenever there was 3 ft or more of snow. On ice, high-explosive bombs and shells shattered without exploding.

German troops suffered severe privations. Many faced these harsh conditions while still in summer uniforms. Even German winter clothing was not adequate for the Russian winter, with one general pointing out that Russian felt boots were much better than German leather boots, while anti-skid soles were also needed. At Moscow, the German Army suffered 10,000 cases of frostbite. Supplies of food and fuel were rapidly exhausted.

The Germans never managed to enter Moscow, and the anti-tank trenches dug in the streets by the inhabitants were never needed. It was here that the position stabilized, and during fierce fighting, the Germans were forced into retreat, so that by the end of January 1942, the front line had been pushed back some forty miles from Moscow. This – if not a complete victory, at least a defeat avoided – encouraged Stalin to take a more positive attitude, considering the relief of Leningrad and retaking of the Ukraine.

By spring 1942, the German position was still not irretrievable. They had secured the front at Moscow, and after failing to take Leningrad the previous September they had settled into a state of siege. Had they been able to encourage the Finns to renew their offensive against the Soviet Union, the city might just have fallen. By the time the siege was lifted in January 1944, more than 200,000 civilians had died from German aerial and artillery bombardments, and another 650,000 from starvation. Elsewhere, the Ukraine had been occupied.

Further advances were still planned for the Axis forces at this time. The Germans were determined to seize the oilfields in the Caucasus, and Hitler also ordered the capture of Stalingrad (now Volgograd) on the River Volga. Even the Caucasus alone might have been manageable, but the longer lines of communications, compounded by the need for yet more railway regauging, were beginning to tell. Initial Russian resistance was weak, but as the Germans entered mountainous country, the Russian response toughened in terrain that favoured the defence. Soviet strategy at this stage was beginning to work. Rather than fight the Germans on a broad front in open country where the tanks could crush resistance, they fell back, towards the mountains and to Stalingrad. This was when German strategy started to show its weaknesses. In the mountains, the Germans found that their well-tried blitzkrieg tactics were useless. In the cities, as at Leningrad during 1941 and then at Stalingrad a year later, the German advance was brought to a halt amid street fighting. The Germans reached Stalingrad on 19 August and by 13 October they were on the Volga, with the Russians jammed into a narrow perimeter, although they were still able to supply the city across the river. If any one objective could be described as a 'city too far', it was Stalingrad. Here, the besieging forces became the besieged.

The Russians mounted a counter-attack on 19 November, and by 23 November the German Army was in retreat, in heavy snow and with many still not issued with winter uniform. Soon, twenty German and two Romanian divisions were trapped. One German general, Weichs, had withdrawn his forces in time, but General Paulus was ordered to remain by Hitler, after Goering promised to provide 500 tons of fuel and food by air daily, although in reality three times this quantity was needed. Less than half the aircraft available were transports, others were bombers, ignoring the fact that supplies needed more space than bombs. In the Stalingrad air resupply operation, the best daily tally was 289 tons.

Within the area occupied by the besieged Axis forces, the situation became critical. The siege continued while the Germans attempted to mount a relief operation, which was itself checked by the Russians while still 25 miles away. Because the Russians underestimated the number of troops trapped outside Stalingrad, they failed to attack in sufficient force, and instead of a major victory simply chipped away at the edges, keeping the encircled Germans and Romanians within a slowly tightening circle. Within this circle, troops were on less than starvation rations. Among the besieged troops, many quartermasters, uncertain just how long the siege would last and doubtful about the Luftwaffe's ability to provide adequate supplies, reduced rations far more than was necessary, so that when surrender eventually came, the Russians found large quantities of supplies intact amid soldiers suffering from starvation.

The loss of the airstrip at Pitomnik on 16 January 1943 meant the end for the Germans at Stalingrad, and eventually more than 94,000 surrendered. More than 147,000 were estimated to have died within the city, and more than 100,000 outside it.

Defeat at Stalingrad led eventually to a second battle for the Ukraine, starting in December 1943, and ending with German defeat the following May, by which time a growing confidence in the Soviet forces had already seen the siege of Leningrad lifted. Losses of men and equipment meant that the demoralized Axis armies were forced back into a long and cruel retreat.

The Germans had given little quarter during their advance, slaughtering civilians and maltreating Russian prisoners of war, and they received none in retreat. Typical of the times at Stalingrad was the example of a German Army padre, who was bending over a wounded man yet was shot in the back of the head by a Russian officer. Prisoners were left to starve after being robbed of personal possessions, and especially their watches. Attempts to help the sick – of which there were many due to the poor diet and unsanitary conditions – and wounded, were few and far between. The cruelty displayed by both sides prolonged the conflict. Unaware of Nazi attitudes to the Jews, many Russian Jews had welcomed the advancing Axis forces as liberators, but were soon disillusioned. Even so, the Germans did find Russians willing to fight alongside them against the Soviet regime. One reason for the prolonged resistance by the Germans and their allies was that they hesitated to surrender to the Russians for fear of the consequences.

The Balkan campaigns had delayed Operation Barbarossa for too long. Even so, Germany had fatally overreached itself by invading the Soviet Union. Losses were such that they could not be replaced. It became increasingly difficult to stop the advancing Russians, the more so as Allied bombing raids increased in intensity, then Italy surrendered and Allied forces started to advance through France and towards the Fatherland. Germany still had a mighty war machine, but it was falling into a state of disrepair, while those of its opponents were still growing in strength. Most of all, German confidence in the outcome, and morale, crumbled.

Twelve

EMPTY GESTURES: PETSAMO AND KIRKENES, 1941

Germany's invasion of the Soviet Union completely changed the war, with the Soviet Union suddenly moved from pariah to ally.

Germany's invasion of the Soviet Union had changed the war. The Soviet Union, which had been regarded as an ally of Germany at the outset, was now an ally of the British. But it was an unreliable and uncertain ally; the two nations, one might almost say the two great empires, had nothing in common. Russia was a demanding ally. Having failed to prepare for a German invasion, despite the warnings and despite the signals which gave little scope for misunderstanding German intentions, it expected the hard-pressed British to demonstrate their commitment to her survival. The British, for their part, and not without some cause, were concerned that Russia might try to reach an accommodation with Germany – ceding parts of the Soviet Union's territory was considered by Stalin before and immediately after the German invasion.

In these circumstances, the British felt compelled to take action to demonstrate their commitment to the Russians, and to encourage Russian resistance. Opportunities for doing so were limited – and so the idea of an attack on German shipping in the ports of Petsamo and Kirkenes, north of the Arctic Circle, was born. The only way such an attack could be carried out was through using carrier-borne aircraft. By 1941, the Fleet Air Arm was an invaluable part of the Royal Navy. During the Norwegian campaign, it had sunk the German cruiser

Konigsberg, operating from a shore base on the mainland of Orkney, the group of islands to the north of Scotland. Later that same year, it had crippled the Italian fleet with its well-conceived and daringly executed raid on the naval base at Taranto. Modern aircraft were still needed, but the new fast armoured carriers were in service and the Fleet Air Arm's elderly aircraft had been highly effective.

Both ports were north of the Arctic Circle. Kirkenes was in German-occupied Norway. Petsamo, or Pechenga to the Russians, had changed hands on a number of occasions. Originally part of Russia, it became part of Finland as the Finns seized their independence in the wake of the Bolshevik Revolution, but it was one of the towns lost again as the price of peace in the Russo-Finnish War of 1940–1. When Germany invaded the Soviet Union in Operation Barbarossa in June 1941, Finland was drawn into the orbit of the Axis powers, largely for national preservation on the basis that 'my enemy's enemy is my friend'. German possession of these ports made it more difficult for Russia's new allies to send supplies to her, since the most direct route, through the Baltic, was completely impracticable.

From the start of the German invasion, the Soviet Union's dictator, Joseph Stalin, was pressing his new allies to take action against the Germans to ease the pressure on his forces. The question of what could be done was a difficult one. German forces advancing into the Soviet Union were even further beyond the reach of the RAF's heavy bombers than when they had invaded Poland. There was no opportunity for the British Army to engage the enemy anywhere to help Russia's plight. Later, Stalin would demand a premature invasion of France to draw German forces away from Russian territory, but in 1941 the only possible means of making an impact lay with the Royal Navy, and especially with naval air power.

The Commander-in Chief, Home Fleet, Admiral Sir John Tovey, was urged by Britain's wartime leader, Winston Churchill, to carry out an attack which would be 'a gesture in support of our

Russian allies to create a diversion on the enemy's northern flank'.[1] Still fresh from its victory at Taranto, the Royal Navy deployed one of its newest aircraft carriers, and its oldest, for the operation. The new vessel was HMS *Victorious*, a sister of HMS *Illustrious*, the victor of Taranto, while the other ship was HMS *Furious*, the first aircraft carrier. Aircraft still included the veteran Fairey Swordfish biplanes, but this time they were joined by Fairey Albacore torpedo-bombers, and escorted by Fairey Fulmar fighters.

It must have been tempting to consider this as a repeat of the mission against Taranto, but with supposedly more modern and more capable aircraft. It wasn't, and it couldn't be. In the almost twenty-four-hour summer daylight of the far north, the passage of the two ships northwards was spotted, and their intentions guessed, by German reconnaissance aircraft shortly before the aircraft were flown off on a late July afternoon in 1941.

Victorious was to send twenty Albacore torpedo-bombers to Kirkenes, escorted by Fulmar fighters, while *Furious* was to send nine Albacores and nine Swordfish, again escorted by Fulmars, to Petsamo, or Pechenga. The aircraft from *Victorious* had to fly over a German hospital ship on the way in to the target, and were ordered not to attack this, although, of course, those aboard could warn those ashore.

Neither port had the mass of shipping found at Taranto. Instead of attacking from the sea, at Kirkenes the aircraft had to fly over a mountain at the end of the fjord before diving into the bay, where they found just four ships. After enduring heavy anti-aircraft fire from positions on the cliffs, the attackers were themselves assaulted by German fighters, and most of them had to jettison their torpedoes in a desperate bid to escape. They managed to sink only one cargo vessel of just 2,000 tons, and set another on fire. The slow and lumbering Fulmars did well to shoot down four Luftwaffe aircraft. At Petsamo, the harbour was empty, and the frustrated aircrew could do nothing more than loose their torpedoes at the wharves.

In the operation, *Victorious* lost 13 of her aircraft, while *Furious* lost 3. Altogether, 44 aircrew were lost, 7 of them killed, the remainder taken prisoner.

Tovey's reaction to this debacle was clear. 'The gallantry of the aircraft crews, who knew before leaving that their chance of surprise had gone, and that they were certain to face heavy odds, is beyond praise. . . . I trust that the encouragement to the morale of our allies was proportionately great.'[2]

The operation had no bearing on the course of the war, in contrast to Taranto, where the raid stopped the Italian Navy from using the port for the duration of hostilities as well as inflicting heavy, tangible, losses. Aircraft and their even more valuable and difficult to replace aircrew were lost.

Opinion is polarized between those who believe support was necessary to keep Russia in the war, and those who argue that the Soviet regime deserved little help, and that the Russian winter should have been left to do its worst. This is the old argument that 'General Winter' is Russia's most successful general! Which of these would have been right is difficult to assess. Stalin could have negotiated an armistice and ceded the Ukraine to Germany, releasing German forces for operations in western Europe and North Africa. Whether or not the Germans would have felt at ease reducing their presence in the Ukraine, and risking Russian retaliation at a later stage, is a moot point.

NOTES

1. *Daily Telegraph*, 30 October 1996.
2. Ibid.

Thirteen

FIGHTING THE WEATHER AND THE GERMANS: THE ARCTIC CONVOYS, 1941–4

The sudden ending of the uneasy alliance between Germany and the Soviet Union meant that the Russians had an insatiable appetite for war material of all kinds.

Invaded by Germany, the Soviet Union changed sides in the Second World War. In her time of need, the Soviet Union turned shamelessly to the much-despised west for aid – expecting the shortfall in her defence needs to be met by British and, later, American output. Terrific moral pressure was brought to bear on the other Allies by the single-minded insistence of the Russians to be given the necessary support. At its most extreme, there were the almost hysterical demands for a second front although, as many of the Nazi leaders later claimed, the Allied bombing campaign was indeed the second front.

Stalin worked hard to convey the impression that while Russia suffered, her new allies were doing nothing. Insult was added to injury as later Russian records failed to note the achievements made possible by western aid. Researchers scan official Russian accounts in vain for the mention of British and American equipment supplied.

War between Germany and the Soviet Union had highlighted Russia's lack of preparation, and the weaknesses of Soviet industry. Russia suddenly needed the means with which to fight war, and especially aircraft, tanks, guns and ammunition. Soviet industry had not developed sufficiently after the revolution, and at the onset of war, both industry and the products provided were far behind those of the west. Russian industry had also suffered tremendous upheaval and disruption in the evacuation of heavy manufacturing industry east of the Ural Mountains. The movement of industry east was a necessary step, although it made it difficult to copy the British system of shadow factories, which did so much to increase British war production.

In an attempt to allay Russian concerns and enable them to resist the German advances, a system of convoys was introduced, sailing from Scotland and Iceland, where ships assembled from British and American ports. The route was round the North Cape, to Murmansk and Archangel. At any time of the year, this was hard going, and never more so than in winter, with almost constant darkness, extremely bad weather and sub-zero temperatures.

Convoys to the north of Russia faced some of the worst weather to be encountered on any major sea route. The Germans had the whole of the heavily indented Norwegian coastline in which to hide their ships, including the pride of the German Navy, the battleship *Tirpitz*. Ashore, they had Norwegian air bases. If this combination of weather, surface ships and air power was not enough, the U-boat fleet could also be deployed against convoys. Bad weather favoured the U-boat.

It is impossible to overestimate the problems. Gale force winds could tear an aircraft from the flight deck of an aircraft carrier, while the wind frequently exceeded the flying speed of the Fairey Swordfish biplane, at first the Fleet Air Arm's main defence against enemy submarines. In winter, the sea shipped in a storm would freeze on the deck and superstructure of a ship. Bad weather contributed to fatigue among the crews of the merchant ships and their escorts. One naval officer, having difficulty eating a meal as his cruiser rolled to angles of 30 degrees, consoled himself that life was much worse aboard the smaller escort vessels, which rolled to 50 degrees, and occasionally even more. On watch, frostbite was a danger, even to one's nose, and touching metal with a bare hand meant the skin peeling off.

Life expectancy once in the sea could be measured in minutes, a thought that could never be far from the minds of the seamen and airmen involved. For those on the ships carrying explosives, life expectancy in the sea was academic. A direct hit, by bomb, torpedo or shell, meant a large flash, and that was it. The noise could be heard through ship's plating, above the noise of ship's machinery, a mile away. Those on the decks of their ships would feel the heat of the blast. Yet, the odds were also high. In his book, *Arctic Convoys*, Richard Woodman points out that 'the sinking of a single 10,000 ton freighter was the equivalent, in terms of material destroyed, of a land battle'. Losing more than one such ship was the equivalent of an army being overrun.

While the passage from Scotland and Iceland to Russia does not seem as exposed as that across the North Atlantic, the weather was far worse. Air cover was also absent. Having occupied Iceland to prevent it falling into German hands and to provide bases for maritime reconnaissance, the Allies had a good forward base. Even so, at best, there was a gap of at least 600 nautical miles between the limit of air patrols from Iceland and the Shetlands, and the limit of those from Russian territory, which usually had to be provided by RAF units based there. The 'gap' without air cover could, at convoy speed, amount to a good four days. The arrival of the escort carrier improved matters, taking anti-submarine and fighter protection with the convoy, although launching and recovering aircraft in bad weather was far from an easy task.

The most notorious of all the Russian convoys was the ill-fated PQ17. Acutely aware of the threat posed by the German battleship *Tirpitz*, which had arrived in Norway in January 1942, the Royal Navy and Royal Air Force tried on many occasions to sink the vessel. Due to the difficulties created by the ship's fjord anchorage, it was not until late 1944 that the RAF managed to sink the *Tirpitz*. Watched by the Norwegian resistance movement, it was a change of berth that caused alarm at the Admiralty in London on 4 July 1942, and caused the First Sea Lord, Admiral of the Fleet Sir Dudley Pound, to order convoy PQ17 to scatter.

The convoy had sailed from Hvalfiordur in Iceland on 27 June 1942. It consisted of 34 merchant vessels, 3 rescue ships and 13 escorts. A close support force of 4 cruisers and 3 destroyers accompanied the convoy. While, in theory, there was protection from the Home Fleet, with 2 battleships and an aircraft carrier, as well as another 2 cruisers and 13 destroyers, these were too far away to offer the protection needed from a concerted German attack. The 4 cruisers accompanying the convoy would not have been able to protect it against the *Tirpitz*, with her eight 15-in guns.

Luftwaffe attacks began on 2 July, and by 4 July, when reports were received by the Admiralty that the *Tirpitz* had sailed with an escort of three cruisers, three ships had already been lost to air attack. Faced with what seemed to be an extremely unfavourable position should the German battleship get within range of the convoy, the order was given for the convoy to scatter, in the belief that the individual ships presented a more difficult prey than a single large convoy. While the German surface vessels did not turn up as expected, over the next five days Luftwaffe and U-boat attacks accounted for the loss of twenty-three merchant vessels and one of the rescue ships. Fifteen ships were lost on one day alone, 5 July. Two-thirds of the cargo for Russia was lost. The Luftwaffe lost just five aircraft.

Naval historians have been divided over whether the decision to order the convoy to scatter was the right one, given the circumstances at the time. Had the convoy had an aircraft carrier close at hand, and possibly a battleship as well, the wiser decision would have been to keep the ships together. Not only were convoys safer than independent sailing – unless a ship was remarkably fast, as with some of the big ocean liners on trooping duties, such as the RMS *Queen Elizabeth* – operational research showed that the larger the convoy, the greater the chance of survival for individual ships.

The next convoy, PQ18, was the first Arctic convoy to have an escort carrier, HMS *Avenger*, as well as a cruiser, HMS *Scylla*. This was an even larger convoy, with forty-one merchant ships and twenty-one escorts, including the carrier and cruiser. One of the merchant vessels also carried a catapult-launched Hawker Sea Hurricane fighter. There were four rescue ships, including three minesweepers being delivered from the United States to the Soviet Union. *Avenger* carried three Fairey Swordfish equipped with radar for anti-submarine operations, and twelve Hawker Sea Hurricane fighters, although some of these were dismantled and carried in her hold as a reserve.

Once again, there followed the pattern of repeated attacks. While still at Iceland, *Avenger* was attacked by a Luftwaffe Focke-Wulf Fw 200 Condor maritime-reconnaissance aircraft, and then again on 8 September, once the convoy was at sea. Thick overcast cloud then kept the convoy safe until 12 September, when it was discovered by a German Blohm und Voss Bv 138 flying-boat, which managed to escape back into the clouds before the Sea Hurricanes could be scrambled. A day or so later, the Swordfish discovered another flying-boat laying mines ahead of the convoy.

On 13 September, the Luftwaffe made its main attack. Sixty-six aircraft, mainly Junkers Ju 88s but with a substantial number of Heinkel He 111s, made a bombing and torpedo attack, having waited until the Sea Hurricanes were back aboard their ship for refuelling. Within fifteen minutes, eight ships had been lost for just five Luftwaffe aircraft. One, the *Empire Stevenson*, filled with ammunition, disappeared in a single big explosion.

U-boats were also in the area. One U-boat escaped attack from the Swordfish that had discovered it, but was sunk shortly afterwards by a destroyer. Increasingly, a pattern emerged of the Swordfish being intimidated by the German reconnaissance aircraft so that they were forced back towards the convoy. When an assault on the carrier itself was detected, the Sea Hurricanes, by now on constant patrol, managed to fight it off and with support from anti-aircraft fire, eleven German aircraft were shot down. In a further attack, the Sea Hurricanes were forced into their own anti-aircraft fire, and three out of the four on patrol were shot down, although the pilots were all rescued. Later, another ammunition ship was blown up.

Relief came for the convoy on 16 September, when it came under the protection of RAF Consolidated Catalina flying-boats based in Russia. From this time on, improved convoy protection and the growing use of escort carriers saw losses on the Arctic convoys fall.

The Russian convoys were either a necessity to keep the Soviet Union in the war, or a waste of men and equipment. But there is another way of looking at this. Many who went with the convoys were to find aircraft parked, unused, on Russian airfields. It was all too commonplace to find that the Russians were either not using, or were being slow at putting into service, better aircraft than had been made available to those charged with protecting the convoys.

The question is whether the manpower, ships and aircraft used to protect the Russian convoys could have been put to better use elsewhere by the Allies. Could the same be asked about the equipment sent to Russia? If the Soviet Union had ceded the Ukraine to Germany, and even if the Germans had then redeployed the forces so released back to France and Italy, how long would it have been before the Soviet Union would have been compelled to renew hostilities to retake the Ukraine? Given the poor preparation of the Germans, was Allied intervention necessary at all?

During the first six months after the German invasion of the Soviet Union, at least 200 Hawker Hurricane fighters were sent to the Soviet Union; these aircraft could have made a difference when Japan invaded Malaya. The cruisers and aircraft carriers might not have fared too well against the Japanese, but they too could have made a difference elsewhere, especially in the North Atlantic, and perhaps also in the Mediterranean. A Soviet Union forced to fight on its own would eventually have been compelled to do so. Furthermore, German forces inadequately prepared would sooner or later have been broken. The consequence could well have been that German defeat would have come from the Red Army racing across eastern Europe towards Berlin, but with British and American forces taking Germany and perhaps even liberating Poland and Czechoslovakia. The people of these countries could have been saved almost half a century of virtual slavery.

Fourteen

THE VICTORY THAT NEVER
WAS: PEARL HARBOR, 1941

*The Japanese attack on Pearl Harbor on 7 December 1941 is often
presented as a major American failure rather than a major strategic
blunder by the Japanese.*

On 7 December 1941, 353 aircraft flying from 6 Japanese
aircraft carriers sprung a surprise attack on the US Pacific
Fleet at its base at Pearl Harbor, in Hawaii. This was the
outcome of a plan prepared by Admiral Isoroku Yamamato, and
was intended to end the imbalance between the Imperial
Japanese Navy and its foe, the United States Navy. As with the
Russo-Japanese War almost forty years earlier, the attack was
made in advance of the formal declaration of war.

Pearl Harbor has usually been presented as a great Japanese
victory. Like the North Koreans less than a decade later, the
Japanese attacked on a Sunday morning, in the well-justified
belief that this would find the defences at a low ebb, with most,
if not all, commanders away from their posts, and their
subordinates at rest; the army and navy commanders were
spending the morning playing golf together.

Japanese forces had the advantage of surprise, sailing through
a tropical storm and launching their aircraft in conditions that
would have seen exercises cancelled. Even though the Americans
knew that the Japanese fleet was at sea, they had convinced
themselves that it was headed for South-east Asia. When a radar
operator at the radar station on the northern tip of Oahu Island
reported blips, the duty officer, Lieutenant Kermit Tyler, simply

replied, 'Well, don't worry about it.' To be fair, he was expecting a flight of B-17 bombers. The radar station itself was about to close down for the day.

Even if Tyler had sounded the alarm, the attack could not have been stopped, but the defences would have been prepared and those men aboard their ships or at their shore stations could have gone to action stations. Fighter aircraft could have got off the ground. The Japanese had expected to have to fight their way to the target and were surprised to find that they reached it unscathed. Despite the rising tension between the two countries and Japan's known friendliness towards the Germans and Italians, the ships in the harbour did not even have torpedo nets in place – which the Japanese had expected to find.

There was nothing new about American suspicions over Japanese intentions. The Russo-Japanese War had been fought because of conflicting ambitions on the Asian mainland, where Japan had already seized Korea. Much of the allied intervention in the Russian Civil War, which could have foiled the Bolshevik Revolution, floundered as the Japanese tried to pursue their own agenda and the Americans endeavoured to stop them. As the century moved on, Japanese aggression and Chinese weakness presented an unhealthy combination, not conducive to stability in the Far East.

While at first the Americans were reluctant to act, with many favouring a policy of isolationism, to some Japanese war with the United States seemed inevitable. American opinion changed as the extent of Japanese ambitions became clear. Japanese atrocities in China could not be ignored, especially after the rape of the former Nationalist Chinese capital of Nanking, which fell to Japanese forces in December 1937. The signing of a non-aggression pact between Japan and the Soviet Union further emphasized Japanese ambitions, and left French Indo-China under threat.

In December 1940 the United States imposed an embargo on the sale of scrap metal and war materials to Japan. This was followed by the freezing of Japanese assets in the United States in July 1941, after Japan invaded Indo-China. The United Kingdom followed, denying Japan the currency with which to purchase oil and raw materials. Japan was left with a strategic reserve of 55 billion barrels of oil, enough for eighteen months of war. The only way to extend this was for Japan to find another source of oil, by invading the Netherlands East Indies.

Despite many Japanese seeing war with the United States as inevitable, others fully appreciated the enormity of the task, and some at least of these were opposed to war. One realist was none other than the Commander-in-Chief of the Imperial Japanese Navy's First Fleet, Admiral Isoroku Yamamoto. He fully realized that Japan would not be able to match the United States either militarily or, no less important in modern warfare, in industrial output. Yamamoto's view was that Japan could win a major victory during the first year of war, but that by the second year, the United States would have recovered and could move to the offensive. Although the Imperial Japanese Navy was superior in strength to the United States Navy in the Pacific, it was weaker than the combined strength of the United States Pacific and Atlantic Fleets.

Regardless of Yamamoto's opinions, the government of Japan was in the hands of the army-dominated pro-war faction. The inability to buy crude oil also meant that Japan had either to abandon its plans for what amounted to an Asian empire, the so-called Greater Asia Co-Prosperity Sphere, or go to war and achieve its needs by conquest.

Japan had few friends. The Soviet Union and the United States saw her as a dangerous rival, the British Empire also viewed her as a threat; and Germany and Italy were too far away to be able to provide any worthwhile assistance.

Yamamoto's orders were clear: he had to find a solution to the problem. He chose to strike a crippling blow at the US Pacific Fleet by attacking its main base at Pearl Harbor, on the Hawaiian island of Oahu. If Pearl Harbor could be knocked out and major units of the Pacific Fleet destroyed at the same time, it would take time for the United States to re-establish a significant naval presence in the area. Given the vast distances involved in the Pacific, control of the seas had to take precedence over everything else. The successful British raid on the Italian fleet at Taranto had proven that an attack on Pearl Harbor was feasible.

The Japanese were able to devote far greater resources to the operation than the British had managed at Taranto. Instead of 1 aircraft carrier with 21 obsolescent biplanes, they were able to use 6 aircraft carriers with 423 aircraft, and not a single biplane among them. The aircraft were modern monoplanes, including the famous Mitsubishi A6M, the 'Zero', but this was a fighter, and the real work was to be done by dive-bombers and torpedo-bombers, and the so-called 'level bombers', aircraft which dropped bombs in the conventional manner. They also had an even greater advantage of surprise than that enjoyed by the British at Taranto. Britain and Italy had been at war for some months by the time Taranto was attacked; Japan intended to attack without first declaring war on the United States. Circumstances aided the Japanese. The fleet approached the flying-off position through a tropical storm, so remained undetected. The United States Pacific Fleet had its battleships and cruisers in harbour, at peace on a Sunday morning. As already mentioned, the radar watch was lacking in many respects, and was not maintained continuously. Contrary to Japanese fears, the fleet did not even have torpedo nets around those ships that could have been vulnerable to such attack. There were no standing fighter patrols or ships on picket duty.

The Japanese sent 353 of their aircraft to Pearl Harbor. Rather than fighting their way to the target, as they had expected, the first wave of 183 aircraft was unchallenged, and even had the benefit of the local weather forecast from a radio station at Hawaii. Flying at 10,000 ft, the first wave passed over the northernmost point of Oahu at 0730 hr; Mitsuo Fuchida, leading the raid, called out 'Tenkai', ordering his aircraft into their assault positions. At 0749 hr, the attack began, Fuchida calling out 'Tora! Tora! Tora!' or 'Tiger! Tiger! Tiger!' – the code for surprise.

And surprise it was, with no anti-aircraft fire at first, and the sky completely clear of fighters. Freed from any need to defend the bombers, the Zeros dived down and raced across the dockyard and the airfields, firing at anything in their sights. Dive-bombers swooped down on Ford Island, their bombs causing fires and sending debris into the air. Torpedo-bombers flew so low when attacking Battleship Row that observers thought that they would never clear the towering superstructures. To many senior Japanese naval officers, like their counterparts in other navies still adherents of the 'big gun' navy, success was to be measured by the scale of the losses suffered by the Pacific Fleet.

By the time the level bombers started their bombing run over Battleship Row, anti-aircraft fire had started. Fuchida's own aircraft was hit, and then shaken by a near miss. It was only when he landed back on his ship, the carrier *Akagi*, that he found his aircraft had been severely damaged and had only just missed being shot down. Meanwhile, he remained to watch the second wave mount its assault. This time, the Zeros had to attack American fighters as they struggled into the air. The strike aircraft in the second wave consisted entirely of bombers and dive-bombers, as torpedo-bombers were seen as being too vulnerable once the defences had been alerted; later experience at the Battle of Midway was to prove this assessment of the dangers facing torpedo-bombers correct. As it was, almost all of the twenty-nine Japanese aircraft shot down over Hawaii that morning belonged to the second wave.

From his vantage point, Fuchida could see the battleship *Arizona* blazing 'like a forest fire', while the *Oklahoma* had capsized, along with the target ship *Utah*, counted by Japanese intelligence as an active battleship, while both the *California* and *West Virginia* were settling. The light cruiser *Helena* had been crippled. The *Pennsylvania* and two destroyers, all in dry dock, were all damaged.

In a stroke of bad luck for the Japanese, the commanding officer of another battleship, *Nevada*, decided that his ship would be safer at sea than sitting as a target in Battleship Row. The Japanese dive-bomber pilots realized that this was their chance of sinking the ship in the harbour mouth and blocking the port, and dived down onto the ship in the face of heavy anti-aircraft fire. The commanding officer did well to beach his ship, keeping the base functional and saving the *Nevada*.

On his return to the *Akagi*, Fuchida found the task force leader, Vice-Admiral Nagumo, impatient for news. Fuchida reported to the bridge: 'Four battleships sunk. I am confident of this from my personal observation.' He was asked about the other four. 'There hasn't been time to check results precisely, but it looks like three were seriously damaged, the other somewhat damaged, although not quite so badly.'[1] Fuchida described the other ships sunk or damaged. Asked whether the Pacific Fleet would be able to operate from Pearl Harbor for six months, he confirmed that although this was likely as far as the main force was concerned, many smaller vessels and the shore installations were still functional. He urged a further attack, at least a third wave, if not a fourth. The targets would be the remaining ships and, even more important, the shore installations and airfields.

As Fuchida completed his report, the hangar and flight deck crews were rearming and refuelling aircraft, including the torpedo-bombers that would be needed should American warships give chase. The Japanese were all too well aware that the big disappointment of the morning had been the absence of the American aircraft carriers from the ships assembled at Pearl Harbor. Torpedoes were more effective than bombs in the open sea, where there was often the problem that bombs would bounce off the heavy armour of a battleship.

While Fuchida lunched off rice crackers and bean paste, the decision was taken against a further strike. Nagumo ordered a withdrawal to the north-west. Angered by this action, Fuchida did the unthinkable for a Japanese officer, by storming to the bridge and bypassing the chain of command to ask Nagumo directly why an attack was not being ordered. Nagumo didn't reply; his Chief of Staff, Kusaka, abruptly told Fuchida that the raid's objectives had been met.

Any chance of victory had been lost by the Imperial Japanese Navy's failure to return to Pearl Harbor. The only possible justification would have been an attack on the Panama Canal to delay reinforcement of the Pacific Fleet. At no time was Pearl Harbor unavailable to the United States Navy. The airfields ashore were quickly repaired. The American carrier force remained at sea until it was safe to return, and then started the series of attacks that brought the Japanese to battle, and ultimately, to defeat.

A further raid on Pearl Harbor would have given the Japanese the breathing space they so desperately needed. The position of Pearl Harbor was crucial to the successful operation of the United States Pacific Fleet, whose next significant base was at San Diego, on the West Coast of the United States, and more than 2,000 miles away. Even given the US Navy's proficiency in refuelling and replenishing its ships while under way at sea, the lack of a forward base would have been a crippling blow. The problem was more than one of supply, or of an extra three days' steaming time for even the fastest ships, it also meant that badly damaged ships would have had further to sail before they could be repaired.

In not completing the attack and causing further devastating damage, the Japanese had failed miserably. They had done nothing more than awaken a giant and start a conflict that they could not win. The loss of the battleships was a blow to the United States Navy, but mainly because of the loss of experienced men and the impact on national morale. The war that had been started did not need battleships. They were already obsolete.

NOTES

1. Gordon W. Prange, Donald M. Goldstein and Katherine V. Dillon, *God's Samurai* (Washington DC, Brassey's, 1990).

Fifteen

THE PRICE OF COMPLACENCY: THE FALL OF SINGAPORE, 1942

Singapore was the British Empire's 'island fortress' in the Far East, positioned on the major shipping route through the Straits of Malacca, it was a major naval base.

On 7 December 1941, Japanese troops landed in Malaya (now Malaysia), and Siam (now Thailand), hitting the British Empire on the same day that they had attacked the United States in Hawaii. Their objective was Singapore, the key to control of the Far East. A strong naval base and supposedly also an island fortress, Singapore was linked to what was then known as Malaya by a causeway and a railway line, which ran north to Kuala Lumpur and on to Bangkok in Thailand. Singapore guarded the Straits of Malacca, the shortest and most direct route between the Indian Ocean and the South China Sea.

Britain had not identified the need for a strong base in the Far East until 1919. The reasons for this were not too difficult to find. The neighbouring territories were either also British colonies, or in friendly hands, in this area mainly Dutch, Portuguese or French. In addition, Singapore was not too far distant from India or Australia, while Japan had been an ally during the First World War. British sympathies during the earlier Russo-Japanese War had been with the Japanese but, by 1918, it was becoming clear that Japan's support could not always be relied upon. This was borne out by Japanese behaviour during the Russian Civil War. It was clear that Japan now had her own national agenda, one that did not coincide with that of the United Kingdom or her allies.

While the need for the base was identified in 1919, it was not seen as a desperate need. Despite concerns over Japanese intentions, there did not seem to be an immediate threat. The interwar period included the years of the great Depression, so the strict financial parsimony applied by successive British governments between the wars meant that completion of the defences to create a true 'island fortress' was forever being delayed. The irony of the situation was that the alternative location for a major naval base, Sydney, was ruled out because it was too far from Japan to be effective.

Singapore needed more than just fortifications. The island had been aptly described by the First World War naval veteran, Lord Jellicoe, as 'a haven only for a strong fleet' but, as war in the Far East approached, Singapore's defences suffered from the absence of that strong fleet. The major units of the Royal Navy were concentrated in the Atlantic and Mediterranean. This was nothing new; from the start of the twentieth century, the growing naval power of Germany had meant that the might of the British fleet had to be concentrated in home waters, in the North Atlantic and in the Mediterranean. Jellicoe's remarks accepted the danger to Singapore from an attack overland. The strong fleet would be needed to deny enemy forces access to the Malay Peninsula. At this stage few understood that the strong fleet was no longer enough on its own, but also needed strong air cover.

In theory, Singapore was well defended when war broke out in the Far East, but the reality was different. The defences depended heavily on five huge 15-in gun batteries. The myth has grown up that these gun batteries could only fire to seaward, and were of no help in countering an attack over land. This was untrue. Although the guns could have fired at the invading Japanese, they were only supplied with armour-piercing shells, of little effectiveness against Japanese infantry.

Preparations for the defence of Singapore reflected Britain's colonial complacency. They ignored growing alarm in Australia and New Zealand over the increasing belligerence of Japan, and that country's expanding military might, some of which had been with the assistance of a British Naval Mission in the 1920s. Both countries had to be satisfied with guarantees that, if war threatened in the east, the bulk of the Royal Navy would arrive within seventy days. Such promises were valueless, given the way in which events unfolded in the early years of the Second World War. Such a difficulty could have been foreseen. It was inevitable that Japan's boldness would be intensified by the conflict in Europe, which preoccupied the British and had seen the French and Dutch overrun by the Germans.

Recognizing the threat from Japan, the Admiralty had requested that there should be light- and medium-calibre field artillery able to defend the causeway, but the installation of these guns was opposed by the RAF, which wanted the available money spent on air defences instead. The RAF's argument was that any battle would be fought either over the sea or over Malaya. This was proved to be right, but the air defences were to be inadequate against the Japanese invasion.

To the end, the British deluded themselves. Britain's wartime leader, Winston Churchill, insisted that Singapore, with a garrison of 20,000 men, '. . . could only be taken by an enemy of at least 50,000 men. . . . As Singapore is as far away from Japan as Southampton is from New York, the operation of moving a Japanese Army . . . and maintaining it during a siege would be forlorn. Moreover, such a siege, which should last at least four or five months, would be liable to be interrupted, if at any time Britain chose to send a superior fleet to the scene.'[1] This might be forgiven as political rhetoric, intended to bolster morale. What cannot be forgiven was the refusal to send additional aircraft. The RAF had wanted 556 aircraft to defend Malaya and Singapore following the collapse of France, because support from forces in the French colonies could no longer be counted on. The British Chiefs of Staff had scaled this down, and suggested that Malaya and Singapore needed at least 336 modern aircraft for their defence, in addition to 48 infantry brigades and 2 armoured brigades.

The reality on the ground and in the air was that Singapore and Malaya had just 33 infantry battalions, not all fully trained, and no armour. As for aircraft, just 141 were present in 1940. The best of these were 41 Brewster Buffalo fighters, which were no match for the Japanese Zero. The rest included a mixture of elderly Vickers Wildebeeste torpedo-bombers; Bristol Blenheim bombers, already proving to be ineffectual in Europe; Bristol Beaufighter night fighters; a handful each of Swordfish and Shark biplanes; and some Lockheed Hudson patrol aircraft. Singapore was not receiving the attention it deserved. In the six months that preceded Pearl Harbor, at least 200 Hawker Hurricanes, many of them of the latest mark, were sent to the Soviet Union.

Japan's assault on Malaya came quickly, with the first troops landing on the evening of the day Pearl Harbor was attacked, taking Kota Baharu on the east coast near the border with Siam in order to seize the airfields. The invasion transports had been spotted on 6 December off Cape Cambodia, but at first their destination was not clear and, short of a pre-emptive attack, which would have started the war, nothing could be done. The main assault came the following day, 8 December 1941. Troops landed in the north of Malaya, although the main force attacked through neutral Siam and was able to establish a strong foothold there.

Attacking Malaya was strategically sound; the colony was difficult to defend. The terrain consisted of dense jungle, with swamps and mountains, and, inevitably, ground communications were poor. The British had made a number of strategic errors. They had failed to invade neighbouring Siam, because this assault on a neutral nation could have offended the United States. This was an interesting argument, since once committed to war, the United States showed little reluctance in invading neutral Iceland.

British strategy depended on defending the roads and railways running north–south throughout the Malay Peninsula, but the troops were not trained to fight in the jungles and swamps. Many airfields had been built for the defence of Malaya, but for too few aircraft, and these had to be defended to stop them falling into the hands of the Japanese, who already had plenty of aircraft. RAF planners had built the airfields, with no less than three at Kota Baharu, with little thought as to how they could be defended from ground attack. The Japanese had already shown that they favoured assaulting major harbours from the land, as at Port Arthur during the Russo-Japanese War.

Usually, an attacking force should outnumber the defenders, but in this case the defenders outnumbered the invaders. The British commander, Lieutenant-General Arthur Percival, had 88,000 troops under his command. These included 19,000 British, 15,000 Australians, 17,000 Malays and, inevitably in the Far East, the largest contingent came from India, which provided 37,000 troops. This force was ill-equipped, and lacked tanks. Its training had been for the pre-emptive invasion of Siam in Operation Matador, which, had it been put into effect, could have changed the situation. There was also an echo of Churchill's overconfidence. Even the RAF believed, with just 141 aircraft in the area, that they could sink 70 per cent of an invasion force before any troops could be landed. The Japanese invasion force consisted of just 35,000 men, but they also had 211 tanks and 560 aircraft.

British troops belatedly tried to advance into Siam, but were driven back by a combination of Japanese armour and air power. It took the Japanese just two days to push across the Malay Peninsula to the west coast. That same day, 10 December, Japanese aircraft sank the new battleship, HMS *Prince of Wales* and the elderly battlecruiser *Repulse*, gaining complete control of the seas. The loss of these two ships was another British blunder. Had they been operating as a properly constructed task group with a couple of aircraft carriers with high-performance fighters, the outcome might have been different. The plan had been for the two ships to operate with just one carrier, the new *Indomitable*, but she had run aground and was not available. The force commander, Rear Admiral Tom Phillips, thought that they could attack the invasion fleet, and discounted the threat of aerial assault. He even maintained radio silence, making it difficult for the RAF to offer air cover. Lacking such cover, it would have been better for both ships to have stayed away.

Contrary to popular belief, few, if any, of the Japanese troops were jungle-trained. It was the presence of armour, artillery and air power that made the difference. The defenders lacked good artillery, mobile anti-aircraft units, and, perhaps most telling of all, good anti-tank weapons. The Japanese also gained much-needed battlefield mobility by the simple expedient of seizing bicycles in captured Siamese and Malay territory.

Pre-invasion proposals for a series of defensive lines had been rejected on the grounds that they would be bad for morale, suggesting to the local population that not all of Malaya could be defended. Manuals describing how tanks could be knocked out without anti-tank weapons were kept at headquarters, while officers were forbidden to disseminate the information to their troops. After the invasion, successive attempts to establish a defensive line failed. A stand on the road at Jitra on 11 December was swept aside by Japanese tanks, supported by artillery. The decision was taken to start a general withdrawal, which rapidly descended into chaos, with many Allied troops becoming lost in the jungle. Again, an attempt to check the advance on the River Perak failed for the same reasons. When the defenders attempted to make a stand at Kampar, and finally succeeded in establishing a strong position, the Japanese used captured small craft to land behind the lines, outflanking the British Empire forces. These moves down the west coast were accompanied by steady progress down the east coast.

Lieutenant-General Pownall arrived on 23 December, taking over from Air Chief Marshal Brooke-Popham as Commander-in-

Chief of British forces in the Far East. He decided on a new plan, yet another stand, but on this occasion on the River Slim, still some distance north of Kuala Lumpur, the capital of Malaya. This was when the Japanese took to the jungle. They discovered an abandoned jungle track and used this to bypass the roads being covered by the defending forces, to mount a surprise attack on the bridge over the River Slim on 8 January.

Another change of command occurred on 10 January 1942, when General Wavell took over as Supreme Commander. There was also a change of strategy. The gradual fighting withdrawal wasn't working, and heavy losses were being suffered. Central Malaya was evacuated, with Kuala Lumpur taken by the Japanese on 11 January, while a new defensive line was established with fresh troops from Singapore at the River Muar. Once again, the Japanese bypassed the defensive line, landing at Batu Pahat to cut off the defending Australian and Indian troops. A final attempt to hold the Japanese at Johore failed. On 31 January 1942, the remaining British Empire troops fell back into Singapore.

Following the rout of the defending forces in Malaya, Singapore's garrison was inflated by those troops who had managed to withdraw to the island, giving a force of 85,000 troops, of whom no less than 70,000 were combatants. While the original force in Malaya had been poorly equipped, what little equipment there had been was abandoned. Eventual defeat seemed inevitable, no matter how many troops were on the ground. Faced with this inevitable outcome, the British sent additional troops. This decision was taken under pressure from the Australian government, which felt that to abandon Singapore would show that Britain had failed to keep her promises of the interwar years.

There was no air power left to the defenders at this stage. The 15-in guns were fired at the Japanese, but their armour-piercing shells had little serious impact on the advancing troops. Fragmentation shells would have been more successful against infantry, but there weren't any. These guns were meant to fight off an invading fleet, hitting the battleships and cruisers, and no other situation had been considered.

The key to Singapore was the causeway linking the island with Malaya, and this was heavily defended. The Japanese mounted a heavy air and artillery bombardment to damage the defences, before again bypassing the fixed defences and landing 13,000 assault troops along some eight miles of waterfront. This action forced the defenders of the causeway to withdraw, or risk being cut off by the invaders, and so the main route into Singapore was wide open and unprotected. Further Japanese landings followed, allowing them to build up their forces to some 30,000 men. At this stage, the final defensive line was abandoned, with most of the supplies. A last-ditch attempt was then made to defend Singapore City itself, but this could not be sustained due to a shortage of water. On 15 February, Percival surrendered 130,000 men to the Japanese commander, General Yamashita.

Malaya's loss and the fall of Singapore, believed to have been at the cost of less than 10,000 Japanese troops, established the Japanese in a strong position throughout South-east Asia. It paved the way for the attacks on New Guinea and Burma, which were to mark the limits of the Japanese advance. Before Singapore fell, the Netherlands East Indies was already substantially under Japanese control, with many of the oil refineries being seized intact. The Japanese captured many of the 98,000 Dutch troops in the region. At the Battle of the Java Sea, on 27 February, the Japanese scored yet another victory due to the absence of air cover for the Allied ships.

It is open to question whether the Japanese assault could have been rebuffed by better equipped defenders with air power and armour, as well as anti-tank weapons. Given the area that had to be defended, to some extent the advantage was always with the attacker. Yet, many military theorists believe that a successful assault generally needs a three-to-one margin of numerical superiority, and in Malaya and Singapore, this margin was reversed. Sending major capital ships to sea without naval air cover was a complete waste of men and ships at a crucial period. The Japanese gave the impression at this stage of the war of always being in control of the situation, but this only happened because they were allowed to be.

In the longer term, the outcome marked the end of the European empires. The Japanese had wanted to deprive the Europeans of their colonies in the Far East, and in the end, this was the result. The indigenous populations discovered that the European empires were too big to be defended successfully, and that their military power had severe limitations. Any myth about European superiority was cruelly crushed by the Japanese victories. Yet, the Japanese were also making the same mistake. Their new empire was also stretching their resources to the limit. Although the capture of the Dutch oil refineries was a great boost to national morale and to the war economy, which could no longer be harmed by British and American sanctions, communications became so stretched that they were vulnerable to attack by American submarines. The Japanese failed to institute a convoy system for their merchant vessels, and this was proved to be a fatal flaw in their conduct of the war.

NOTES

1. L. Allen, *Singapore, 1941–2* (London, Davis & Poynter, 1977).

Sixteen

MEDITERRANEAN CROSSROADS: THE FAILURE TO INVADE MALTA, 1940–3

Malta controlled the shipping routes through the Mediterranean, but the RAF and the British Army felt that it could not be defended against attack, or invasion.

During 1940–1, that first winter of Italian involvement in the war, the Luftwaffe's *Fliegerkorps X* was in Sicily, building up its strength to 450 aircraft by March 1941. No fewer than 200 of these were transport aircraft, which had one purpose, the invasion of Malta. Italian and German air power was tightly coordinated, through a joint liaison staff, *ItalLuft*, established by the Luftwaffe and the Regia Aeronautica in June 1940, as soon as Italy had joined the war on the side of Germany.

Malta sits in one of the two most important strategic positions in the Mediterranean Sea. It is almost exactly halfway between that other vital strategic position, Gibraltar, and the Suez Canal. The island, or small group of islands of which Malta itself is the largest, is also situated on the most direct route between Italy and North Africa. In effect, Malta stands at a crossroads of the Mediterranean. Long known as a major naval base, even before the outbreak of the Second World War, Malta was renowned for its dockyard facilities. It was the base for the Mediterranean Fleet, whose ships were to be seen in the Grand Harbour and Sliema Creek. Naval bases seldom exist in isolation, and Malta also had a substantial army garrison, including locally raised troops, while inevitably, the Royal Air Force also had bases on the island. On an island group of just 127 square miles, with the traditional bases confined to the main island, during the Second World War the RAF and Fleet Air Arm had three airfields and a flying-boat station between them. Newest of these was the airfield at Ta Kali, near the ancient capital of Mdina, which had been planned as an aerodrome for Imperial Airways.

Given the proximity to Italy, and that country's interest in North Africa and her close association with Germany, it seemed inevitable that Malta would be in the front line if Italy entered the war on the side of Germany. Perhaps the only surprise was that this was delayed until 10 June 1940, when the Battle of France was almost over.

The Chiefs of Staff of both the British Army and the Royal Air Force were agreed that once hostilities started, Malta could not be defended. Just 60 miles from Sicily, they felt that the island was vulnerable to air attack, bombardment from the sea, and to a naval and air blockade. There was little room in which to fight should enemy forces manage to land, and the speed at which the Germans had silenced the Belgian forts could not be overlooked.

A contrary view was that of the Royal Navy. In the inevitable inter-service discussions and submissions to the British War Cabinet, the Royal Navy insisted that Malta could be defended. The Admiralty even went further, pleading that Malta should remain as a base for submarines and light forces, which could attack the Axis supply lines to North Africa. The naval arguments won the day.

Italy's air force, the Regia Aeronautica, wasted little time after the declaration of war before starting to bomb Malta, concentrating on the capital, Valletta, and, across Grand Harbour, the dockyard, set amid the historic 'three towns', as well as the airfields. Malta itself was not the sole target; the other primary targets were the convoys bringing fuel, food, ammunition and, above all, aircraft to the island and to British forces in Egypt, protecting the Suez Canal.

At first the outlook was bleak and the threat of an invasion real. In 1941 and 1942, the siege almost brought the island to its knees. Fighter defence initially consisted of just three obsolescent Gloster Sea Gladiator biplanes left behind by the aircraft carrier HMS *Eagle*. These were the famous *Faith*, *Hope* and *Charity*. A Home Defence Force was established to support the Army, which included Maltese units, and this eventually became the Malta Volunteer Defence Force.

Convoys to Malta were wiped out by persistent Italian and German aerial attack. British forces in Egypt, guarding the Suez Canal, had to be supplied by ships taking the long and circuitous route around Africa and through the Canal from the south. At one stage, the main means of supplying Malta was by using the three fast minelayers, HMS *Abdiel*, *Manxman* and *Welshman*, capable of a 40-knot dash. These were augmented by specially modified submarines, which had to submerge in the harbour during daylight to avoid enemy bombing, and unload their cargo of fuel at night. The new British airline, the British Overseas Airways Corporation (BOAC), formed by the 1940 merger of Imperial Airways and British Airways, used obsolescent converted bombers to ferry supplies.

Fighter aircraft could only be sent to the island by being flown off at extreme range from aircraft carriers, including the USS *Wasp*, which made two such trips after the United States entered the war. The Spitfires and Hurricanes were attacked as soon as they landed, but fortunately, as time passed and the island's defences improved, it later became possible to mount air patrols to coincide with the new arrivals, which were quickly refuelled and returned to the air.

The island's position began to improve as the Allies started to make progress in North Africa, progress which was helped by the constant attacks on the Axis convoys by Malta-based submarines and light naval forces. The turning point is frequently regarded as the convoy, Operation Pedestal, in August 1942. Nevertheless, it was not until the Allied invasion of Sicily the following year that the strain began to ease on the island and the siege could truly be regarded as having been lifted.

Malta was as obvious a base for the Germans and Italians as it was for the British, and an invasion of Malta was planned, Operation Hercules. Taking Malta and using it as a forward base for aerial operations against British forces in North Africa made good sense. It would have removed a thorn from the side of the Axis forces as they sought to keep their troops in North Africa supplied. Finally, it would block any attempt by the British to re-establish their supply routes across the Mediterranean to Egypt. Taking Malta held the prize of control of the Mediterranean.

So, what happened? Why didn't the Germans and Italians seize Malta? One problem was that the war was not going to plan elsewhere. Germany's new allies, the Italians, had failed to take Greece and Yugoslavia, and on 6 April 1941 the Germans were forced to launch Operation Marita, the simultaneous invasion of both countries. Yugoslavia surrendered on 17 April, followed by Greece on 20 April. German airborne forces had to be deployed in an attempt to cut off the retreating British, Australian and New Zealand forces in the Peloponnese, and managed to capture some 10,000 of the 50,000 troops. The remainder of the British Empire force was evacuated to Crete, which became the next priority for the Germans.

Attention turned away from Malta to Crete because the Germans saw two advantages. The first would be the capture of the island and the British troops. The second would be a stepping stone for an invasion of Cyprus, which would finally put German air power within reach of the Suez Canal. This became a greater priority than the taking of Malta. The big obstacle to an invasion of Crete was the Royal Navy's domination of the eastern Mediterranean. The Luftwaffe had aerial supremacy, but only within range of its airfields. It was the Luftwaffe that decided on a paratroop assault on Crete, since these troops belonged to it, and the decision was taken without any reference to the army High Command. It is still a matter of debate whether the plan to invade Crete was simply a question of inter-service rivalry – of the Luftwaffe trying to show how all-powerful it had become. It could equally well have been a reflection of the 'Führer system', under which the service chiefs were largely unaware of the problems faced and advantages enjoyed by their colleagues in other arms. There is also the possibility that it could have been an attempt by the Luftwaffe chiefs to further defer the start of Operation Barbarossa, already delayed due to the invasion of Yugoslavia and Greece, beyond a date when it would have been a practical proposition. Finally, the Luftwaffe, after its failure in the Battle of Britain, needed a success.

Once the idea was sold to Hitler, army units were ordered to take part. This meant that once the paratroops had secured airfields, air-landed troops could be flown in. A force of 500 Junker Ju 52/3 transports was assigned to *Fliegerkorps XI*, plus 80 DFS 230 gliders, to be supported by 280 bombers, 150 dive-bombers and 180 fighters. The leader of the operation, General Kurt Student, was unaware that instead of an expected 15,000 British and Empire troops, his men would face twice that number, plus 11,000 Greek troops. The defenders had lost most of their heavy equipment in Greece, having little artillery, virtually no radios, and were also short of ammunition.

Despite the difficulties facing the defenders, the invasion of Crete was almost a disaster for the Germans. The first airlift started before dawn on 20 May 1941. Despite one of the gliders containing a headquarters unit, and Sussman, leader of one of the main invasion groups, breaking up in mid-air, the poor state of Crete's defences meant that just seven aircraft were lost in the initial assault. The defenders were convinced that an amphibious attack was likely, and so the main forces were assembled on the coast. As the invasion started things began to go wrong. Later gliders were hit by heavy and accurate machine-gun fire, and many crashed as they came in to land. One of the two main groups was almost wiped out by a well-organized British counter-attack. By nightfall, much of the German force was scattered across the island, fighting as small independent groups.

Congestion on the airfields back in Greece meant that the second wave was late in starting. Casualties were heavier among the transport aircraft this time, and many of the paratroops were shot as they descended, so that afterwards much of the island had the corpses of paratroopers in the branches of the trees.

The battle could easily have been lost by the Germans but for the shortage of radios among the defenders. Had the defending forces been better coordinated, with good communications, the Germans would have been defeated. As it was, fighting continued for several days, allowing all but 5,000 of the defending forces to be taken to safety by the Royal Navy. Having spent the early years of the war with few casualties, the Germans were now faced with more than 4,000 paratroops and air-landed troops killed, including more than 300 drowned, as gliders and aircraft ditched in the sea. Faced with this costly victory, Hitler forbade any further major assaults from the air.

At the time, the decision to leave Malta to the combined tactics of heavy bombing and a blockade of the shipping routes seemed to be the right one. The island was within such easy reach of German forces in Italy, Sicily and North Africa that it was an easy target, all the more so for being densely populated.

An invasion of Malta would have been a different proposition from Crete. Malta could have been easier for the invader. There are no mountains and few trees; however, the island is divided into small fields with dry stone walls, making a decent landing run for a glider impossible. At the time, the forces on the island would have had the equipment, including radios and anti-aircraft guns, to give a good account of themselves. In addition, for the defending forces, movement around the island would

The Japanese battleship Asahi, one of four ships that faced a numerically superior Russian force in the Battle of Tsushima, 1905, and won. (IWM Q41292)

Australian troops using ships' boats and barges to land at Anzac Cove at the start of the Gallipoli Campaign, 25 April 1915. (IWM HU57389)

As the Gallipoli Campaign ground to a halt, an attempt to break the stalemate came with landings at Suvla Bay in August 1915. This photograph clearly shows the lack of any sense of urgency with which these landings started. (IWM Q70703)

During the Battle of Cambrai on the Western Front in 1917 British forces reached the St Quentin Canal, but the tank Flying Fox crashed through the bridge at Masnières, making it unusable for those following. (IWM Q56826)

A recaptured British tank, 1917. This could have been one captured by the Germans when it ran out of fuel, and which was pressed into German Army service. (IWM Q56823)

Russian Don Cossacks are being trained on British equipment, 1919. British intervention in the Russian Civil War was initially intended to keep Russia involved in the war against Germany, and then to provide a force around which White Russian, or anti-Bolshevik, elements could coalesce. (IWM Q75897)

Further north, Karelian troops were also trained by a British contingent. The Karelians are seen here wearing British uniforms, as they joined in fighting that ultimately led to the independence of Finland. (IWM Q73467)

The men of a ski patrol are seen here lying in wait for Russian troops during the Winter War, January 1940. In this war Finnish troops were heavily outnumbered by the Russian invaders, but far better equipped. Ski patrols possessed the mobility that their opponents lacked. (IWM Q55566)

More reminiscent of gun turrets on a warship, these are the heavy artillery of a Maginot Line fortress, waiting for the enemy, but they were by-passed. (IWM MH24417)

Abandoned French tanks in a residential street, following the retreat to Dunkirk and the fall of France, June 1940. (IWM HU8212)

Dunkirk saw the evacuation of the British Expeditionary Force, but equipment had to be left behind. These are abandoned British Army lorries. (IWM HU69731)

Withdrawal from Norway, 1940. Here is the British aircraft carrier HMS Glorious, the day before she was sunk, with the evacuated RAF Hawker Hurricane fighters ranged aft on her flight deck.

The blitz seriously affected many British cities. This is the aftermath of a raid on Portsmouth, close to the city centre (the tower in the background is that of the Guildhall). (IWM HU36197)

Failure to make good use of the carrier saw HMS Courageous *sunk by a German submarine within weeks of the outbreak of the Second World War.*

At first, all went well for the German invasion of the Soviet Union, Operation Barbarossa, in 1941. Here, German soldiers throng a street in the Ukraine, outside a damaged shop. (IWM HU5052)

The Luftwaffe succeeded in the rapid defeat of the Red Air Force during Operation Barbarossa in 1941, but those Russian pilots who did get into the air succeeded in putting up a fight. This is a Heinkel He 111 bomber that survived being rammed by a Russian pilot. (IWM HU39684)

The excesses of the Communist regime meant that not all Soviet citizens hastened to defend their country. Here, German troops are joined by members of a locally recruited militia. (IWM HU8905)

On the Russian convoys survival time in the Arctic waters could be measured in minutes, but for the crew of this ammunition ship, the matter was academic as she blew up after being bombed by the Luftwaffe, taking the bomber with her. (IWM A12275)

Admiral Isoruko Yamamoto was the architect of the attack on Pearl Harbor, 7 December 1941, and among the first of Japan's senior commanders to appreciate that the operation had failed to achieve all of its objectives. (IWM HU36485)

The Japanese Army did not have everything its own way as it raced south through Malaya to Singapore. Here Japanese tanks burn after being ambushed by Australian troops early in 1942. (IWM MH31388)

A German Ju 88 bomber is silhouetted against the Grand Harbour during a raid over Malta, late April 1942. The capital Valletta is seen at the bottom of the photograph with the Admiralty Dockyard top left. (IWM HU40200)

Luftwaffe personnel with German newspapers while off duty in Sicily, enjoying the winter sunshine, mid-February 1941. (IWM HU39457)

During the Second World War the Imperial Japanese Navy had a powerful submarine force, including mine-laying submarines such as I–121, seen here. However, worthwhile targets such as the Pacific portals of the Panama Canal were left alone. (IWM MH6185)

The Battle of Midway in 1942 saw the Imperial Japanese Navy lose four aircraft carriers in a single day. The last to be destroyed was Hiryu, seen here with much of her flight deck blown away as a result of USN bombing. (IWM MH6492)

The mainstay of operations such as those at Nuremberg on 30 March 1944 was the Avro Lancaster bomber, the best heavy bomber of the Second World War. Unfortunately, the majority lacked a ventral turret able to cope with German night fighters with upward firing cannon. (RAFM P016423)

The first conflict in which the United Nations took sides was the Korean War. Here American troops are moving through a British position to the frontline – with some friendly banter between the two armies. (IWM BF168)

A Royal Navy Sea Hawk races across Egypt during the Suez Campaign of 1956. (FAAM SH62)

Defeat, as South Vietnamese hand in their weapons after the Viet Cong victory in 1975. (IWM HU30978)

Other South Vietnamese struggle to get aboard a helicopter to be flown to American warships and freedom. (IWM HU30996)

British troops examine abandoned Iraqi arms and ammunition in the desert during the Gulf War. (IWM GLF1)

In the former Yugoslavia, armoured fighting vehicles, such as these British Army Warriors, were an essential element, combining mobility and protection from sniper fire for the infantry. These Warriors are in Bosnia. (IWM BOS21)

have been less difficult than on the steep and narrow mountain roads of Crete.

Once the moment was lost, the opportunity for an invasion disappeared. Failure to take Malta at an early stage of the war gave the islands' defenders time to establish increasingly stronger defences. As they did so, the naval forces based on Malta became ever more successful at intercepting supplies for Rommel's Afrika Korps in North Africa. Many of the Royal Navy's most successful submarine operations of the Second World War were mounted from Malta. The next stage was for the island to become the base for a growing volume of offensive air operations against Rommel's forces in North Africa. Surrender of the Afrika Korps in May 1943 left Malta's airfields free to operate the aircraft ready to support the invasion of Sicily in July 1943. Without bases on Malta, the invasion of Sicily would have been much more difficult, and with strong German and Italian forces based on Malta, it would have been impossible.

Seventeen

AN UNCLOSED DOOR: THE PANAMA CANAL, 1941–5

The Panama Canal is the quickest and most direct route for the United States Navy to deploy forces between the Pacific and the Caribbean.

It is tempting for people in Europe to equate the Panama Canal with the Suez Canal; after all, both are international waterways, in effect man-made marine bypasses which save shipping the time and distance of travelling around a continent. Transit time for ships passing through the canals is remarkably similar, around eight to ten hours. Here, though, the similarities end.

The Suez Canal is a relatively simple structure, running without locks from the Mediterranean to the Red Sea. By contrast, the Panama Canal is interrupted by a number of locks, and indeed is not a canal in the accepted sense for all of its length, as it includes the artificial Lake Gatun, a flooded valley. Passing between the Pacific and the Caribbean, ships negotiate the Pedro Miguel Locks and then the two sets of the Miraflores Locks, before passing through Lake Gatun and then down through the three sets of the Gatun Locks. Politically too the situation is different, because the Panama Canal is one means of moving between the eastern and western coasts of the United States, giving it domestic significance to Americans.

Japan's *raison d'être* for the attack on the United States Pacific Fleet at Pearl Harbor was perfectly clear. It was to even up the imbalance in the size of the United States Navy compared to that of Japan, by effectively destroying half the total American naval forces. This would buy Japan time – they hoped for six months at least – in which to establish itself across much of the Pacific and South-east Asia. As far as it went, the logic was impeccable, even though the wiser and more thoughtful Japanese, including Admiral Yamamoto, knew that Japan could not compete with America's industrial power, which would be as important in the final outcome as military power.

Despite the mismanagement of the initial raid on Pearl Harbor, nothing was done to hinder the movement of major units of the United States Navy between the Atlantic and the Pacific. The difference between using the Panama Canal and having to sail vessels past the storm-ridden Cape Horn was tremendous – depending on the port of origin and the Pacific destination of the ships, it could be as much as 9,000 miles. Even for a large, fast aircraft carrier or battleship, this meant an extra two weeks at sea; for smaller vessels and slower supply ships, it would mean much more.

It was not until late in the war that the Imperial Japanese Navy considered attacking the Panama Canal. The plan was to use aircraft launched from submarines, but by then it was too late and the idea was abandoned. It might not have been very successful because such aircraft could only have dropped small bombs, a mere pinprick, especially against such strong targets as lock gates. The American defences of the Canal Zone were, by this time, also a force to be reckoned with.

Could the Japanese have cut the Panama Canal at the outset of the war, delaying reinforcements for the US Pacific Fleet? The Canal would have made a tough target. Canal lock gates are immensely strong, although not as strong as dams; in the case of the Panama Canal the lock gates were all duplicated to allow ships to pass in both directions. That meant that to be really effective, both sets of gates would have had to be destroyed, otherwise shipping would have been delayed, but not too seriously, as the remaining locks were used in both directions.

Although the Japanese aircraft-carrying submarines such as the Type A2 had the range to reach the Panama Canal, with an endurance of ninety days, it seems unlikely that the small aircraft operated from Japanese submarines could have carried sufficient explosive power to damage a lock gate, let alone destroy it. Their bomb load was too small, and they could not carry torpedoes.

At the outset of the war, the Canal Zone was unlikely to have been as heavily defended as later on. An attack by carrier-borne torpedo-carrying aircraft on a ship in the narrow Gaillard Cut could have blocked the Canal for some time while the sunken wreck was either destroyed or refloated. Again, an assault on the locks, destroying the gates in both directions, would have put the Canal out of commission for some time, especially if a ship was caught in the locks, adding to the damage.

Few of the Imperial Japanese Navy's carriers had the range which would have got them to the Panama Canal and back, although the Imperial Japanese Navy did refuel at sea, and had done so on the way to Pearl Harbor. The demands of the raid on Pearl Harbor were such that just two aircraft carriers were available for any other operation, and these were the small *Hosho* and the *Ryujo*. Even with refuelling at sea, it is questionable whether these two ships could have carried a large enough strike force for a successful operation against the Canal.

The carriers heading for Pearl Harbor had managed to escape detection, through a combination of good fortune, bad weather and American complacency. It was highly unlikely that a similar force heading for the Panama Canal could have succeeded in getting close undetected, even before the outbreak of war. The most direct route from Japan to the Panama Canal would have taken the ships past Hawaii, and near to the mainland of the United States.

The alternative would have been for three or four of the best ships involved in the raid on Pearl Harbor to have retired to the Caroline or Mariana Islands for refuelling, and then to have pressed on to the Panama Canal. This would have been risky, and it would have taken ten days to achieve, but it would have seriously crippled the US Navy's recovery. It is unlikely that the Japanese carriers would have been able to return to Japan, despite refuelling, as the Pacific Fleet's carriers and shore-based aircraft from California could have been expected to hunt them down.

The Japanese emphasis on attack suggests that such a mission might have had its supporters among senior naval officers, and it would have been politically acceptable as well. Japan had a substantial submarine fleet, apart from the aircraft-carrying submarines. The 'Long Lance' torpedo had a very high speed and range. Had two or more submarines been deployed at the Pacific end of the Panama Canal to coincide with the raid on Pearl Harbor, sinking ships in the short sea level stretch of the Canal, the objective could have been achieved. Further disruption could have been caused by minelaying in the approaches to the Canal. Even in 1939, the Imperial Japanese Navy had fourteen minelaying submarines, and more were added in the time before the outbreak of war in the Pacific.

The failure to do anything to hinder movement through the Panama Canal must rank alongside the failure to send a third, and even a fourth, wave of aircraft to Pearl Harbor as the greatest missed opportunities by the Japanese at the outset of the war in the Pacific. They not only left the United States Navy with an operational forward base, and with its Pacific Fleet carriers intact, they also ensured that reinforcements could be moved from the Atlantic to the Pacific within days, the transit of the Panama Canal itself taking just eight hours or so. These failures were a factor in the early reversal of Japanese fortunes, and contributed to the outcome at the Battles of the Coral Sea and Midway.

Eighteen

THE DANGER OF SECRECY: THE CHANNEL DASH, 1942

Renowned for its audacity and for the bravery of the Swordfish pilots who attempted, in vain, to intercept them, the dash by German ships through the English Channel showed the danger of too much secrecy.

On 12 February 1942, three German ships succeeded in a dash through the English Channel, on their way from Brest on the French Atlantic coast – where they had been confined by the Royal Navy and bombed by the RAF – to safety in Germany. To reach their destination, they had to sail within range of heavy guns at Dover, and risk the possibility of encountering British warships, and being bombed or torpedoed by British aircraft. Yet they got away with it.

The daring of the Germans was a massive blow to British morale. For the latter people, the English Channel has always been seen as a very special stretch of water. It is an international waterway, even though it passes through both British and French territorial waters, but the British in particular have always felt very possessive about it. It is the 'English Channel' to them, while to the French it is 'La Manche', the sleeve!

The Channel has saved England and indeed Britain from invasion, and played its part in the creation of an island race. Over the centuries the feeling that nothing could pass through this stretch of water without British acceptance has grown. This confidence ended on that bleak and wintry February day in 1942.

The Germany Navy's action was a gamble taken at the very top of the Nazi hierarchy, by Adolph Hitler himself. As with his opposite number, Britain's wartime leader, Winston Churchill, the German Führer could not resist meddling in military questions, and with both of them, the results were often mixed. Hitler, in particular, was probably more often wrong than right, but on this occasion he gauged the British reaction correctly.

Unlike the German Navy in the First World War, the fleet created in the 1930s was not looking for a decisive naval engagement. The Germans knew from experience just how successful commerce raiding could be. To the forefront of this campaign were the U-boats, but for the Second World War they also decided to deploy larger surface units, including battlecruisers. They also knew the value of such ships in tying down large numbers of an opposing fleet's ships.

Rebuilding the German fleet between the wars was more difficult for the Germans than rebuilding the air force. Ships took longer to build than aircraft, and there could be no equivalent of the 'flying clubs' and aircraft factories in foreign locations in which progress could be made while waiting for the right moment. Warships could not be developed in the guise of commercial vessels in the way that some of Germany's bomber designs were developed on the pretext of being airliners for Deutsche Luft Hansa, the national airline and predecessor of today's Lufthansa. Even so, some possibilities did lie in the terms of the Versailles Treaty that permitted Germany a small navy. This allowed the building of the famous pocket battleships, built to a restricted tonnage on the pretext of being replacements for the coastal battleships granted by the Treaty.

Something bigger was needed for the possibility of war. In 1933, Germany announced that instead of building a 'fourth' pocket battleship, a 26,000-ton battlecruiser would be built. The explanation given was the need to possess a rival to a French ship, the *Dunkerque*. Germany's choice of a battlecruiser gave some indication of official thinking. These ships had the armament of a battleship, but sacrificed armour for speed. In effect, this meant that the ships were fine for commerce raiding, but could come off worse in a fleet action – with an opponent's shells falling onto a lightly armoured superstructure – and were far more vulnerable to heavy aerial attack, if the bombers could hit a fast-moving target. The result was the *Scharnhorst*, but while she was being built, the Germans managed to construct a sister ship in secret, the *Gneisenau*, laid down in 1934. As was common with many major warships ordered by the Axis powers, the tonnage was understated, and on completion these ships displaced 31,800 tons each.

An unusual feature for both ships was the choice of 11-in guns rather than the more usual 15-in of major capital ships (although 14-in, 16-in and even 18-in guns were not unusual). This was because the warship building programme had envisaged six pocket battleships, with two triple turrets each, and these had been ordered. It was decided to fit the six spare turrets for the last three pocket battleships to the two battlecruisers, giving them three turrets each. This was another feature likely to put the two ships at a disadvantage in a major fleet action, when they would be outgunned by their opponents, and so provision was made to upgrade the armament to 15-in guns at an appropriate time.

At first, the two sister ships enjoyed a successful war. The *Scharnhorst* sank the British armed merchant cruiser *Rawalpindi* in November 1939, and she and *Gneisenau* came together again the following June to sink the aircraft carrier HMS *Glorious* and her two escorting destroyers, although *Scharnhorst* was damaged by a torpedo from one of the destroyers. The following year found the two ships actively engaged against the North Atlantic convoys, and between them accounted for twenty-two ships totalling 116,000 tons. Nevertheless, the Royal Navy persisted in hunting them down, finally forcing them to take refuge at Brest in occupied France, along with the heavy cruiser *Prinz Eugen*.

Prinz Eugen had been one of three heavy cruisers being built for the German Navy on the outbreak of war, and the only one of the three to be completed. Heavy cruisers differed from light cruisers in having 8-in guns rather than 6-in. As a cruiser, *Prinz Eugen*'s role was secondary, and she escorted the battleship *Bismarck* in 1941. Some believe that it was a shell from her 8-in guns that accounted for the loss of the British battlecruiser HMS *Hood*.

Scharnhorst and *Gneisenau*'s sojourn at Brest was not a comfortable one. The three ships were subjected to heavy aerial bombardment by the Royal Air Force, and while there seemed to be little danger of any of the three being sunk by the high-altitude bombing techniques of the day, they were damaged. The German Navy decided to move the three ships home to Germany for safety in an exercise known as Operation Cerebus. Hitler decided that rather than take the most obvious route, out into the Atlantic and round the west of Ireland, the direct route through the heavily defended English Channel and the Straits of Dover would be more likely to succeed.

Britain's service chiefs were well aware that the Germans would eventually attempt to move the three ships. Whether they would sail to attack merchant shipping, or simply seek to return to German waters was to some extent irrelevant, just so long as they were caught at sea and sunk. Many judged a return to Germany as being the more likely eventuality. Together, the RAF and Royal Navy produced a plan to stop any escape – Operation Fuller. It was kept strictly confidential, and only a few senior officers in each service as well as a number of others who were likely to be involved knew about it. On news being received that the ships were leaving Brest, the word 'Fuller' was intended to put the plan into action. A close watch was kept on the three ships, with frequent reconnaissance flights over Brest in addition to the bombing sorties. Operation Fuller involved extensive plans involving the RAF's Fighter, Bomber and Coastal Commands, as well as the Royal Navy's Home Fleet and the Fleet Air Arm, which had a number of suitably positioned shore bases as well as those aircraft aboard the aircraft carriers.

Fuller encountered problems, even at the planning stage. The Commander-in-Chief Home Fleet, Admiral Sir Dudley Pound, refused to send major units of the Home Fleet south to engage any breakout through the English Channel. Not only did he not want his ships to be drawn away, leaving opportunities for the *Tirpitz* in northern waters, but there was the risk from mines and aerial attack in the more confined and relatively shallow waters of the southern end of the North Sea. There can be little doubt that his thinking was influenced by the losses of the *Prince of Wales* and *Repulse* to Japanese air attack the previous December. Six elderly destroyers and a number of motor torpedo-boats were to be the Home Fleet's response.

As for the RAF, the main effort was expected to fall on Coastal Command, whose head was Air Chief Marshal Sir Philip Joubert. He had a squadron of Bristol Beautorp torpedo-bombers based in Cornwall to stop a breakout into the Atlantic, and some aircraft at an air station on the south coast of England. His main force of Beautorps was being kept at RAF Leuchars, near St Andrews on the east coast of Scotland. The idea was that a squadron could be moved forward to a base in Norfolk. A fast twin-engined torpedo-bomber based on the Beaufighter design, the Beautorp was seen as the main means of attack. This was because torpedo-bombers were usually far more effective than bombers against warships under way at sea, as these were extremely difficult to hit accurately with bombs. While the RAF has been criticized for not producing a planned 300 heavy bombers to attack the German ships, it was highly unlikely that these would have greatly damaged the ships. A final line of opposition lay in the guns around Dover, intended for coastal defence, but capable of hitting warships attempting to pass through the straits.

Operation Cerebus was set for the night of 11/12 February 1942. The *Scharnhorst, Gneisenau* and *Prinz Eugen* were expected to cope with any major surface threat themselves, but they were given a heavy escort of ten destroyers, several of which were more powerful than anything the Royal Navy possessed, as well as a substantial force of E-Boats, German motor gunboats. The

Luftwaffe was to play its part, with 280 fighters allocated to the operation, so that a standing air patrol of 30 aircraft could be maintained above the ships. This fighter cover was expected to keep bombers of any kind at bay. For their part, having lost the *Bismarck* in an operation in which torpedo-bombers had played a significant part, the Germans feared this type of attack and mines most.

Late in the afternoon of 11 February, RAF Wellington medium bombers attacked Brest, causing no damage to the three ships. Unknown to them, while they were overhead, the ships had their engines working. As soon as the Wellingtons had gone, under cover of the smoke from shore installations damaged in the raid, the three ships started to move. In itself, this wouldn't have been too serious. No one could be expected to hang around over Brest itself. RAF Coastal Command had planned for any movement by the three ships, with radar-equipped Lockheed Hudsons on patrol. It just happened that the Hudson covering the sector closest to Brest suddenly found that it had attracted the unwelcome attentions of a German night fighter, and the crew switched off its radar, whose signal was assisting the enemy aircraft. When the fighter had gone, the crew attempted to switch the radar on again, but it didn't work. After several attempts, they returned to base, where the ground crew attempted a repair, without success, although the radar had simply blown a fuse. The crew switched to another aircraft, which wouldn't start. They then transferred to a third aircraft, and eventually took off to resume their patrol. Too late; the German ships were clear of their sector. The Hudson patrolling the next sector also had problems with its radar, and the ships continued to escape detection.

So far, everything could be put down to sheer bad luck. What happened next, though, was nothing short of incompetence. One of the RAF's 'Chain Home' radar stations, which played such a great part in the success of the RAF in the Battle of Britain, detected the fighter escort flying above the German ships. Indeed, they soon discovered the ships. They weren't interested, however – after all, ships had nothing to do with the RAF. Had the fighters been escorting bombers, that would have been a different matter. Eventually, someone decided to contact the Royal Navy, only to be told that the Navy wasn't interested in aircraft.

By this time, it was after dawn on 12 February. The German ships were in a fine position for an attack. By chance, two Spitfires from RAF Kenley and another two from RAF Hawkinge were in the air. The first pair saw the German ships. Their orders were to maintain strict radio silence, and forgetting the maxim that orders were to be disobeyed if common sense demanded it, they continued to maintain silence and returned to base. The two aircraft from Hawkinge broke radio silence, contacting the major base at Biggin Hill, where nobody would believe them.

The catalogue of blunders continued. When one of RAF officers who had seen the three ships landed back at his base and demanded a book on warship recognition so that he could confirm their identity, it was found to be on the other side of the airfield. An airman was sent to fetch it, riding a bicycle, and on the way back, he stopped for refreshments. Then someone tried to telephone the Royal Navy at Dover, but they couldn't get through. An attempt on their secure 'scrambler' line was no more successful. The two telephone lines were connected to the same local lines, allowing anyone in Dover to hear top secret wartime communications. Next, an attempt was made to contact Fighter Command's Air Vice-Marshal Leigh Mallory. They were told that he was inspecting Polish units and presenting medals. Nothing, it seemed, was sufficiently important to disturb the great man.

By this point, more time had passed. Coastal Command seemed to be unaware of what was happening. Fighter Command wasn't interested. Bomber Command, which was originally to have provided up to 300 aircraft, was without a Commander-in-Chief, having seen Peirse depart, and was still awaiting the arrival of Harris, his successor. When Dover was finally contacted, it could only be via the major naval base at Portsmouth. The guns at Dover could do nothing, as a thick fog had descended and the gunners couldn't see the ships. Fortunately, the naval officer in command at Dover had brought a squadron of elderly Fairey Swordfish biplanes forward to the air station at Manston on the North Kent coast. These aircraft had not been included in the original plan for Operation Fuller. The Beautorps that were in the plan were grounded at RAF Leuchars by snow, and could not be flown to their forward base in Norfolk. No one seemed to consider moving the squadron based in Cornwall.

This action and inaction was taking place without any reference to the plan for Operation Fuller. No one even knew where it was. Few knew any of the details because of the secrecy surrounding it. They now needed to be able to check the plan and issue orders. At this stage, the British attempt to stop the German ships moved a few steps beyond farce. One officer who knew about Operation Fuller contacted the Air Ministry in London, and barked 'Fuller' down the telephone, believing that he was activating the plan; he was simply told that there was 'no one of that name here'. Eventually, the plan was tracked down, but no one could get at it. An intelligence officer had been so concerned with secrecy that he had locked the plan away in a safe and gone on leave, taking the key with him.

Belatedly, action started to be taken. The six Fairey Swordfish biplanes, the type that had operated so successfully at Taranto and against the *Bismarck*, were put on standby at Manston in Kent. They were promised the protection of sixty Supermarine Spitfire fighters; these were essential if the Swordfish, which lumbered along at 90 miles per hour, were to press home their attacks in the face of resistance by Messerschmitt Bf 109 fighters. Just ten Spitfires turned up.

Nevertheless, the attack had to go ahead. The ships were moving at a steady 28 knots, more than 30 miles per hour. In the gloom of a late winter's afternoon, Lieutenant-Commander

Eugene Esmond RN took his six aircraft into the air. Despite the poor light, they soon found the German warships, and their fighter escorts. Caught in a hail of fire from the fighters above and the warships below, they pressed home a torpedo attack. His aircraft badly damaged, with pieces being knocked off it in the heavy fire, Esmond managed to keep his aircraft in the air just long enough to launch its torpedo, after which the aircraft crashed into the sea. The target for his torpedo, the cruiser *Prinz Eugen*, was able to avoid it, while all six Swordfish were shot down, with the loss of the lives of Esmond and twelve others of the eighteen aircrew on the mission. Esmond was awarded a posthumous Victoria Cross.

Finally, awakened to the danger, the British put 700 aircraft on alert while confusion continued to reign. Seven Beautorps at RAF Thorney Island, in Sussex, were ordered to attack. When they in turn asked for fighter cover, they were told that the fighters were covering an attack by Swordfish. Two of the seven aircraft had been loaded with bombs rather than torpedoes, and a third aircraft had mechanical trouble. Rather than send just four aircraft, they waited for the bombs to be replaced by torpedoes, and the faulty aircraft fixed, losing yet another hour. When they eventually arrived over Manston, the airfield was operating on morse code, the aircraft on radio telephony, so neither could contact the other. Eventually, some of the aircraft landed for instructions. Only two of these aircraft ever found the ships, and when they launched their torpedoes, they also missed the target. Meanwhile, some of the Beauforts from RAF Leuchars had reached Norfolk. The squadron commander hadn't been told anything about the operation, other than his squadron's forward operating base. The aircraft arrived in Norfolk armed with bombs rather than torpedoes. Torpedoes were demanded from a munitions depot, but the nearest one able to provide torpedoes was on Humberside, some distance away. Despite bad weather and icy roads, the torpedoes could have reached the Beautorp squadron in three hours with a police escort, but by the time the torpedoes arrived at a stately pace, the German ships had reached Kiel. The only damage suffered during the entire trip from Brest to Kiel was to the *Gneisenau*, which hit a mine towards the end of her epic voyage.

Once in Germany, the warships were less of a threat than they would have been had they remained at Brest. *Scharnhorst* was later sent to Norway, where after much delay, she finally sallied forth to attack a convoy, and was sunk by a British battleship while preoccupied with a gunfight with two British cruisers. *Gneisenau* was badly damaged by explosions following a bomber attack on Kiel, and was taken to Gdynia for repairs and to have the long-awaited 15-in guns fitted. Eventually, after work stopped due to a shortage of materials, she was scuttled in the harbour entrance to delay the approach of Russian forces. A happier fate awaited the last of the trio, the heavy cruiser *Prinz Eugen*. This ship had the distinction of being the largest unit of the German Navy to be taken intact and undamaged at the end of the war.

The whole episode showed how excessive secrecy and inter-service bureaucracy could undermine the best of intentions. Technical failures were inevitable with technology, such as radar, then in its infancy, and the early sets were probably not robust enough to cope with the environment inside an aircraft, especially in the middle of winter. Accelerated wartime training of ground crew probably accounted for the delay in fault-finding and repair of equipment.

What cannot be excused was the secrecy that resulted in aircraft being fitted with the wrong weapons. It is also impossible to overlook the attitude that aircraft were the RAF's problem, and ships were the Navy's problem. The RAF was able to coordinate its fighters to good effect during the Battle of Britain – and did this so well at the onset of the blitz that the Germans were forced to resort to night bombing – yet, even after more than two years at war, couldn't find Spitfires to escort Swordfish. It had two squadrons of Beautorps in Scotland, but couldn't spare one of these early enough to be positioned in Norfolk ready for use. The Royal Navy's Fleet Air Arm had a different problem: it had twenty-four Swordfish ashore at HMS *Daedalus*, the shore station at Lee-on-Solent, between Portsmouth and Southampton – but no pilots.

As for the Home Fleet, Pound, its Commander-in-Chief, was overworked and unwell. Acutely aware of the setbacks suffered from enemy aircraft elsewhere, he was scared of committing his ships anywhere where they could be vulnerable to air attack. Yet the North Sea was not the coast of Malaya. In home waters, the Royal Navy had at least one aircraft carrier at the time, and surely could have demanded RAF fighter cover. This could have been the one classical fleet action for the Royal Navy of the Second World War, able to outgun its opponents, who also would have had the disadvantage of poor armour protection. After all, enemy warships destroyed would have been far better than enemy warships bottled up, for these would have had to be watched.

Nineteen

THE DAY JAPAN LOST THE WAR: THE BATTLE OF MIDWAY, 1942

Midway was the last chance for the Imperial Japanese Navy to demonstrate its superiority.

On 4 June 1942, less than six months after the Japanese attack on Pearl Harbor, the Imperial Japanese Navy had a strong force of aircraft carriers ready for an attack and invasion on Midway, a US base in the Pacific. The battle which ensued was to finally settle the outcome of the war in the Pacific.

In terms of the numbers of ships lost by each side, the Battle of the Coral Sea in May had been a draw. It had been a warning to the Japanese that all was not going their way. They had sunk the USS *Lexington* and severely damaged the *Yorktown*. The Americans had sunk the *Shoho*, admittedly only a light carrier, but they had badly damaged the *Shokaku*, one of the Imperial Japanese Navy's best carriers. The *Shokaku* was so badly damaged that she was not available for operations for some time.

From start to finish, the Battle of Midway was to prove to be a disaster. It was marred from the outset by over-optimism and the selection of an objective that hardly justified the attention. These problems were compounded by poor reconnaissance, and then finally settled by indecision and inadequate management of their carrier flight decks and hangars on the part of the Japanese.

Even senior officers in the Imperial Japanese Navy were divided over whether or not Midway was worth the risk. Among those at

Imperial Headquarters in Tokyo, many favoured isolating Australia from the United States. Others were taking a more defensive line, following the Doolittle raid on Japanese cities. At Midway, the objective was twofold: to occupy the island and lure the US Pacific Fleet beyond the atoll so that it could be destroyed.

Midway is not just a single island but a coral atoll and two islands, some 1,300 nautical miles north of Honolulu, with a total area of just 2 square miles. Although annexed by the United States in 1867, a naval air base was not established until 1941, just in time for the outbreak of war in the Pacific. In happier times, the islands had been a useful staging post for the Pan American World Airways (later Pan Am) flying-boat services across the Pacific to Hong Kong, developed before the war.

There were other objections to the plan. Even before the Battle of the Coral Sea, Nagumo's Chief of Staff, Kusaka, had objected to the operation because the ships were not ready. They needed to refit, and retrain new aircrew to combat readiness. Two of the most experienced airmen in the Imperial Japanese Navy also objected. Those veterans of Pearl Harbor, Mitsuo Fuchida and his friend on the staff, Minoru Genda, considered that the base on Midway was not worth taking. They also felt that too many experienced aircrew had been taken from the carriers after the campaign in the Indian Ocean, and that they needed to recover from their losses off Ceylon.

The carrier force was to be divided, with a raiding force and two carriers sent to the Aleutian islands, off the coast of Alaska, leaving four for the Midway operation. Many naval officers objected to this splitting of the available forces. The Japanese would have been even more concerned had they realized that the Americans had already broken their codes, and were aware of their plans.

At Midway, the Japanese were hoping for a decisive victory, despite having sent two carriers, the *Ryujo* and *Junyo*, to attack Dutch Harbour in the Aleutian islands, close to Alaska. The Midway force was under the command of Vice-Admiral Nagumo, the same man who had failed to make the most of his tactical advantage at Pearl Harbor, and in so doing had shown a lack of strategic sense. Meanwhile, the Americans were concentrating their naval forces to defend Midway Island, on which the United States Army Air Force (USAAF) had based fighters and heavy bombers, including the new Boeing B-17 Flying Fortress.

It was at this stage that a combination of good intelligence and a sound grasp of strategy began to tell. The Americans were not distracted when Japanese carrier-borne aircraft attacked the Aleutians on 3 June 1942. Instead, their energies were concentrated on finding the main Japanese fleet, including not just the inevitable aircraft carriers, but the troop transports as well. Having located the Japanese forces, Boeing B-17s were dispatched from Midway on the afternoon of 3 June to bomb the landing fleet, but without scoring any hits on the ships – ships moving at speed at sea are difficult targets for high-altitude bombers.

The Japanese were to open their attack on 4 June. The original intention was that the attack on Midway would be led by Mitsuo Fuchida, the veteran of the raid on Pearl Harbor. After Fuchida was confined to the sick bay of the carrier *Akagi*, having had an operation for appendicitis, another officer, Lieutenant Tomonaga, took his place. Fuchida was determined to be present for the operation and had refused the offer of a destroyer to take him to hospital. This determination led him to rise from his sick bed on the morning of the attack and make his way to the flight deck. This was no easy task, and especially for someone who had only had his stitches removed the previous day. Warships 'closed up' for action stations, and this literally meant closing off watertight doors in the bulkheads to give the ship a chance of survival if seriously damaged. Fuchida had to open a small manhole in each watertight door, using a wheel, climb through, and then close the door behind him, securely, again using the wheel. He had to do this ten times between leaving the sick bay, which was below the waterline, and reaching his cabin, where he rested briefly before shaving and changing into his uniform. While Fuchida had remained with the fleet so that he could help with the planning of the operation, his advice had not been sought. This led to the first mistake by the Japanese. The search patterns being flown by the fleet's reconnaissance aircraft were badly planned, leaving large areas of sea uncovered, with the danger that an American force could approach undetected.

On 4 June, at dawn, Nagumo sent 100 aircraft to Midway, to destroy the island's defences. Almost immediately, the fleet came under heavy attack from USAAF and shore-based USN aircraft from Midway. The attackers managed to disrupt the formation of the fleet and were able to strafe the carriers' decks, killing and injuring many crewmen, before being chased off by the fleet's Zero fighters for the loss of seventeen American aircraft. One USAAF Martin B-26 Marauder, as it was shot down, almost hit the *Akagi*'s bridge, and just missed the *Hiryu*, before crashing into the sea.

By this time, the aircraft from the Japanese carriers were over Midway, inflicting heavy damage to the shore installations. After the attack, the airfield and anti-aircraft defences were still operational, and Tomonaga passed this information back to the fleet by radio. On this occasion, Nagumo accepted that a second strike was necessary, but the remaining aircraft aboard the four carriers had been loaded with torpedoes, expecting an attack on American warships. Nagumo ordered that the torpedoes be taken off and exchanged for bombs, quickly! The armourers were engaged in this task when a reconnaissance aircraft radioed that it had seen ten American warships. Nagumo changed his mind. Midway could wait. The American warships posed the more serious threat to his ships and to the troop transports. Nagumo reversed his earlier order, so that now the bombs had to be removed and aircraft once more fitted with torpedoes. Aboard the Japanese carriers, the hangar decks were scenes of frantic activity, with each aircraft having what amounted to two warloads on or near the aircraft, with bombs for the attack on Midway and torpedoes for the strike against the American warships. At this stage no mention had been made in the reconnaissance reports of the presence of American aircraft carriers.

Rather than scramble those aircraft that now had torpedoes fitted, Nagumo decided to hold them back until the aircraft of the first strike, now returning from Midway and short of fuel, had been recovered aboard the carriers. At 0900 hr, while the Japanese were still waiting for the first strike to return, one of their reconnaissance aircraft reported sighting an American aircraft carrier, thought to be the *Yorktown*. This came as a surprise to the Japanese, who had assumed that there were no American carriers in the vicinity because of the lack of fighter cover for the earlier attack on their ships. It was too late to change the orders, the first strike had arrived and aircraft, short of fuel, were circling waiting their turn to land. All Nagumo could do was wait for these aircraft to land, have them struck down into the hangars as quickly as possible, and get the second strike aircraft away.

Aircraft for the second strike were on the Japanese carrier decks, ranged ready for take-off, when the first wave of American carrier aircraft attacked. The entire force of aircraft from two carriers, the *Enterprise* and *Hornet*, had been put into the air, while the *Yorktown* had sent half her aircraft, so that a total of 156 aircraft had been dispatched to attack the Japanese fleet. The first wave consisted of forty-one Douglas Devastator torpedo-bombers. These suffered heavy losses as they ran into make their assault, flying low over the waves towards the Japanese carriers. Thirty-five of these aircraft were shot down by heavy anti-aircraft fire from the fleet, and from the few fighters which had managed to get airborne from the carriers. Whole squadrons disappeared. Many of the aircrew had no time to escape from their low-flying aircraft before they crashed into the sea.

The ease with which this attack was fought off, combined with their earlier successes against the aircraft attacking from Midway, put the Japanese into a jubilant mood. Morale had suffered as a result of the setbacks at the Battle of the Coral Sea, but now they were confident that they were on the verge of yet another victory.

There was a paradox in what was now happening. Had the Japanese carriers been depending on radar, they might not have spotted the low-flying Devastators until it was too late, but they would have noticed the second wave, which consisted of high-flying dive-bombers, in good time. But it was too late. At 1022 hr, the first of the second wave of Douglas Dauntless dive-bombers was already plunging down from 19,000 ft towards the first of the carriers. Each aircraft carried a 1,000-lb bomb. The dive-bombers had arrived while the Japanese were still preoccupied with the torpedo-bombers and the aftermath of their ill-starred attack. Eyes were cast down to the sea, rather than looking into the air. Even the Zero fighters were still flying around, pointlessly, low over the sea. Aboard the ships, the flight decks were still full of armed aircraft ready to assault the American ships. In the hangars, aircraft were being refuelled, while the bombs for the Midway strike lay on the hangar deck, for in the confusion there had been no time to send them back to the magazines.

The first bombs hit the *Kaga*, which took four direct hits from the twelve bombs aimed at her. Four direct hits were more than enough. The bombs crashed through the flight deck and exploded in the hangars among the aircraft being refuelled and rearmed and the bombs left on the hangar deck. The ship was abandoned almost immediately.

Aboard the flagship *Akagi*, the first bomb missed, but only just, for when it exploded black water was washed over everyone on the ship's bridge. Then the ship was hit by two 1,000-lb bombs. The first bomb crashed through one of the lifts, while the second plunged through the flight deck. Both bombs exploded on the hangar deck, hitting stacks of 1,750-lb bombs intended for the airfield at Midway and setting them off in a chain reaction. Fully armed aircraft burst into flames, again in a chain reaction as one aircraft exploded and set the one nearest to it ablaze, before that too exploded. The hangar became a blazing inferno, and soon flames were sweeping across the flight deck. Those working below in the engine rooms and sick bay were cut off.

A third carrier, the *Soryu*, was also on fire by this time. Three 1,000-lb bombs had hit her flight deck in a straight line, and again crashed into the hangars. Only *Hiryu*, ahead of the rest of the fleet, was still operational.

The dive-bombing raid was over in just four minutes. Faced with a crushing defeat, Nagumo wished to go down with his flagship. He was persuaded to transfer his flag to a cruiser, the *Nagura*. This he did, followed by Fuchida, who broke both his legs in the transfer.

In an attempt to strike back at the Americans, an assault was mounted from the *Hiryu*, but just eight Japanese dive-bombers managed to penetrate the *Yorktown's* fighter screen and anti-aircraft fire to drop three 500-lb bombs on the carrier. The first of these bombs exploded among parked aircraft on the carrier's deck, setting these on fire. The second went down the funnel, a lucky shot for the Japanese, and blew out the fires under five of her six boilers. The third penetrated three decks to ignite the carrier's aviation fuel. These hits could have been fatal for the carrier, but prompt damage control and effective firefighting extinguished the burning aviation fuel with carbon dioxide, while as a precaution the magazines were smothered in foam.

Early in the afternoon, *Hiryu* sent a further strike against the *Yorktown*. Again led by Tomonaga, who had survived the earlier raid and the disaster aboard the *Akagi*, this assault had just ten Nakajima Kate torpedo-bombers and six Zero fighters. Once the Japanese aircraft were sighted, the *Yorktown* stopped refuelling aircraft and drained her aviation fuel system – a precaution against pipelines being ruptured during an attack. Her fighters were waiting to be refuelled after an earlier scramble, but even though very short of fuel, six Grumman Wildcat fighters were scrambled to intercept the assailants, and managed to shoot down five of the torpedo-bombers.

Four of the torpedo-bombers managed to get within dropping range. Crippled by the earlier attack, the *Yorktown* could not manoeuvre easily, but she managed to avoid two of the torpedoes before two hit her on the port side. Three bombs also struck the ship. Badly damaged by this fresh assault, the *Yorktown* had to be abandoned shortly afterwards, but her six fighters managed to land aboard the *Enterprise* before they ran out of fuel.

A combination of poor reconnaissance and intelligence, and inadequate debriefing of aircrew, meant that the Japanese now believed that they had attacked two different carriers, and that neither ship was now operational. They also believed that the Americans had just two carriers in the Pacific, so that they must now be without a strike capability. It was time for them to inflict a crippling blow on the rest of the American fleet, using aircraft recovered from the other Japanese carriers and currently embarked aboard *Hiryu*.

As the Japanese prepared for a final all-out strike on the American fleet, with the surviving aircraft ranged on the flight deck of *Hiryu*, the ship was attacked by more Dauntless dive-bombers. As she turned sharply to avoid their bombs, the Americans scored four direct hits, and four near misses. Near misses can sometimes be as fatal as hits, the reverberation causing damage inside the hull, especially to fuel lines and plating. Once again, a Japanese carrier was suffering from an outbreak of aviation fuel fires. The Japanese carrier force had been destroyed. After this attack, the *Soryu*, still burning, blew up, followed later by *Kaga*. *Akagi* had to be sunk by Japanese destroyers to prevent her falling into US hands, who also attacked *Hiryu*, which survived this, and a further attack by Midway-based B-17 bombers, before sinking the following day.

As they withdrew from Midway, a Japanese heavy cruiser was sunk by American aircraft, while another heavy cruiser and two destroyers were badly damaged. The Americans failed to catch the seven Japanese battleships that had accompanied the invasion force, for these had been kept safe far distant to the carrier fleet. Many Japanese airmen had argued against the decision to leave the battleships so far behind the carrier force, believing that the assault on Midway would have been more successful with gunfire added to the bombing of the carrier aircraft. The decision was wrong, but for another reason. Experience later in the war was to show that the presence of battleships and cruisers among aircraft carriers was useful because of the far heavier volume of anti-aircraft fire put up by the battleships, which meant better protection for a fleet.

Yorktown, despite the punishment received, was still afloat, and was attempting to reach Pearl Harbor with an escorting destroyer on 7 June, when the Japanese submarine *I-168* discovered her and sank both ships using her torpedoes, in one of the rare successes for Japanese submariners of the Pacific War.

Had Japanese intelligence been better, incorrect assumptions would not have been made about the strength of the United States Pacific Fleet at Midway. And had the reconnaissance from the carriers been more thorough, even this intelligence defect could have been corrected. The initial strike might not have been against Midway, but against the American carriers. Even if Midway had still been the initial target, the assault on the American carriers could have been undertaken before the Midway strike returned, possibly preventing the launch of the first American carrier-borne attack. At the very least, it would have ensured that armed and fuelled aircraft were not caught at a disadvantage on the carrier decks and in the hangars. The danger of having bombs sitting on the hangar decks would also have been avoided.

Better still, with four carriers to play with, Nagumo could have ensured that one ship was always ready with a free flight deck ready to launch fighters, and he could have maintained fighter patrols, which would have caught the American dive-bombers. Of course, with either angled flight decks or short take-off and vertical-landing aircraft, modern carriers should not be caught out, and are able to launch and recover aircraft at the same time. But it is easy to be wise after the event. If one carrier deck had been kept free at all times, it would have limited the number of aircraft sent on any one strike. As it was, aircraft were sent in waves on major operations because of the limited size of the flight deck, which meant that only a certain number of aircraft could be launched at any one time, before the next wave was brought up from the hangar deck.

The feeling remains that the Japanese bungled this operation. That Midway itself was hardly a prize worth fighting for makes the loss so much less understandable. Despite having had continuous control of its own naval aviation, the Japanese did not seem to have aviators at a senior level. This is something that can be excused in the wartime Royal Navy, which only regained control of its aviation in 1937, but it is impossible to excuse the Japanese for this. Where were the senior officers who understood aviation, its strengths and limitations, and its requirements, those who would have been able to reason with their peers brought up in the 'big-gun' navy? Never again would the Japanese be able to face the United States Navy on equal terms. The carrier was the weapon of choice for the war in the Pacific, followed closely by the submarine. The Japanese failed to make good use of either. Worse, they had sacrificed the best of the carrier fleet in two major battles within six months of the attack on Pearl Harbor.

After Midway, defeat was just a matter of time for the Japanese, for the outcome of this battle ended any lingering hope of victory, or even of a stalemate with a negotiated compromise. Final defeat was only delayed by a brutal attitude, which showed itself not only in their refusal to surrender, even when the odds were overwhelming, but in shooting women and children in the back if they attempted to do so.

Twenty

A Lost Opportunity: Japan's Failure to Understand the Submarine, 1941–5

Between the wars, the Japanese created a substantial force of submarines.

A mbitious plans for expansion of Japanese power and the massive potential of a large modern fleet did not mean that attitudes in the Imperial Japanese Navy of the interwar period differed greatly from its European and American counterparts. Japanese senior officers were as likely as those in any other navy to believe in large ships with big guns, and in the primacy of gunnery in war. Junior officers showing an interest in the newer forms of warfare, such as the aeroplane or submarine, were quietly advised against them, if they wanted to enjoy a rewarding career and make full use of their potential.

It would be fair to say that the United States Navy had the most progressive attitudes in terms of incorporating new technology into warfare, and that they were even better at this than the German Kriegsmarine. The Kriegsmarine knew how to make good use of the submarine, but was locked in argument with the Luftwaffe over the control of naval aviation, a fatal argument, since the Germans failed to complete either of the two aircraft carriers under construction. At least, after the early disappointments, the Royal Navy learnt fast.

Japan created opportunities for its fleet, and then wasted them. The Imperial Japanese Navy had established a powerful

177

carrier force with fine naval aircraft, as well as a strong submarine force. Their mistakes with the aircraft carrier have been demonstrated earlier, but the Japanese also wasted the submarine force, ignoring the opportunities it offered as the American advance across the Pacific produced many good targets and extended supply lines. Given these failings, perhaps it should not be too surprising that they also failed to protect their own shipping from the American submarines. Even as the threat from the American submarines grew, Japan failed to create a proper convoy system. They could see for themselves what the Allies were doing; they knew about American escort carriers; and they had the German experience to benefit from, but they ignored everything.

At the outset of the Second World War, Japan possessed a powerful and balanced fleet, of which the submarine component was an integral part. A glance through the pages of *Jane's Fighting Ships 1939* tells an interesting story. The Imperial Japanese Navy is shown as having twenty-four large submarines classified as 'ocean-going', and the same again classified as 'sea-going'. The inference is that the ocean-going submarines were superior to their sea-going counterparts, but the sea-going submarines were certainly a force to be reckoned with, since some of them had an operational radius of 16,000 miles. This meant that, if extended through the use of refuelling at sea, such attractive targets as the San Diego naval base in California and the Pacific portals of the Panama Canal were within range.

This was not all. The Japanese had minelaying submarines, and coastal submarines as well. It is highly likely that the tighter security enjoyed by the Japanese may well have meant that *Jane's* understated the position, and a great deal can happen between a reference book closing for production, and publication. Japan had plenty of time before they attacked the United States Pacific Fleet at Pearl Harbor, and submarine building continued apace.

In addition to the conventional submarines, the Japanese ignored the unfortunate, but very limited, British experience with the aircraft-carrying submarine, and created a fleet of these boats (submarines are boats, not ships) able to carry one, and in some cases two, aircraft. The Type A2 submarine, some of which could carry two aircraft, had an endurance of ninety days. Some of the aircraft-carrying submarines lost their hangars and aircraft when modified to carry Kaitan suicide midget submarines; the submarine equivalent to the kamikaze suicide aircraft.

If this significant force was seldom used to good effect, the other side of the coin in the Imperial Japanese Navy's conduct of the war was its refusal to see the submarine as a menace. Scant regard was given to the establishment of a convoy system. When they did consider convoys it meant, typically, that up to eight merchantmen would be escorted by a single destroyer. British and American experience had been that larger convoys suffered proportionately lower losses than small convoys, provided that they were given adequate protection. When the mighty First Fleet had the chance to provide cover for a convoy, the request was refused on the grounds that the First Fleet's independence of action was sacrosanct; compare this with the provision of carrier and cruiser support for Allied convoys, and when called for – as in some of the Malta convoys – full-sized carriers rather than just escort carriers.

Despite a balanced fleet at first glance, closer examination showed that Japanese provision for anti-submarine warfare was almost non-existent on the outbreak of war. Under pressure, ships were made available, but training in techniques was ignored. The officers and men were often those brought out of retirement, or considered unfit in some way for service with the First Fleet. Typically, a Japanese escort vessel would chase down the track of a torpedo to find the American submarine. Depth-charge technology was primitive. Sonar technology was as good as any at the start of the war, but failed to keep up with advances elsewhere as the war progressed.

The paradox was that in the 'Long Lance' torpedo, the Imperial Japanese Navy had the world's best and most potent torpedo. By contrast, at first the USN suffered from torpedoes which wouldn't run straight, and when they did, persistently ran deeper than intended so that they shot under the target. When, despite all the odds, American torpedoes did hit the target, they failed to explode. One outstanding example of this occurred when the American submarine, the USS *Tinosa*, had to break off an attack on a Japanese whale factory ship, the *Tonan Maru*, after expending no less than fifteen torpedoes, none of which exploded, although one did a somersault after hitting the ship.

Popular belief has been that the Germans were the masters of submarine strategy and tactics during the Second World War, until escort carriers and longer-range maritime reconnaissance aircraft combined to make operations hazardous. This has always been an oversimplification. While the British also had their moments of glory, especially in the Mediterranean, the greatest run of successes belonged to the Americans. The United States Navy could not at times believe its own success: when, for instance, the new aircraft carrier *Shinano*, the pride of the Japanese fleet and the largest aircraft carrier built outside the United States, was sunk by the USS *Archerfish*, the USN refused to accept it at first.

America used its powerful industrial capacity to the full during the war years. The submarine service benefited as much from this as did any other branch of the armed forces. At one stage, five submarines a month were being completed, and these craft were reliable and had up-to-date radar and night vision equipment. Racing ahead at this pace meant that long before the war was over, construction programmes could be scaled down. The Japanese targets were disappearing as the 'empire' contracted to the home islands and the main merchant shipping routes were abandoned. As with other American warships, long range, good sea keeping and high standards of crew comfort (at least by the standards of other navies) were characteristics of the American submarine. The United States Navy had in mind the long distances between bases in the Pacific, and the often storm-tossed nature of the world's largest ocean.

Before the outbreak of war, American attitudes to submarine warfare had been ambivalent to say the least, and even naive. President Hoover had attended the London Naval Conference of 1930, and advocated exempting ships carrying food from submarine attack. In doing so, he not only seemed to forget that during the American Civil War, the Confederate States had been starved by a Unionist blockade, but also overlooked the impossibility of enforcing such a measure in wartime.

It would be wrong to pretend that the United States Navy was a wholehearted supporter of the submarine, just as it would be to suggest that every Second World War USN admiral was a fan of the aircraft carrier. The Americans had their share of believers in the supremacy of the 'big gun' battleship. It took changes to the command of the submarine service before it was taken seriously by other naval departments, including the Ordnance Department, who were responsible for rectifying the problems of torpedo reliability.

American submarines packed a big punch. While the Royal Navy's 'T' class with ten 21-in torpedo tubes might have led the field, in the American submarine fleet, eight tubes were commonplace. No less important, many of them also had two 5-in guns (as opposed to the 4.5-in guns of British destroyers) as well as an anti-aircraft armament of 20-mm Oerlikons and 40-mm Bofors. These craft usually had two periscopes, but some had three, and the radar was periscope-mounted. A Plan Position Indicator meant that captains could control night operations from the conning tower rather than from the bridge, using the PPI's guidance to avoid firing at too great a range – a pitfall of attack using night vision.

In preparing for war, the Imperial Japanese Navy had allocated just 200 vessels to the protection of merchant shipping, probably no more than one-tenth of the number required. Of these

200 ships, just 10 were destroyers, and the rest were smaller craft. There were no cruisers or aircraft carriers assigned to convoy protection. Late in the war, plans were laid for a class of frigates, the *Kaibokan*, intended as convoy escorts, but although 263 were planned, these were still too few and too late.

Sonar operation and performance is a science in its own right. Different levels of salinity, water pressure or sea-water layers of different temperatures can all affect the performance of sonars. This was another Japanese weakness. The urge to attack was so strong in the Japanese psyche that even once a submarine was detected, the escorts would give up rather than persist with the hunt over the period of several days that it might demand.

Japan began the war with a merchant fleet of 2,528 ships, of which 40 per cent were allocated to army and navy use, leaving a number barely adequate for the communications needs of a vast and growing empire, or for the losses which should have been seen as inevitable. On a tonnage basis the situation was worse, for out of a total merchant tonnage of 6.34 million tons, the civilian share was just 2.44 million tons, giving the military 60 per cent of the tonnage. Captured vessels as the empire expanded helped to compensate for the shortfall in shipping.

No one took responsibility for the protection of shipping. It was not until spring 1942, less than six months after the war started in the Pacific, that action was taken, prompted by mounting losses. The First and Second Escort Groups were formed. While the first convoys were introduced, these would not have been regarded as such by the Allies, with a single destroyer looking after perhaps eight merchant ships. Not surprisingly, Japanese losses continued, reaching 172,000 tons of merchant shipping in September 1943, and then 300,000 tons in November, and 350,000 tons in January 1944, the year that saw a total of 3.9 million tons of Japanese shipping sunk.

Long before the end of the war, the Japanese were forced to bow to the inevitable and started to withdraw many of their convoy routes. Allied carrier raids forced the withdrawal from the route between Truk and the Marshall Islands in December 1943, while Allied advances also saw Truk–Rabaul end that same month. Even the route to Shanghai lost its escorts in January 1944, although shipping continued unescorted, as escorts were transferred to the vital route between Japan and Formosa. The Hong Kong route lost its escorts in August 1944, so that protection could be increased on the Singapore route. In its turn, the Singapore route had to be abandoned in January 1945, because of a shortage of tankers, before American submarines virtually closed Singapore off from many of the other territories in South-east Asia. Even routes linking the home islands were at the mercy of the submarine. When the war did end, Japan's total tanker tonnage was just 250,000 tons, but even this figure disguises the true state of affairs, since more than half the ships were out of action.

Japan's failure over the submarine had two consequences. The first of these was that Japanese shipping was left largely unprotected from this potent weapon. The Americans learnt from this as the war continued. They improved their equipment, especially the torpedoes, but they also experimented with tactics, which were varied between allowing commanders to operate on their own initiative, or giving them firm target directions, which was soon abandoned. For a short period, the United States Navy operated a looser form of the wolf pack tactics favoured by the Germans. The Japanese had needed the raw materials of the conquered territories, including fuel, rubber and food, and had an empire which stretched from beyond Tokyo to Singapore, itself a distance of more than 3,000 nautical miles, but took little care to defend its communications. As the end of the war approached, Japan was desperately short of fuel, and had to conserve stocks to have enough for the final grand kamikaze attack being planned for the invading American and British forces. The population was starving, and malnutrition was widespread.

The second consequence was the inability to inflict real damage on the Americans, especially early in the war when mines laid outside Pearl Harbor and the Panama Canal could have done much to impede the revival of the USN's forces in the Pacific. Mines or a submarine blockade at other important places such as the San Diego naval base and the commercial port at San Francisco could have done much harm. It might not have won the war for Japan, but it would have provided the six- to twelve-month breathing space that Japanese strategy demanded.

When the Japanese did use their aircraft-carrying submarines, they confined themselves to two bombing attacks on the forests of Oregon, a heavily forested state on the West Coast of the United States. The idea was to cause a forest fire, but it failed. Perhaps the bombs didn't go off, or perhaps the autumn attack found the forests too damp, but the impression which remains is that this was a futile attempt, and feeble as well. In this, as in other examples, the Japanese failed to make use of the advantages at their disposal. The potential was there, but it was neglected. Usually the reason was that the commanders did not encourage originality of thought or individuality in their subordinates, while the traditionalists held sway over those versed in more modern warfare. Throughout the war, the Imperial Japanese Navy was obsessed with the need for a major fleet action, a repeat of Tsushima, but only on a larger and far grander scale. They tried to arrange this at Leyte Gulf, and failed. The truth, which they could not recognize, was that the days of capital ships engaging each other in naval gun battles were long over. Fleets no longer met, their aircraft did, or they encountered one another's submarines.

Twenty-One

NO ACCIDENT: THE RAF RAID ON NUREMBERG, 1944

By 1944, RAF Bomber Command had succeeded in cutting the level of losses on missions over enemy territory.

On the night of 30/1 March 1944, the RAF suffered the worst losses of any air force on a single night as heavy bombers were sent to attack the German city of Nuremberg. The losses were far in excess of those suffered on the ill-starred bombing raids during the early years of the war, and came at a time when attrition rates had been reducing, due to concentration of the bomber stream close to the target. Bombing accuracy had also improved over the years, with most bombers now reaching the correct target area, and then able to hit the target with often devastating effect. Yet, on the Nuremberg raid, accuracy was to be another victim. The root of the problem lay in German technical developments, although this was only one of the difficulties facing RAF Bomber Command that night.

War is a game of measures and countermeasures, and nowhere more so than in the air. A combination of the Monica radar, intended to warn British bombers of the presence of German night fighters, and the H2S blind-bombing device, was to prove the undoing of the increasingly successful British bombing raids over Germany. The Luftwaffe put airborne radars, known as Naxos, into service, which could detect the course, and therefore the intended target, of the bomber streams up to ninety miles away, giving as much as twenty minutes warning.

The Junkers Ju 88 night fighters' Lichtenstein radar system was able to home in on the Monica radars.

It took a stroke of luck, good for the British, bad for the Germans, for this problem to come to light. A Ju 88, short of fuel, landed by mistake at an RAF base in Suffolk in July 1944, the crew believing that they were over the Netherlands. As the Ju 88 was short of fuel, had the crew attempted to cross the North Sea, they would have had to ditch, and their aircraft, with its precious information, would have been lost. The find led the head of Bomber Command, Air Chief Marshal Harris, to order the removal of the Monica system from the RAF's bombers.

It is easy to believe that had this information been available to the British at the time of the ill-fated Nuremberg raid some four months earlier, all would have been well. However, this is not the case as there were other problems, most of all with Harris himself. Harris is sometimes seen as a genius and a great leader, but he also had his weaknesses. He could be very stubborn. He had been opposed to the raids on the Ruhr Dams, and to the so-called 'bouncing bomb', or mine, offered for the raids. He was not alone. Despite the newness of the RAF, many senior officers had fixed minds. When, earlier in the war, shortly after Dunkirk, the 10-ton bomb was proved to be a realistic proposition by the British inventor, Barnes Wallis, it took the British Air Ministry three years to accept the idea. While the Luftwaffe used Triolin, an aluminium additive, in their bombs, almost doubling explosive power, the Air Ministry rejected this.

It remains difficult to understand why Nuremberg was chosen for a major air raid. The town had a symbolic appeal for the Nazis, who had chosen it as the venue for great rallies of the 1930s, but it had no significant armaments industry and was very much picture-postcard 'old' Germany. If there were no compelling reasons why Nuremberg should be bombed, there were several reasons why it would be good to avoid it, for the town was deep into Germany, further even than Berlin, and the route would be mainly over enemy territory.

Timing was also wrong. On the date chosen, the night of 30/1 March, the moon would not set until 0148 hr. Meteorological reconnaissance showed that the hoped-for cloud would not materialize. The route was too direct, with a 265-mile leg from Charleroi in Belgium to Fulda in Germany, before the turn south to Nuremberg. The bombers would be flying over the Ruhr, including many of the heavily defended areas, and past Cologne, with its new beacon for night fighters. All of these facts were known to the High Command, and even to the bomber crews. The announcement of Nuremberg as the target, and the route chosen, created uproar. When Air Vice-Marshal Sir Robert Saundby put the weather reports and other information to Harris, he expected the raid to be called off, but this did not happen.

On top of these known problems, the Germans had kept secret a nasty surprise. New German night fighters had upward firing machine guns, able to strike into the unprotected underbellies of the British bombers. American bombers had a ventral turret for just such an eventuality. The Lancaster Mk II was delivered with this feature, but in most cases it was removed to save weight, with the exception of some Royal Canadian Air Force aircraft.

Expecting carnage, the bomber crews took off, trusting in the concentrated fire of the bomber stream to see them safely through. The Pathfinder crews spearheading the attack to mark the targets were especially worried, but the leading bombers and the Pathfinders escaped almost unscathed. On this operation, the bombers flew in five waves, and those at the rear were able to react to the threat. It fell to the second, third and fourth waves to bear the brunt of the night-fighter attack.

On the cloudless, bright moonlit night, the night fighters didn't need their radar as their bomber targets glinted in the moonlight. The upward firing guns caught the bomber crews by surprise. The heavy German cannon just cut many aircraft in half, leaving little or no time to escape from the stricken aircraft.

On this operation, there was just one instance of an entire crew of a bomber managing to escape. Many bomber aircrew did not wear parachutes throughout the flight, as these were bulky in the confined interior of a bomber, and nowhere more so than in the gun turrets.

Harsh experience had proven that the concentration of aircraft into a dense bomber stream was usually the best means of defence against night fighters. On this night, the bombers who survived from the three middle waves were those who broke the rules and abandoned the stream to find their own way to the target. The German night fighters knew that they had such a good chance of shooting down the bombers in the stream that they had no need to go hunting for stray bombers.

During the outward flight to the target, 41 Avro Lancasters and 18 Handley Page Halifaxes were lost in just 60 minutes. A further 10 were shot down on the approach to the target. Having flown most of the way to the target in a clear moonlit sky, the remaining bombers eventually reached cloud cover as they neared the target, and as a result most of the bombs were dropped well away from Nuremberg. The combination of fighter attacks on the way to the target and dense cloud cover close to it also meant that the concentration of bombers over the target failed to materialize. At 0110 hr, the main force should have been attacking the target, but instead of 47 planes per minute, just three arrived in the first minute and another 30 in the next five minutes.

Nearby, the small town of Lauf received the worst damage, and fire engines were sent from Nuremberg to help as the larger town could spare them that night. In one of the misfortunes of war, many bombs fell on a prisoner of war camp holding Russian prisoners, among whom a heavy toll of fatalities and serious injuries was inflicted. So-called 'friendly fire' in war has always been an emotive subject, and had the POWs been British or American, the outcry would have been deafening.

The irony of the situation was that a number of aircraft wandered over Schweinfurt, a target rejected by Harris.

Schweinfurt was home to important ball-bearing factories, and the aircraft that dropped their bombs there were the ones to inflict the most damage to the German war effort that night. Elsewhere, to escape the carnage over Germany, some aircraft commanders chose the night's optional target, Ostend in Belgium. Even here, disaster struck. Two aircraft missed the docks, by this time of little use to the Germans, and hit a civilian area of the Belgian town, killing thirty-six Belgian civilians.

Given the distance to and from Nuremberg, inevitably some aircraft were lost on the homeward leg in addition to the 69 lost on the way to the target. Others would have suffered over Schweinfurt, which was heavily defended. The final tally was the loss of 94 aircraft out of the 795 bombers deployed, of which 702 managed to get near the target, an attrition rate of 11.8 per cent. No air force has ever suffered such heavy losses on a single operation. By contrast, on the night of 26/7 March 1944, out of 705 aircraft sent over Essen, 695 reached the target and losses amounted to just 9 aircraft, an attrition rate of 1.3 per cent.

The heavy wastage of aircraft and aircrew has remained controversial to this day. Some argue that Harris was under pressure and running out of good targets, while committed to mounting heavy raids night after night. Others have suggested that the choice of Nuremberg was symbolic, because of its past Nazi connections. The cynics suggest that Harris was attracted to Nuremberg because the older cities burned more readily, and this was part of the plan to undermine German civilian morale.

It will never be known which of these was true. It is known that Harris was warned of the risks to his crews, and rejected the advice. Other targets were available, and in many cases even if this meant a repeat visit to a target only recently bombed, the raid would have had an impact on the work of reconstruction. Schweinfurt itself was an important target, and one visited by the Americans, which could usefully have been bombed that night.

Twenty-Two

NO DETERRENCE ENCOURAGED INVASION: THE KOREAN WAR, 1950–3

An uneasy peace existed between the former Second World War Allies and the Soviet Union.

Without any warning or declaration of war, North Korean forces invaded South Korea on 25 June 1950, a Sunday morning. Finding South Korean forces unprepared, they were barely challenged as they raced southwards. This was the first major hot spot of the so-called Cold War between Communist east and democratic west in the aftermath of the Second World War. This was the start of a three-year war, which on at least one occasion came close to seeing the use of nuclear weapons.

Optimists may have looked forward to a new era of world peace on the ending of the Second World War, but the more realistic could see new threats emerging, even while the war was at its height. Peace saw many changes on the international front, not the least of which was the creation of many new nations and the rise of new totalitarian regimes, usually supported by the Russian and Chinese Communists and committed to a policy of expansion.

There had also been a change among the democracies. The colonial powers no longer held their former authority. The United States had emerged from the war as undoubtedly the most powerful nation on earth, with its armed forces deployed around the world, supposedly on the watch for sudden Communist attack.

One part of the world that had changed almost out of all recognition as a result of the war, and civil war in China, was Korea. A small peninsula running south from mainland China, which had been taken and operated as a Japanese colony early in the twentieth century, Korea was liberated at the end of the war, but it was a country divided. After the Soviet Union had belatedly entered the war against Japan, on 8 August, it was agreed that the United States would take the surrender of Japanese forces in the southern part of the country, leaving the Soviet Union to take Japanese surrender in the north. An arbitrary line was drawn between the two zones at the 38th parallel.

Soviet forces entered the northern part of Korea on 26 August; United States forces did not land in the country until 8 September. Officially, the object was a new and independent Korean state, and a United Nations Temporary Commission on Korea was to supervise elections for a new national assembly, which would lead the way to a government. The Soviet Union rejected the Commission and refused it access to the northern zone, in which they had already established a puppet government similar to those installed in the 'liberated' eastern European nations.

The scene was set for confrontation. Korea was to be one more area of postwar tension. The warning signals were overlooked. On a Sunday morning, a sudden invasion by North Korea of its southern neighbour found few senior commanders at their posts, leaving the North Koreans free to sweep south, supported by strong air cover. Much of the blame can safely be laid at the door of one man, General Douglas MacArthur. He had been in command of the Philippines as the Japanese swept across Southeast Asia during the first half of 1942, and had been responsible for the unsuccessful defence of the Bataan Peninsula. As Allied Supreme Commander in the south-west Pacific, he was later responsible for land forces used in the recovery of territory captured by the Japanese, including New Guinea, the Solomon Islands, New Britain and the Philippines. Throughout the war, MacArthur had pressed for the defeat of Japan to be accorded priority over the defeat of Germany, and although this did not happen, he had the satisfaction of taking the Japanese surrender on 2 September 1945.

A vain and arrogant man, MacArthur's sanity was also doubted by many, while he increasingly showed his contempt for politicians. In mitigation, some point out that, at the time of the North Korean invasion, he was aged seventy, and too old for the shock of a sudden invasion and the stresses and strains of a front line command. Age had little to do with it. Churchill hadn't been much younger when he became Britain's wartime Prime Minister. MacArthur certainly was no politician, lacking the finesse to handle the political problems that were inevitable in this type of war.

Unable to operate in what was to become North Korea, the United Nations monitored an election for an assembly in the rest of the country in May 1948, from which Syngman Ree became president of the new Republic of Korea in July. With UN backing, the new republic claimed jurisdiction over the entire country on both sides of the 38th parallel. A rival Soviet-backed government emerged in August in North Korea, which became known as the Democratic People's Republic of Korea, with Kim Il Sung as Prime Minister. The Democratic People's Republic of Korea also claimed to have jurisdiction over the whole country.

In December 1948, the United Nations General Assembly recognized the Republic of Korea, and called for the withdrawal of both United States and Soviet forces. The Soviet Union staged a withdrawal on 25 December 1948, gaining a propaganda coup by being first, leaving the United States to withdraw the last of her forces the following July. Soviet willingness to withdraw reflected the different policies pursued north and south of the border regarding Korean armed forces. The Soviet Union had armed North Korea, while the United States had failed to do this for South Korea. MacArthur was to blame for this state of affairs. He had effectively treated South Korea as a colony, rather as the Americans had regarded the Philippines before the outbreak of the Second World War. He had turned down proposals for the creation of an air force for South Korea, leaving the country with an embryonic air arm operating training aircraft, and little else.

On the ground, the situation was scarcely better. The Republic of Korea (RoK) Army, trained and equipped by the United States before withdrawal of its own armed forces, was not much more than a gendarmerie. It had 95,000 men in 1950, nominally comprising eight divisions although only half of these were up to strength. It had war-surplus American equipment, including rifles and light mortars. The few anti-tank mortars and guns were obsolete and ineffective against modern armour. Ammunition stocks were limited.

MacArthur, and therefore the United States, believed that Korea had no strategic value in the confrontation that had emerged between east and west. It was thought that any North Korean aggression against the South would be restricted to terrorist attacks. By contrast, North Korea was heavily armed. Its armed forces included the North Korean People's Army (NKPA), with eight full-strength divisions and another two at half strength, with at least 135,00 men under arms. An armoured brigade had 150 T-34 tanks provided by the Soviet Union. Each division had a towed artillery regiment and a battalion of self-propelled 76-mm guns. This relatively substantial force had been in training since 1945, and contained a cadre of seasoned troops who had fought either with the Russians or, more usually, against the Chinese Nationalists.

The Korean People's Armed Forces Air Corps included a number of fighter types, the most modern of which were piston-engined Yakovlev Yak-9 fighters, as well as Ilyushin Il-10 ground-attack aircraft. The Yak-9 would not have been a match for the North American F-51 fighter-bombers that had been proposed for the putative RoK Air Force.

The United States had pulled out without making anything other than the most rudimentary preparations for the South Koreans to defend themselves. It was argued that creating stronger RoK armed forces, including an air force, would add to the tension in the area. This overlooked the point that tension had become a fact of life already. Emerging from these policies was a serious military imbalance, amounting to a complete failure of deterrence. None of this would have mattered had the United States still maintained forces on the ground in Korea. How much this was due to United Nations pressure and how much to MacArthur, who had claimed that he could handle the Communists with one hand behind his back, is uncertain. Most of the USAF's equipment in the region was by this time deployed on Okinawa, one of the smaller Japanese islands, and in the Philippines.

When the attack came, on 25 June 1950, no one was prepared for it. The North Koreans maintained that they had repulsed an invasion from South Korea, but this was a blatant piece of propaganda. It was bad propaganda, since no army has ever succeeded in rejecting a serious invasion immediately – there has always been a period of delay and retreat before the line could be held, counter-attacks mounted, and territory recovered.

The United States Far East Air Force, whose component air forces included the Twentieth in Okinawa and the Thirteenth in the Philippines, was not at the state of readiness that could have been expected given the tension in the area. This reflected similar slackness in Korea, so that US FEAF's headquarters in Japan did not receive notification of the invasion until 0945 hr, almost six hours after it had started. Most of its personnel were away for the weekend. No decisions were taken for some time, as confusion and indecision reigned early on. At first, the priority lay not in attacking the invaders, but in evacuating US nationals. This took time to organize, and did not start until 0330 hr the morning after the invasion, with the air evacuation not starting until 27 June. Initial orders were that the US FEAF

194

could only make an assault on North Korean forces if the evacuation itself was attacked.

While this was going on, South Korean ground forces continued to be pushed back by the invaders, although they had managed to slow the pace of the advance. After a preliminary skirmish on 26 June, fighter combat flared up on 27 June between Yak-7s and Lockheed F-82 jet fighters. The first US FEAF bomber sorties were the following day.

Due largely to the Soviet boycott of the United Nations, the Security Council was able to declare that a 'breach of the peace' had occurred, and called for an immediate ceasefire and the withdrawal of all NKPA forces back to north of the 38th parallel. Two days later, a resolution called on all member states to give military assistance. This was to be the first, and for many years the last, conflict in which the United Nations formally deployed troops, due largely to a Russian boycott of the Security Council, which meant that the Soviet Union's veto could not be enforced.

Substantial forces from both sides of the east–west divide had to be deployed to rectify a situation which would not have occurred if South Korea had been equipped with one of the basic requirements of a nation state, the ability to defend itself, or if outside assistance had been timely. Wars can often be ascribed to a failure of deterrence, but this resulted from a complete absence of it. The signals sent to the Soviet Union and Communist China were that they could get away with the annexation of South Korea.

After the initial series of defeats, MacArthur achieved successful landings at Inchon, in occupied South Korean territory, although many commentators believe that he took unjustifiable risks in the process. His performance afterwards was decidedly uneven, ranging from risk-taking to inaction, to underestimating his enemy to overestimating them. He also had his own agenda, which was to reunite Korea by removing the Communist leadership, bringing him into conflict with the UN's stated aim to simply recover lost South Korean territory.

Ignoring Chinese warnings, MacArthur pushed the UN forces northwards through North Korea to the River Yalu, beyond which lay China itself. The Chinese crossed the Yalu and inflicted a devastating defeat on the UN forces. Many observers record that this period saw MacArthur undergo a series of violent mood swings in which he first refused to believe that China could threaten American forces, and then believed that they were about to be overwhelmed by Chinese forces. His inaction allowed Chinese forces to cross the Yalu and surround his positions, leading him to demand to be able to use nuclear weapons against the Chinese, or to saturate large areas of Korea with radioactive material so that the Chinese could not occupy it. In the end, he was relieved of his command and retired, leaving his successor General Ridgway to stabilize the position.

When peace eventually did come, any chance of remedying the divide between the two halves of Korea had disappeared. The consequence has been an armed stalemate for some fifty years. The passing of North Korea from a zone of Soviet influence to that of the Chinese also meant that the area has missed out on the benefits that followed the end of the Soviet Union, and which allowed the countries of eastern Europe to enjoy independence and self-determination.

Twenty-Three

MAKING A HERO OF NASSER: SUEZ, 1956

Britain and France reacted to Egyptian nationalization of the Suez Canal.

Egypt's nationalization of the Suez Canal in late July 1956 resulted in a major operation by British and French forces the following November, in an attempt to retake the Canal. The delay of slightly more than three months, and collusion with Egypt's neighbour, Israel, which offended even moderate Arab opinion, saw international support for the action fade away. This was to be one of the defining episodes of the postwar world, revealing British and French military and economic weakness.

The crisis had its origins in the distant past. Nominally an independent kingdom, Egypt had been almost as good as a British colony for many years. Substantial British armed forces occupied the country in 1882, mainly through concern for the security of the Suez Canal, which had been built by the French. The Khedive was bankrupt and sold his share in the Suez Canal Company to the British, to whom it was invaluable as a means of fast communication between the United Kingdom and India and Australia. During two world wars, the strong British presence had kept the Canal safe.

Britain's occupation was anathema to Arab nationalists, even though it had allowed Egypt to leave the Ottoman Empire earlier than her neighbours, with a constitutional kingdom being established in 1922, and had held at bay the German and Italian threat to the country during the Second World War. The removal of any obvious threats after the war, and the creation of the state of Israel, meant a realignment of Egyptian strategic interests, and loosened the ties between the two countries. In 1946, Britain agreed to pull out of Egypt, although troops remained in the Suez Canal Zone until 1954. Before the British left, a military coup overthrew the monarchy in 1952, deposing the corrupt and complacent King Farouk. A new leader emerged, the arch-Arab nationalist, Colonel Gamal Abdel Nasser, who established himself as a dictator.

Relations between Britain and Egypt deteriorated after Nasser's arrival. Britain continued to run down her military presence, and joined the United States in funding the Aswan Dam on the Nile, which Nasser saw as a potent symbol of national regeneration. Britain, however, in particular objected to a military dictatorship in the region. Nasser's procurement of sophisticated weapons from the Soviet Union and her satellites also disturbed western opinion. Eventually, Britain and the United States withdrew their support for the Aswan project.

Egyptian nationalization of the Suez Canal on 26 July 1956 outraged British and French opinion – as the two countries owned the international waterway – and alarmed the Israelis, who saw this as a threat to Israeli shipping by one of their hostile Arab neighbours. The move was seen as retaliation for the ending of support for the Aswan Dam, and as a blow to British prestige throughout the Middle East. France was by this time also estranged from the Egyptians because of Egyptian support for Algerian nationalists in an increasingly bloody war for independence from France, and the nationalization of the Canal was the final blow. The Israelis were also concerned at Egypt's growing military strength.

At first, world opinion was on the side of Britain and France, who agreed to take military action to regain the Canal. Had both countries been able to act decisively in July, all might have been well, but the time for action passed, and support faded.

Many countries, including the United States, were far more concerned about establishing good relations with the new regime than supporting the British and French. The Americans at the time had relatively little use for the Canal, but couldn't really afford to take a high moral tone given that they had run Panama for many years to protect their investment and strategic interest in the Panama Canal.

Britain's Prime Minister, Sir Anthony Eden, in deciding on military action, had failed to ensure that he had the forces available. The British armed forces, still overstretched in the twilight of the colonial era, and with a massive new postwar commitment in the occupation of part of what was then West Germany, did not have the manpower. The armed forces also lacked suitable equipment. For a start, they did not have sufficient landing craft, and many of those that were nominally available in reserve were found to be unseaworthy. This was just part of a list of deficiencies, which included an absence of tank transporters. The tanks had to be moved to Southampton, where the British Army had its own docks at Marchwood, close to the main port area, by Pickfords, a commercial haulier better known for its household removals but which, fortunately, also included a fleet of low loaders. Many of the weapons equipping the British armed forces were found to be unsuitable for desert conditions.

The plan the British and French developed centred around an Israeli pre-emptive offensive against Egypt in Sinai, which would be followed by Anglo-French intervention in the Canal Zone. Successive British governments have denied British complicity in the Israeli attack, but the French started a re-equipment of Israel's armed forces. As time passed, British and French forces established a joint command and redeployed naval and air forces to the central and eastern Mediterranean. The United Kingdom had the advantage of a major naval base at Malta, with airfields in both Malta and, even closer to the Canal Zone, Cyprus. Reservists were mobilized and a fleet assembled.

International opinion started to move in favour of Egypt, and swung against any military operation by Britain and France. Despite this, preparations continued, slowly but steadily. There could be no element of surprise as the intentions were increasingly obvious, and could be seen at many British bases, including the naval base at Portsmouth.

On 29 October, Israel launched her attack against Egypt, and two days later, British and French shore and carrier-borne aircraft launched an attack, code-named Operation Musketeer, bombing Egyptian military targets. The landings did not start until 5 November, by which time world opinion was strongly opposed to the action. The operation was notable not just for the paratroop operations by both countries, but for the use of helicopters to ferry Royal Marine commandos ashore from two British aircraft carriers, HMS *Ocean* and *Theseus*.

The operation was condemned by the United States, and by a number of countries in the British Commonwealth. American refusal to continue to support the pound sterling and the French franc led to an almost immediate ceasefire. Some 15 per cent of Britain's gold and currency reserves had been withdrawn during the operation, so that she had to seek a loan of US $1.5 billion (£530 million, at the rate of exchange then prevailing) from the International Monetary Fund to maintain the value of the pound. The loan could not be obtained without American support.

Had British and French forces been able to respond as quickly as Britain did after the Argentine invasion of the Falklands, all might have been well. The delay, and the bungled operation, showed just how weak both countries had become. Not all Arabs were supporters of Nasser, and indeed many feared the nationalists. British and French weakness strengthened the hand of the nationalists and dismayed the traditional allies of the two countries. Worse still, British and French collusion with the new state of Israel angered Arab opinion of all shades.

If Britain lost influence in the world at large, and in the Middle East in particular, the outcome for France was more tangible, and much closer to home. Within two years, the Fourth Republic ended and General Charles de Gaulle, the wartime leader of the Free French, assumed power. Encouraged by the display of weakness at Suez, Algerian nationalists had increased their campaign against the French armed forces and the French settlers. It was left to de Gaulle to bite the bullet, overriding much public opinion in France to arrange for Algerian independence.

From this time onwards, influence in the Middle East came to be shared between the two big superpowers, the United States and the Soviet Union. The US managed this without compromising on guarantees to Israel. Before Arab nationalism was overtaken by the spectre of Islamic fundamentalism, 'revolutions' saw other countries follow Egypt's lead, including first Iraq and then Libya, where monarchies were also overthrown. These countries moved from maintaining relatively small armed forces, posing no threat to their neighbours, to a more aggressive stance.

Twenty-Four

COUNTER-REVOLUTION DOOMED TO FAILURE: THE BAY OF PIGS, 1961

Members of the Cuban émigré population in the United States planned a counter-revolution to regain control of their country.

Invasion of their home country on 17 April 1961 by a force of Cuban exiles expecting support from the United States was to result in disaster. Inadequately equipped and poorly trained, not only did the expected support not materialize but, unknown to the invasion force, the plans had been changed at the last moment. The United States had been tempted to support this action after Fidel Castro's victory in the Cuban civil war in 1957 had two unwelcome side effects. The first was that the United States had a revolutionary Communist dictatorship on its doorstep, ready to destabilize Latin America and also possibly provide a base for Soviet forces, as indeed was attempted later. The second was that the United States had become home to the many Cubans who had fled the revolution, losing their homes and businesses. All this was in addition to the many American businesses that had lost subsidiaries on the island.

Most of the Cuban refugees had settled in Miami in Florida, less than a hundred miles from Cuba. They were hoping and waiting for a counter-revolution. By 1959, they had become a sizeable force, and the Eisenhower administration, keen to resolve the difficulties which could arise from having a Soviet satellite state so close, encouraged a group of exiles in their plans to overthrow the Castro government. In 1960, President Eisenhower himself approved the training and equipping of a Cuban 'army of liberation' composed of exiles. The plan extended to the provision of sixteen surplus Martin B-26 Marauder bombers, which would be flown by pilots recruited from among the exiles, operating from bases in Nicaragua to avoid any embarrassment to the United States. The arms available to the exiles would also include artillery. The would-be liberators were led to believe that once they were established ashore, they would be supported by the United States as soon as they had acquired a sufficiently large area on which to rally supporters and declare a provisional government.

Thus far, all looked good, and it is probably true that, had Eisenhower's administration been followed by one with a similar political viewpoint, the operation would have gone ahead as planned. But a new president was elected, and when President John F. Kennedy took office in 1961, he was unhappy with the proposal. His mistake was in not stopping the venture, but allowing it to continue.

There were many uncertainties. As with all Soviet satellites, the Cuban armed forces were substantial and heavily armed, although they had yet to obtain modern equipment. It would not be until later that the Cuban Air Force, or Fuerza Aerea Revolucionaria, would acquire MiG-15 and MiG-17 jet fighters from the Soviet Union, by which time these aircraft would also be obsolete. The Soviet Union seemed to have grasped the fact that, at the time, there were few Latin American air arms with modern equipment, and that up-to-date equipment could be deployed elsewhere in the world.

In Washington, the Joint Chiefs of Staff (JCS) reviewed the plan and came to the obvious conclusion that the outcome depended on the initial landings going well and then on sufficient support coming from the local population – a mass uprising would be ideal. Strangely, no one had attempted to assess the strength of any local support. The need for substantial outside assistance was also regarded as important.

On no objective assessment whatsoever, the JCS report then continued to suggest that the plan stood a fair chance of success. This was despite the fact that a mere 1,400 exiles would be involved, fewer than one-tenth of them with military experience, and would face total Cuban regular and militia forces of 200,000. It was also likely that the Lockheed T-33 jet trainers and ex-British Hawker Sea Furies still operated by the Cubans would make light work of the invasion force of just five ships.

Faced with the likelihood that the invasion would be seen as an attempt by the United States to overthrow a foreign government, Kennedy stressed that there could be no direct military support from the United States. This was a major setback since both the exiles and, more important, the CIA, had by this time convinced themselves that American support could be taken for granted. To them, US support was inevitable. To any objective observer, it was essential. To anyone conscious of the demands of diplomacy and international law, overt US support was unlikely.

At this stage, the wise course would have been to abandon the plan, or find dissident groups within Cuba and see to what extent the planning could embrace them. Neither course was adopted. One reason for this was that the Cuban exiles, training in Guatemala, were strong enough to cause problems if their hopes were dashed, even though not sufficiently strong for the projected operation. The official options presented to the President suggested that if the mission failed, the Cuban exiles could take to the mountains and set up a guerrilla movement, but the mountains were some eighty miles away from the proposed landings at the Bay of Pigs, with swamp and jungle lying in between. This also ignored the not unimportant fact that the exiles had not been trained for guerrilla warfare. They expected an invasion followed by early American support and a quick overthrow of the Castro regime. Longer-term guerrilla warfare was a means that had not been considered by the exiles, or their CIA supporters.

Seeking a way out, Kennedy sought advice, and requested a report from a United States Marine Corps officer. When this proved encouraging, the operation was allowed to go ahead. Even so, there remained the problem of the air strikes. This proved to be a chicken and egg situation. The State Department took the cautious view that air strikes before the exiles landed might be seen to suggest American involvement, while the Pentagon's view was that without air strikes the invasion was doomed to failure. It was finally decided that part of the B-26 force should bomb the Cuban air bases before the landings, pretending to be rebel Cuban Air Force pilots attacking Cuban aircraft on the ground. The B-26s were a good choice. Many Latin American air forces at this time operated obsolete piston-engined aircraft dating from the Second World War. While a B-26 would be no match for a Sea Fury, a fighter type that had shot down a MiG-15 during the Korean War, it could maintain the fiction that the US was not involved.

The air raid went ahead on 16 April 1961, in an atmosphere of total delusion, so that it was claimed that the Cuban Air Force had been wiped out, when just five aircraft had been hit. A second attack was planned for the following day at dawn, to coincide with the arrival of the invasion force. At the last moment, Kennedy, anxious about the likely international reaction to the operation, banned the second raid. This change of plan occurred while the invasion force was still at sea, having left Nicaragua on 14 April. It arrived off Cuba on 17 April, expecting air cover. Their arrival found not just a change of plan, but that the initial planning was not simply over-optimistic but marred by incompetence. The captains of the five elderly ships chartered to transport the exiles had been given packets of nautical charts, but with two vital charts missing. They were not allowed to open the packets containing the charts until after leaving port, when it was too late to do anything about it. Instead of the sandy beaches on which the exiles had trained, the chosen landing spot, close to the town of Playa Giron, had a coral reef offshore, which ripped out the hulls from two of the ships and left the exiles struggling in the sea. Then, of course, instead of being out of action for the landing, the Cuban Air Force had aircraft in the air and ready to attack the invaders.

As the exiles struggled ashore, Cuban Sea Furies made their assault. They blew up the ship carrying the ammunition and the communications equipment, all of which was lost. Had the dawn raid gone ahead, this might not have happened. News of the landings reached the Americans and, in a panic, consideration was given to sending six unmarked aircraft from the aircraft carrier *Essex* to cover a further raid by the B-26s, a plan which Kennedy, in a complete about face, approved. The Cuban émigré B-26 pilots then refused to fly a second mission, claiming exhaustion, and their place had to be taken by American pilots, provided by the CIA. Unfortunately, no one had remembered the time difference between Nicaragua and Cuba, so when the B-26s finally arrived over the island they were an hour too early for their jet escorts, and several were shot down, resulting in the deaths of four Americans.

Castro, alerted by the first, and in effect the only, air raid by the B-26s had rounded up 200,000 people suspected of having counter-revolutionary tendencies, the very section of the populace to which the exiles had hoped to appeal, and directed 20,000 troops equipped with armour to the landing zone. In a little over two days after landing, most of the exiles were rounded up, with the exception of the few who escaped. All in all, 114 exiles were killed and another 1,189 captured.

The operation ended any chance of a rapprochement between the United States and Cuba. While it showed US determination to resist the spread of Communism into its own sphere of influence, it was to take on the Cuban missile crisis before US policy could be judged to be firm and decisive enough to resist Soviet attempts at domination. What then resulted was a tacit agreement between the United States and the Soviet Union, each accepting the other's zone of influence, with the Americas for the US and eastern Europe for the Soviet Union. This left the fate of Africa, the Middle East and South-east Asia undecided.

Twenty-Five

A War Lost Far from the Battlefield: Vietnam, 1964–75

The United States sought to stabilize the political situation in South-east Asia after French withdrawal.

American interest in Vietnam started almost as soon as the French, the colonial power, departed, although at first this was a low-key affair. It took a new president, John Kennedy, to authorize a formal United States involvement so that, starting in 1964, the United States found itself embroiled in yet another war in South-east Asia, in Vietnam. While it is tempting to look for similarities between the situation and Vietnam and that of Korea, the differences outnumbered the similarities.

One of the most significant differences was that the Korean War had ended in stalemate, with the two opposing sides back where they started. This meant a democratic, capitalist, South Korea, and a Communist dictatorship in North Korea. Such an ending would have been regarded by many in the United States as a happy outcome to the Vietnam War, but it was not to be.

A former French colony, Vietnam had been part of French Indochina. Communist-backed guerrillas started fighting even before the Korean War ended, attempting to wrest the countries in the region away from French domination. Despite deploying substantial forces, including paratroops, air resupply and ground and carrier-based aircraft, the French eventually withdrew in 1955. Their old colonies in the area were divided into Laos,

Cambodia and Vietnam. A conference at Geneva divided Vietnam into two states, Communist North Vietnam and democratic South Vietnam, with unification proposed for 1956, following elections. The elections were never held in North Vietnam.

At no time did the United Nations demand military support for the government of South Vietnam. This was largely because the Soviet Union had discovered just how dangerous boycotting the United Nations could be and would oppose any UN support. Another factor was that the composition of the United Nations itself was changing, as more former colonies gained independence and membership; often these states suspected western motives.

One similarity with Korea lay in the attitude of the sponsoring powers to defence. While the Soviet Union rapidly built up the armed forces of North Vietnam, South Vietnam had just the equipment left by the departing French. In the North, a Vietnamese People's Air Force was established with Soviet assistance. The South was left with a Vietnamese Air Force that initially consisted of Dassault communications aircraft and Morane-Saulnier trainers. Grumman Bearcat fighter-bombers, Douglas C-47 transport aircraft and light aircraft were soon added to the new air force, as South Vietnam was driven into the US sphere of influence by the threat posed by its northern neighbour. Neighbouring Laos and Cambodia maintained a vague neutrality, especially at first, although they were to be drawn into the war as the Communist-backed Viet Cong guerrillas used their territory for supply routes and refuge from South Vietnamese forces.

United States military assistance started in 1955, initially providing South Vietnam with equipment and training, including military advisers. As Communist incursions continued, the number of American military advisers increased, until by the early 1960s they were more akin to regular troops in number and activities. In 1963, the new US President, John Kennedy, decided to commit regular US forces to South Vietnam to counter the growing Communist threat. This decision reflected the US State Department's belief in the 'domino' theory, which decreed that as one state fell to Communism, it then posed a threat to its neighbour. The logic of the domino theory dictated that Communism had to be checked in South Vietnam, otherwise Laos and Cambodia would be threatened, followed by Thailand and Malaysia.

Kennedy encouraged America's allies to support the fight. Britain was preoccupied with Indonesia's threat to the newly created Federation of Malaysia and Singapore at the time, as well as trouble in the Aden Protectorate, and could not spare any forces. The war also became increasingly unpopular among some British politicians. In this war, in which American involvement lasted longer than in the two world wars combined, America's staunchest ally was South Korea, although, at first, Australian and New Zealand forces were also involved. Operations by the Australian Army were to be reported by media commentators as 'being particularly successful'. This was largely because their tactics, based on British experience in postwar Malaya and elsewhere, were based on keeping the terrorists moving, so that they could not regroup for an attack. The Australians had also trained in jungle warfare, and brought their experience of operations in Malaya and, later, Malaysia, with them.

Throughout the war, American enthusiasm waned. Increasingly, anti-war protests erupted across the United States, possibly encouraged by earlier protests in Australia having succeeded in ending that country's involvement in the war with the departure of the last Australian units in 1970. While American involvement continued, the level of military activity fluctuated. American troops deployed in South Vietnam were mainly conscripts, with limited experience and little training in jungle warfare. The same media people who praised the Australian Army also reported that some American patrols proceeded with transistor radios playing. Any chance of surprise was lost, and the danger of ambush was intensified. Another problem for the Americans was that they were heavily dependent on locally recruited labour for a number of support duties. The result of this was that infiltration of their bases by Communist guerrillas was easier than with the Australians, for example, and this gave rise to a number of incidents in which lives were lost, and morale undermined.

The classical guerrilla war moves from isolated attacks, including urban terrorism, to the creation of areas in which guerrilla forces have domination, aided by local sympathizers or people forced into providing food and hiding places. The next stage sees heavier and more concentrated attacks, eventually building up to pitched battles with government forces.

In Vietnam, American policy was generally to assault concentrations of guerrillas to make the final stage impossible to achieve. Sweeps were also mounted to eliminate areas of Viet Cong control. In addition, the guerrilla supply lines were attacked, and then the sources of supply in North Vietnam. The attacks on the supply routes moved from within South Vietnam, and then North Vietnam, to those re-routed to run through Laos and Cambodia. Guerrilla hiding places in these two countries were also attacked. Each escalation of the war brought renewed protest, in the United States and abroad.

Probably the most controversial aspects of the Vietnam War centred around the air war. Partly, this was a feeling that using aircraft against ground forces and civilian targets was unfair, forgetting that this was the nature of war in the twentieth century. It was compounded by the use of defoliant weapons, intended to remove foliage from trees and expose the Viet Cong to attack, at least in theory. Another controversial feature was the extensive use of napalm – jellified petroleum – which resulted in media pictures of badly burnt children. The use of chemical defoliants arose from an attempt to remove the Viet Cong threat to US Navy river patrols. These patrolled the many waterways threading through the jungles of South Vietnam, but they were easily ambushed as the jungle came right up to the edge of the waterways. When the decision to use defoliants was taken, American sailors engaged on the river patrols were suffering casualty rates of 70 per cent in their one year tour of duty.

Opponents of the air war conveniently overlooked the occasional aerial combat between the opposing sides, and the extent to which North Vietnam had been equipped with surface-to-air guided missile systems and extensive anti-aircraft artillery, or 'triple A', by the Soviet Union. Unfortunately, in the conduct of the air war, the United States government all too often ignored the way in which air power could have made a difference, had repeated attacks been allowed on the main entry point of supplies into North Vietnam, at the port of Haiphong. When assaults on Haiphong were mounted, they were then eased off for long periods at a time. Given the port's proximity to Chinese territorial waters, a classical naval blockade could not be mounted, leaving air power as the sole instrument for stopping supplies. On occasion, American warships did bombard North Vietnamese positions, but, as in Korea, there was a shortage of suitable targets.

Some of the air attacks were in retaliation for North Vietnamese attacks on American naval vessels. The most notable of these was the Gulf of Tongking incident on 2 August 1964. This had seen the American destroyer *Maddox* attacked by three North Vietnamese gunboats while still in international waters. Four torpedoes were fired at the *Maddox*, but all missed their target, although the destroyer was hit on her superstructure by 14.5-mm gunfire. One of the raiding craft was damaged by fire from the *Maddox*. Four fighters from the aircraft carrier *Kitty Hawk* were in the air, and attacked the gunboats, sinking one of them. Two nights later, a second strike was mounted by the North Vietnamese Navy, this time against the destroyer *Turner Joy*, again without damage. On this occasion, sixteen aircraft from two carriers, *Ticonderoga* and *Constellation*, came to the aid of the destroyer.

These incidents led to an attack on 5 August by sixty-seven aircraft from the two carriers against the North Vietnamese naval bases at Ben Thuy, Hon Gay, Quang Khe and Lach Chao, and an oil storage facility at Vinh. In warfare, these were legitimate targets. The strike resulted in the loss of seven North Vietnamese Navy gunboats, while another ten were badly damaged, for the loss of two aircraft, with one pilot dead and another taken prisoner. In return, the North Vietnamese Navy had almost half of its thirty-six gunboats lost or damaged.

There were two main types of air attack. Precision strikes against a specific target and area bombing. The latter was designed to break up concentrations of Viet Cong or North Vietnamese troops, usually involving the large Boeing B-52 bombers, which provided the media with pictures of scores of bombs falling from the bellies of these aircraft. American losses on the precision raids were very heavy, although later in the war these eased off considerably with greater use of 'smart', or guided, weaponry, such as stand-off bombs and air-to-surface missiles. These had the dual advantage of reducing aircraft losses due to missile and triple anti-aircraft fire, and increasing accuracy.

Innovations of the war included the use of 'gunships', which in this conflict meant transport aircraft equipped with a large number of machine guns, able to fire downwards into the jungle to catch Viet Cong and North Vietnamese troops moving along the jungle trails.

Unfortunately, air power was often expected to win the war for the Americans and the South Vietnamese. As in Korea, good, hard targets against which bombers could excel were relatively few. Porters and mules on jungle trails were difficult targets for air power, and all too seldom was any real attempt made to ambush them, in effect turning the tables on the terrorists. Also lacking was a determined effort to win the 'hearts and minds' of the local population, especially in areas frequented by the terrorists, along the lines of the successful campaign mounted by the British in Malaya during the early 1950s.

Counter-insurgency operations have always been manpower intensive. It takes at least six or seven soldiers, some put the figure even higher, to counter a terrorist because the advantage of surprise is usually with the terrorist. In guerrilla warfare, the ability to strike is only part of the advantage; keeping the authorities guessing over where and when, and even how, is even more important. Even so, the reluctance to sanction repeated raids on Hanoi and its port, Haiphong, ensured that the flow of supplies into North Vietnam was seldom interrupted for long.

The Americans and South Vietnamese did eventually begin to regain control of the situation on the ground in South Vietnam. By 1971, the North Vietnamese were beginning to lose ground in the south. The growing experience of the South Vietnamese forces, increasingly to the fore in the ground war, meant that the Viet Cong was no longer the force it had been. Local support for revolutionary activity was declining, helped by the provision of new strains of rice that increased production, and local prosperity.

North Vietnam had one last card to play, a conventional invasion through the demilitarized zone, timed to coincide with the run up to the 1972 American presidential elections. They needed Soviet blessing and support for this operation, and they got it.

A conventional invasion should have played straight into American hands. In many ways it did, with the American and South Vietnamese forces soon checking the invaders, who also failed to have in place the support facilities essential for such an undertaking. A week was wasted before air power could be authorized against targets in the north, but then smart bombs destroyed the transformer house of the Lang Chi hydroelectric plant, without civilian casualties and without damage to the nearby dam, cutting 47 per cent of North Vietnam's electricity. The use of smart bombs meant that the Thanh Hoa bridge, to the south of Hanoi, which had been the objective for more than 800 sorties between 1965 and 1968 without being touched once, was destroyed. Within weeks of using smart weapons, no bridge was left intact. These late successes finally 'bombed Hanoi to the negotiating table'.

213

International pressure for a settlement in Vietnam was reinforced by domestic pressure. American politicians wanted out of Vietnam. The war had reached a stage where an end could not be seen. It was also souring attempts by successive American administrations to improve relations with the Soviet Union and Communist China. The plight of the growing number of American prisoners of war in North Vietnam was a growing embarrassment to the United States. The POW question was made all the more difficult because almost all were commissioned aircrew, in other words, men from educated, politically aware, middle-class backgrounds, whose friends and families were adept at lobbying politicians. These factors undermined American resolve. The delay of a week before President Nixon had authorized the renewal of the bombing campaign in the wake of the North Vietnamese invasion was another symptom of this.

Whenever efforts were made to secure a negotiated peace, Hanoi always refused to talk unless the bombing stopped. Every time it stopped, restarting it became more difficult, politically. It was a classic example of the difficulties faced by a free society in dealing with unscrupulous and manipulative opponents.

US involvement in South Vietnam, which had started officially in August 1964, officially ended in January 1973. After this, the term was 'Vietnamization', with the armed forces of South Vietnam taking more of the burden. Both the United States and the Soviet Union were supposed to reduce support for their respective client states at this stage, but only the United States did so. Neither side was to receive replacements for combat losses, but the Soviet Union continued to supply North Vietnam. The inevitable result was that morale and military activity started to collapse in the South. Viet Cong and regular North Vietnamese units started to advance, encircling the capital of South Vietnam, Saigon. As defeat appeared inevitable, the United States Seventh Fleet was assembled off Saigon for the evacuation of Americans and those South Vietnamese who had fought alongside them; a total of nine aircraft carriers was assembled for this sad task on

214

20 April 1975. Two days later, 7,000 United States Marines were put ashore to protect the evacuation, including 130,000 South Vietnamese who had emigration clearance in the United States. It took until 29 April to complete the operation.

Amid scenes of chaos, a routine was established. A South Vietnamese helicopter would arrive aboard one of the warships, discharge its passengers, have its doors ripped off so that it would sink more quickly, and would then be flown into the sea by its pilot, who would be picked up afterwards. There was no room for all of the aircraft provided to South Vietnam to be taken away, although in the end the American warships managed to take away a substantial number. These were classed as military aid, and still officially United States property, but that didn't stop the new regime from demanding their return – without success, however.

Vietnam has largely recovered from its ordeal. It could even be said that the consequences of the war were felt worst of all in Cambodia. There the Khmer Rouge conducted a barbaric campaign against the population after taking power, killing an unknown number in an enforced 'return to the country', where many more starved or were beaten to death. That life for those South Vietnamese left behind was hard can be judged by the numbers who later attempted to flee across the sea to the then British colony of Hong Kong, a difficult trip in often overcrowded and frail small craft across the South China Sea. The passage was made worse by the appearance of tropical typhoons, which must have overwhelmed many craft, and by the predatory pirates, often operating from bases in Communist China, who robbed, raped and killed their victims.

The big danger of America's humiliation in South Vietnam was that the country would return to its isolationist past, but fortunately, this did not happen. However, it took until the Gulf War in 1990 for American self-confidence in a military solution to return.

Yet, the defeat was due not so much to failings of American and South Vietnamese arms, but for the blind faith that allowed the Americans to believe, against all of the evidence, that after the defeat of the invasion, all would be well. There was the naive belief that if the United States kept the South Vietnamese at arm's length, the Soviet Union would do the same to North Vietnam. As for Vietnam, the country was unified. The death of the North Vietnamese dictator, Ho Chi Minh, and the collapse of the Soviet Union eventually paved the way for a less oppressive regime, and the renewal of diplomatic and trading links with the west.

Twenty-Six

BAD TIMING: THE FALKLANDS, 1982

Responding to the Argentine invasion of the Falkland Islands and South Georgia.

Argentine troops invaded the Falkland Islands, a British colony in the South Atlantic, on 2 April 1982. All the evidence suggests that the Argentine leadership, a military dictatorship, fully expected to encounter nothing more than diplomatic protests from the British following their conquest against small numbers of lightly armed Royal Marines based on the Falklands and South Georgia. The response was far different from that expected.

The Argentines had long laid claim to sovereignty over the Falkland Islands, known to them as Islas Malvinas. The islands had never been colonized by Argentina, although Spanish and Argentine explorers had reached the islands before the British, but it was the British who were first to maintain a permanent presence in both the Falklands and South Georgia. While the settlers on the Falklands mainly farmed sheep, the attractions of the islands to Argentina lay in fishing rights and, still more important, the strong possibility of valuable oil and natural gas resources. While the Argentines made much of the Falklands being part of the South American continental shelf, this was irrelevant given that they were still 400 miles off the coast. They also implied sovereignty over South George, 1,500 miles away.

Instead of resisting the claim and refusing to negotiate, Britain had been looking for a compromise for some years, to the dismay of the population of the Falkland Islands. In fact, it was Argentina that remained committed to its insistence that the islands must be handed over, and which refused to compromise. Governed by a military dictatorship, the Argentine lacked the checks inherent in a democracy. Diplomatic pressure having failed, Argentine forces eventually invaded the Falklands on Friday 2 April 1982. Even for a dictatorship, this was a political gamble, risking arousing adverse world opinion. Militarily, the situation was different. They knew that all that stood in their way was a small detachment of seventy Royal Marines, protecting the population of almost 2,000, spread over an area about the size of Wales. The operation was encouraged by the fate of Argentine scrap metal merchants on South Georgia, whose arrival had gone unchallenged by the British, who had a small detachment of twenty-two Royal Marines on the island.

The situation indicated to Argentina that there seemed to be every possibility that the British would do little more than mount diplomatic protests. Recovery of the islands once occupied seemed, to the Argentine military, almost impossible. The Falklands were some 8,000 miles from Britain. Small, insignificant, with a very small population, the Argentine dictatorship had gained the impression that the islands meant little to the British. To some extent they were right in these assumptions. A substantial number of British people had no idea where the Falklands were. Some even thought that they were somewhere off the coast of Scotland.

From the Argentine perspective, the British armed forces had suffered repeated reductions in their strength and capability over the years. It seemed unlikely that they had the capacity to recover the islands. They were also confident that American assistance could be ruled out, for despite a close alliance between the United Kingdom and the United States, American interests also involved friendly relations with as many Latin American countries as possible. The Americans would also be inclined against anything that smacked of colonialism, for after all, they were undermining the United Kingdom's continued claim to Northern Ireland, ignoring the wishes of the majority of the inhabitants.

The Argentine reading of the way in which London would react was based on their understanding of British actions. Without actually intending to do so, the British had been sending out the wrong signals, ones that were likely to encourage rather than discourage Argentine adventures. Collectively, these signals amounted to a strategic blunder by the British.

Despite the Argentine claim on the Falklands, the British had sold modern military equipment to Argentina. Over the years, this included two modern destroyers, sister ships of those operated by the Royal Navy. Earlier, Argentina had been sold aircraft, and even an aircraft carrier, and although at the time of the invasion the Argentine Navy's aircraft carrier, *Veinticinco de Mayo*, had been purchased second hand from the Netherlands, the ship was originally British and enjoyed British support to keep her operational. Possibly, these sales could be counted as an attempt to maintain friendly relations and gain influence. The same could not be said of other actions.

A major strategic defence review led the British government to declare its intention of disposing of its ice patrol ship, HMS *Endurance*. Her commanding officer had already reported his suspicions about Argentine intentions, including the landings in South Georgia. These had been ignored. Over the years, successive British governments had moved towards a policy that dictated that the armed forces would only be involved where shore bases were available. There were no shore bases within easy reach of the Falklands. Tristan da Cunha had no facilities at all, and the terrain was unsuitable. There were no alliances in place with any Latin American state, and although Chile was friendly, the Argentines reasoned that they could easily block any operations from any bases that their next-door neighbour might make available. British dislike of South African domestic policies had put the Simonstown Agreement, which allowed British warships to use the South African port, in abeyance.

These policies were once again emphasized by a strategic defence review that proposed further cuts in the Royal Navy. In presenting the review, John Nott, the Secretary of State for Defence, particularly attacked the Royal Navy for the number of aircraft required to support the surface fleet. It was even proposed that one of the two remaining aircraft carriers should be sold to the Royal Australian Navy. The Royal Navy's two assault ships, one of which was already in reserve, were earmarked for disposal.

In fact, even allowing for the Argentines wanting to interpret events in the way that they wanted, their understanding had some logic.

Argentina did not use her aircraft carrier during the Falklands campaign. At first, British observers believed that the ship was being kept offshore, out of harm's way, but later it was discovered that she was being kept in port. Boiler trouble was suspected, but the truth was even more incredible – her steam catapult had been dismantled and was in Britain for overhaul.

Initial landings on the Falklands by Argentine troops were from landing craft and smaller warships, including corvettes. Fierce resistance was met from the Royal Marines, who eventually had no option but to surrender as several thousand troops came ashore. The landing force was followed by reinforcements flown in aboard the Fuerza Aerea Argentina's Lockheed C-130 transports, augmented by chartered civilian Fokker F-27 Friendship airliners. Rather more difficult was the landing on South Georgia. Here the 9,600-ton ice patrol vessel *Bahia Paraiso* was used, with an Aerospatiale Puma and two Alouette III helicopters operating from the vessel. Failing to shoot down the Puma with a 66-mm anti-tank gun, the Royal Marines machine-gunned it until it retreated across a bay and then crash-landed. They then shot down one of the Alouettes, before damaging a corvette with the anti-tank gun. When the twenty-two Marines finally surrendered, the Argentine forces found it hard to believe that they had come close to defeat at the hands of such a small group of men.

When the news reached London, it was greeted with anger and disbelief. The House of Commons sat on the Saturday in an emergency session. It took just seventy-two hours for a task force to be hastily assembled and its first units put to sea on 5 April. The Royal Navy centred this around its two remaining aircraft carriers. The flagship was the larger of these, the elderly HMS *Hermes*, which had been left uncompleted for many years before finally being commissioned in the late 1950s as a light fleet carrier operating conventional carrier aircraft. Later, she had her catapults removed and was converted into a commando carrier, before undergoing another conversion, with a 'ski-jump' fitted so that she could operate the new British Aerospace Sea Harrier and anti-submarine helicopters. Although the Sea Harrier was capable of vertical take-off, it had been found that its performance was vastly improved using a short take-off assisted by the 'ski-jump', leaving the aircraft to land vertically on its return to the carrier. The other ship was the new purpose-designed 'Harrier-carrier', HMS *Invincible*. Between them, these two ships managed to take just twenty Sea Harriers. Yet, less than twenty years earlier, the Royal Navy could have put five aircraft carriers to sea, with two of them almost twice the size of *Hermes*, and added two commando carriers as well.

As it headed south, the task force was joined by the two assault ships *Fearless* and *Intrepid*. These ships had stern docks that could flood so that landing craft could be floated off, and helicopter landing platforms. Fortunately, both ships were still available to join the task force. There were also the inevitable frigates and destroyers. Even here there were signs of future problems and weaknesses. It had been decided to end naval gunnery, closing the gunnery school at Whale Island, just off Portsmouth, and a new generation of frigates was entering service without a main gun armament, just 20-mm cannon and guided missiles. It was essential to requisition merchant ships, including the Cunard liner *Queen Elizabeth II*, and the P&O cruise ships *Canberra* and *Uganda*, the latter later becoming the task force's hospital ship. A container ship, *Atlantic Conveyor*, was modified to carry helicopters. Royal Navy survey ships were pressed into service as hospital ships, later becoming 'ambulance' ships, taking the wounded to the *Uganda*.

Surprise was impossible. The departure of the task force, the core of which sailed from Portsmouth but included ships from other ports, was shown across the world on television.

Even as the task force sailed south, the United States attempted to broker a deal between the United Kingdom and Argentina, but without success, while many American newspapers had started to draw comparisons between the Argentine dictatorship and a democratic ally. Eventually, American support and collaboration was given. New Zealand offered to take over some of Britain's commitments in the Pacific and the Far East to release units for the operation. Chile, secretly, was to provide support, including a refuge for a helicopter and troops involved in an abortive British secret mission against an Argentine air base.

The Argentine gamble had failed. The question was, could the British retake the Falklands and South Georgia, with such a hastily assembled force, so far from their home bases?

Many in the United Kingdom were pessimistic over the chances of regaining the Falklands. One of the most extreme examples was that of a senior officer at the Fleet Air Arm's only remaining fixed-wing shore station, at Yeovil, who told the wives of the pilots that they were to expect heavy casualties, probably as high as 80 per cent. A Labour Party candidate in a by-election, one Tony Blair, opposed sending a task force.

The odds were against the British, but they had a number of factors on their side. In contrast to the Argentine forces, whose army was overwhelmingly composed of conscripts, the British fielded a completely professional force. To the Argentine conscript, the cold, bleak Falklands landscape posed great difficulties. To the British Royal Marine Commandos and the Parachute Brigade, it was hard going, but remarkably similar to much that had been encountered during training, although there was no question of the 'Paras' being able to parachute anywhere, since the Falklands were far beyond the range of their Hercules transports.

Membership of the North Atlantic Treaty Organization (NATO) also had its benefits. The British had been engaged in testing international and inter-service exercises. Even so, there were moments of intense stupidity, even after hostilities had started. Reports in newspapers that members of the British Army's elite Special Air Service Regiment (SAS), and their Royal Marine equivalent, the Special Boat Service (SBS), had landed in the Falklands were premature, and warned the Argentine forces of exactly where to expect a landing. This appeared just before the landings at San Carlos Water. Another British 'own goal' lay in newspaper stories that Argentine bombs had failed to explode, largely because the Argentine pilots had flown so low that the fuses could not arm themselves, which were a warning to the Argentines to either modify their fuses or fly higher. The information came from an official press release from the British Ministry of Defence. What had happened was that three-quarters of all bombs dropped by the Argentinian Air Force and Navy had failed to explode. Sometimes as many as four bombs could hit a warship without sinking it. This announcement on 23 May 1982 could have marked the start of considerable bloodshed among the task force's ships, with loss of equipment and life that could have made this risky operation fail.

Both sides suffered serious losses. The British nuclear-powered submarine, HMS *Courageous*, sank the Argentine cruiser, *General Belgrano*, in an attack that remains controversial to this day. The ship was supposed to be steaming away from the Falklands. The Royal Navy suspected, wrongly, that she had been modified to carry Exocet guided missiles, which posed a real threat to the ships of the task force. In fact, whether or not she was steaming away, or carried Exocet missiles (which can be retro-fitted relatively easily to a warship), was irrelevant. In the open ocean, a large ship can make better progress than a smaller vessel, and she could outgun the British frigates and destroyers. She was a threat to the task force, and the two countries were at war.

The British lost two destroyers, including the class lead ship of the Type 42 destroyers, HMS *Sheffield*, which sank after being hit by an air-launched Exocet missile, and two frigates. In terms of the success of the operation, the worst loss was that of the converted container ship, *Atlantic Conveyor*, which took most of the task force's troop-carrying helicopters with her. This was to compel the British troops to force march, 'yomping' or 'tagging', across East Falkland, the more populous of the two islands.

Nevertheless, on 21 April, a small British force was landed on South Georgia. After initial difficulties due to the severe weather, which necessitated further landings, a force of 120 men took an Argentine force of 200, before moving on to take other Argentine forces on the island. An Argentine submarine, *Sante Fe*, was so badly damaged as South Georgia was retaken that she had to be beached.

At no time could the task force bomb Argentine bases on the mainland of Argentina. The attempts by the RAF to mount long-distance strategic bombing raids using Hawker Siddeley Vulcan bombers were costly, needing twelve refuelling aircraft for each sortie, and did relatively little damage to the runway at Port Stanley, although a radar station was destroyed in one attack. Nevertheless, Argentine use of the base was limited to Pucara light attack aircraft, forcing the air force and naval pilots to operate from Argentina, 400 miles away, and at a disadvantage. Even so, while the Argentine ground forces struggled to cope, their pilots, both from the navy and the air force, showed great skill and courage, earning the respect of their British opponents. Despite this, no Sea Harriers were shot down by enemy aircraft.

In a battle to take Goose Green, a battalion of 600 men from 2 Para of the British Parachute Regiment overcame an Argentine force three times their number, reversing the perceived wisdom that a successful assault requires the attacking force to outnumber their opponents by a ratio of three to one. However, their commanding officer, Colonel 'H.' Jones, was killed in an attack on an Argentine machine-gun post. This success was despite the fact that the British commander had refused the paratroops light armour support, in the false belief that the ground was unsuitable. He later admitted that this was a mistake, and with the benefit of hindsight he should not only have provided armour, but a second battalion of troops as well.

On 15 June 1982, British troops entered Port Stanley and the Argentine forces surrendered. The outcome was, inevitably, a cooling of relations between the United Kingdom and Argentina for many years. Whether or not this display of determination finally persuaded the masters of the old Soviet Union that any plans for an attack in Europe would be equally unwise, that threats would not suffice to encourage a surrender, is something which is open to debate. Nevertheless, it did show that grabbing territory was unlikely to be successful in future.

Later, the Argentines did finally discuss the Falklands. They still demanded the islands, but were refused sovereignty, although the return to democratic government in recent times has meant some thaw in previously frosty relations, and the award of fishing licences to Argentine trawlers.

Bad timing and poor intelligence were at the root of the Argentine failure. Seizure could have succeeded had the Argentines been patient. Had they had their aircraft carrier back in service and present off the islands, and had they waited for the planned reductions in British defence capability to be implemented, it would have been virtually impossible for Britain to retake the islands.

One result was that the planned cuts to the Fleet Air Arm were not fully implemented, eventually leaving the Royal Navy with three modern aircraft carriers, two of which are meant to be available for operations at any one time. The two assault ships were reprieved, and at the time of writing, two replacements, HMS *Albion* and *Bulwark*, are being built. The Royal Navy also gained a helicopter carrier, specifically for commando operations, HMS *Ocean*. Naval gunnery survived as well, and the early Type 22 frigates, which lacked a 4.5-in gun, were later sold to Argentina's neighbour, Brazil.

Sadly, one of the paratroop regiments were among the losers. As they had been unable to use their parachuting skills in the Falklands, a later defence review decided that in future they would become helicopter-borne troops. If implemented, the advantage is that they will arrive more heavily armed than at present. However, only a fool would claim to be able to see into the future, and this could be a case of someone planning to fight a future conflict with an eye on the last one – always a mistake.

Twenty-Seven

UNFINISHED BUSINESS: THE GULF WAR, 1990–1

Iraq had long cast envious eyes at Kuwait, even threatening invasion on occasion.

Iraq invaded Kuwait during the early hours of 2 August 1990. The Kuwaiti forces had no time to react, and little room in which to mount a holding action until reinforcements could arrive. Kuwait City itself was just 75 miles from the major Iraqi centre of Basra, and the flat desert in between offered no natural defensive positions. Overwhelmed by Iraq's superior force, the Kuwaitis could only surrender or flee into the territory of their other, friendlier, neighbour, Saudi Arabia. The invasion was so rapid that a British airliner was caught on the ground during a transit stop, and its passengers and crew taken hostage. In the initial confusion, many residents of Kuwait were able to drive across the desert to safety in Saudi territory.

Iraq had long maintained that the neighbouring small Arab kingdom of Kuwait was an Iraqi province. Repeated over many years, this claim had led to tension in the Persian/Iranian Gulf. In 1961, tension had reached such a pitch, with Iraqi troops gathering on the border with Kuwait, that British forces had to be deployed in the area, reacting quickly and decisively to defuse the situation. The commando carrier *Bulwark* arrived at Kuwait with Royal Marine Commandos, joined shortly afterwards by the aircraft carrier *Victorious*. In addition to her own fighters and bombers, *Victorious* provided fighter control for RAF aircraft deployed to Kuwait. Although a small country, Kuwait is bigger than generally imagined, at just over 9,000 square miles, but the indigenous population is only around 500,000.

While the policies of the Iraqi dictatorship remained unchanged, her neighbours and the West had been lulled into a false sense of security by the prolonged and bloody conflict between Iraq and another neighbour, Iran, which lasted throughout the 1980s. Known as the First Gulf War, most believed that it had left both countries considerably weakened. Iran's fundamentalist Islamic regime had been seen as the more threatening, and during the war with Iran, Iraq had been treated favourably by the west and by its other neighbours.

International anger over Iraq's actions and the break-up of the former Soviet Union combined meant that, for only the second time in its history, the forces that were quickly assembled to liberate Kuwait were under the United Nations banner. The attack on an Arab state also meant that other Arab countries joined the condemnation of Iraq; Arab states rarely condemn any action by one of their number.

Despite deploying troops on peace-keeping missions, the United Nations has never had a military command structure. The command and control mechanisms needed to turn this multinational force into a viable operational command had to be based on those of NATO, which alone retained the experience of combined and multinational operations. The Warsaw Pact no longer existed by this time, and its command and control systems would probably have been unsuitable, based as they were on overall Soviet direction rather than multinational collaboration. This one-off alliance of nations became known as the 'Coalition'.

The operation was in two stages. The first stage concerned protection of Saudi Arabia from possible Iraqi attack and invasion, and this was known as Operation Desert Shield. Within that, the British armed forces described their contribution as Operational Grandby. The second stage, liberating Kuwait, was to be an operation known as Desert Storm. The conflict that ensued has become known as the Second Gulf War, to distinguish it from the earlier conflict between Iraq and Iran.

Assembling the necessary forces took some time. While naval and air forces could be sent relatively quickly, the conflict needed armoured forces and mechanized infantry and artillery. Most of these items had to be moved by sea because of the weight and size of individual items and the sheer numbers involved. Troops were moved by air. The United States Air Force played the major role in moving equipment by air as it was the only air force with large enough aircraft, the Lockheed C-5B Galaxy. During the build-up, an air and sea blockade of Iraq was enforced. This meant 165 ships from 19 navies cooperating to challenge 6,290 ships, which resulted in 832 boardings; 36 of these led to embargo breakers being diverted.

Desert Storm itself was in two parts. The first stage was designed to destroy the Iraqi Air Force, then to deny Iraq use of airfields and port facilities, followed by the destruction of its armies and infrastructure. This was the pattern established during the Second World War. The air war had to start in advance of the ground war, which was to be the second stage. Starting the air war too early could be almost as bad as starting too late. An early commencement could have meant an opportunity for Iraq to rebuild and regroup before the ground war began; a late one would have meant not having enough time to cripple Iraq's defences.

The air war began on 17 January 1991, more than five months after the invasion of Kuwait. This was the first war to be initiated by helicopters, as twelve armed McDonnell Douglas Apache attack helicopters from the United States Army mounted a surprise strike on the two main Iraqi air defence radar stations, destroying these in a missile attack. To evade detection, the helicopters had to fly low and slow. The gap in Iraq's defences opened up by this assault was immediately exploited as some 700 Coalition aircraft flew on the first sorties of the war. The air operation was enormous, with 67,000 sorties between

17 January and the opening of the ground offensive on 23 February. The air offensive enjoyed startling successes, although there were also losses and questions were raised over the tactics employed by some air forces. In particular, the RAF, among others, sent aircraft against heavily defended targets, such as airfields, in small numbers, allowing the Iraqis to concentrate their fire and making losses almost certain. While some Iraqi aircraft were shot down, the Iraqi Air Force quickly arranged to send its most useful aircraft to safety outside the country. Most of these unusual refugees from the war went to airfields in Iran – suddenly in the position of friend – but others were reported as going as far afield as the Sudan.

A novel feature of the war was the first deployment of cruise missiles. These were credited with extreme accuracy, so much so that one newspaper ran a cartoon depicting two cruise missiles studying a road map at a crossroads. Some of the missiles transmitted television pictures of their attacks, later broadcast on television news bulletins. In return, the Iraqis fired their Soviet-built Scud missiles at targets in the Gulf and at Israel, which had not been involved in the conflict for fear of offending Arab sensibilities. The Israelis had to face the attacks with stoicism for fear of inflaming a difficult situation and seeing the Coalition unravel. The United States Army deployed its anti-missile Patriot missiles in Saudi Arabia and in Israel. At first these were credited with shooting down almost all of the Scud missiles, until it became clear that the Scuds, modified by the Iraqis, were suffering from structural problems and breaking up in mid-air. The problem came to light as the warheads from some of the Scuds hit ground targets even though the missiles had broken up. In the Gulf, a British destroyer was also credited with successfully shooting down a Scud missile using a Sea Dart missile, protecting a US cruiser in doing so.

The ground war lasted just three days. The air war had been so thorough that the Iraqi Army quickly broke up and many troops deserted.

With Iraqi forces in full retreat, the Coalition forces suddenly found that they were facing a crisis. The Arab participants were opposed to any invasion of Iraq once Kuwait had been liberated. Not only were these forces a significant element in the Coalition, but also, far more importantly, the main bases on which the Coalition depended were all on Arab territory, many of them in Saudi Arabia, but others in the smaller Gulf states such as Dubai and Bahrain. This reluctance to pursue the Iraqis was shared by many other non-Arab participants. In any event, an invasion of Iraq would also have meant returning to the United Nations for a fresh mandate from the UN Security Council.

Neither the United States nor the United Kingdom wanted the problems of occupying Iraq. Conversely, both wanted to see the Iraqi President, Sadam Hussein, replaced by a moderate regime. They also wanted a demilitarized zone that would effectively act as a buffer between Iraq and Kuwait. Frustrated in seeking a military means to achieving these ends, the Marsh Arabs, living in the south of Iraq near Basra, and who had been subjected to oppression by Hussein's government, were given tacit encouragement to rebel. The rebellion was squashed by the Iraqis, who also took similar action against the Kurdish minority in the north of the country, close to the border with Turkey. The UN reaction to this situation was to create so-called 'no fly' zones in the south and the north of the country, requiring constant monitoring by Coalition air power, in reality, the British and Americans. Economic sanctions against Iraq were also maintained.

Iraq was foiled in her bid to crush Kuwait and threaten the other countries in the region, and Kuwait was liberated, but the western powers failed in their ambition to install a more peaceful regime in Baghdad. Sanctions against Iraq were later eased to allow Iraq to sell more crude oil so that food and medicines could be bought for the Iraqi people, but instead, the funds raised were devoted to maintaining the power and lifestyles of the ruling elite. Despite the bad faith of the Iraqi leadership, the plight of starving and sick Iraqi civilians, especially children, gave Hussein a major propaganda victory, a situation that continues to the present day.

No less seriously, the work of UN inspectors attempting to track down and then ensure the destruction of Iraqi facilities engaged in research and development of nuclear, biological and chemical weapons was hampered repeatedly by the Iraqis. At first, each time this happened, American, and on occasion British, aerial attacks managed to get the inspections operating again. It now seems that little effort is being made to stop Iraqi research that could make it the future dominant power in the Middle East.

It would be wrong to suggest that the Second Gulf War resulted in a pyrrhic victory. After all, Kuwait was liberated. Yet, it can be said to be a case of defeat having been snatched from this very real and tangible victory. Kuwait today is still not completely safe, and once the Iraqis are able to wage war by nuclear, biological or chemical means, no country in the region will be safe.

Hopes of setting up a government in exile or of fomenting unrest within Iraq have come to nothing. Opposition has been so thoroughly squeezed out of the country that a change is unlikely, at least until Hussein is dead, when something might come out of the struggle for power which will surely arise. Yet, the fate of the Marsh Arabs will make many wary of trusting the west too much. Nor can salvation come from the Kurds in the north. They have their own priorities, a Kurdish state, and this is opposed by the three neighbouring countries, including Turkey – a member of the Coalition and NATO – with sizeable Kurdish populations. In any case, for the average Iraqi, the Marsh Arabs and the Kurds are irrelevant minorities.

Twenty-Eight

VICTORY WITHOUT PEACE: SERBIA, 1999

The collapse of the Soviet Union almost coincided with the break-up of another Communist country, Yugoslavia.

On the night of 24/5 March 1999, NATO forces started a campaign of air strikes against Serbian forces in Kosovo, and against strategic targets in Serbia. The move was designed to protect the Kosovo Albanian population, who were suffering from attacks by Serbian forces, often amounting to ethnic cleansing, in an attempt to drive them out of the area. The resulting NATO air campaign over the former Yugoslavia was a substantially different affair to that in the Gulf. For a start, the campaign was not conducted under the auspices of, and with the blessing of, the United Nations, but was purely a NATO operation. There was strong opposition throughout from Russia and China.

Gulf War objectives were clear: removal of Iraqi forces from Kuwait and the restoration of the Kuwaiti government. The campaign over the former Yugoslavia was far more complex because of the political background; it centred on an attempt to curb Serbian ethnic cleansing of the Muslim Kosovo Albanians. Kosovo was not an independent state, but an autonomous province of Serbia, which in turn had been part of the Yugoslav Federation.

The crisis had its origins in the collapse of Yugoslavia following the death of the dictator President Tito. His departure led to demands for independence from Belgrade by many of the constituent parts of the Federation. The roots of the problem dated back more than 600 years but, despite this, Yugoslavia had been a successful multicultural society under Tito, who had managed to suppress ethnic rivalries between the mainly Roman Catholic Croatians, the Orthodox Serbs and the Muslims. The Muslims dwelt mainly in Bosnia and Kosovo, and were a substantial minority in what had been the Yugoslav state of Macedonia. The situation was complicated by resentment against the Croats dating from their support for the German occupation forces during the Second World War. The Serbs also enjoyed support from Russia, another Serbian society.

During the mid-1990s, a United Nations force had been deployed under NATO command to halt ethnic cleansing by Serb forces in Bosnia. The constituent forces were mainly British, American, Canadian and French. Athough these countries had maintained an air campaign, the conflict was finally brought under control by the deployment of Croatian ground forces. NATO troops ensured that supplies were provided for the refugees, and policed a ceasefire once it had been agreed.

In Kosovo, the crisis was provoked by a Serbian attempt to integrate Kosovo into Serbia, a move resisted by the Kosovo Albanian population because they had enjoyed substantial autonomy within the Yugoslav Federation. Kosovan Albanian demands for complete independence followed, with the formation of a Kosovo Liberation Army, the KLA. The Serbs were not alone in not wanting an independent Kosovo; some neighbouring countries feared that this could lead to integration with Albania, in effect a 'Greater Albania'.

The NATO powers attempted diplomacy, with a conference at Rambouillet, outside Paris, through which Kosovan autonomy would be restored. Both sides rejected this. A NATO proposal that their forces should have rights of access not just into Kosovo but throughout the whole of Serbia was also rejected.

Starting on the night of 24/5 March 1999, the campaign of air and cruise missile attacks against Serbian forces in Kosovo, and against strategic targets in Serbia, was controversial, for many different reasons. Not the least of these was that many maintained that the campaign was illegal. Part of the problem was that NATO effectively went to war with Serbia without first declaring war, an omission for which the Japanese have been blamed in the past. The action was outside NATO's remit, as a purely defensive alliance. While this might allow pre-emptive strikes, Serbia did not pose a threat to the NATO members. Then there was the danger that the campaign against the Kosovo Albanians by Serb forces might be intensified. NATO members were also accused of interfering in the internal affairs of a sovereign nation, something that even the United Nations had no right to do. All of these objections were in addition to any that resulted from serious civilian casualties, always a danger in warfare. Finally, there was the point that Yugoslavia was not an area of strategic or economic interest to the NATO countries.

The air campaign started slowly, and showed extremely poor preparedness by NATO. In contrast to Kuwait, there was no build-up of forces before the air campaign started. At the outset, both Britain and the United States committed the extreme folly of publicly rejecting any idea of sending in ground troops, leaving the campaign to be won by air power alone. The Bosnian campaign, after all, had been ended by the deployment of troops.

It took ten days for the air campaign to produce the number of sorties that were mounted on the first day of the Gulf War. As in the Gulf, much use was made of cruise missiles. A further difference was that bomber aircraft were ordered to operate at around 15,000 ft rather than at low level, which reduced the accuracy of their operations and resulted in a number of targets being missed, and in one case a maternity hospital was hit instead of a military barracks.

The reasons for the poor accuracy were not due solely to the relatively high altitude of the attacks. True, many air forces, including the Royal Air Force, train to attack at low level to reduce the time aircraft are visible, either to the naked eye or to ground-based radar, in the area of the target, but a further problem was the weather. In a post-campaign statement to a House of Commons committee, a senior British civil servant explained that they had not anticipated dense cloud, which persisted for all but twenty or so days out of seventy-eight. The thick cloud meant that the laser-guidance for the smart weapons could not always work efficiently, and accuracy suffered as a result. Concerned about the political impact of losses in such a controversial campaign, the British Prime Minister had ruled out low-level attacks beneath the cloud base. Low flying in Yugoslavia below dense cloud would have had an added element of danger because of the mountainous nature of the country.

United States Army Apache helicopters were once again deployed, but almost immediately found that their base was too muddy. Reports then began to circulate that the Apache couldn't carry a full warload over the Yugoslav mountains. Then the story was that the crews had not been trained to operate in these conditions. The real reason emerged after the campaign: the Apaches were not used because the American President didn't want the political fall-out of any losses over the former Yugoslavia.

As the campaign developed, plans eventually had to be made for involving ground forces. The initial refusal to consider sending these was finally recognized as encouraging Serb resistance. The plight of the Kosovans appeared to be worse, not better, as the Serbs retaliated against the civilian population. Air strikes eventually damaged or destroyed all of the bridges across the River Danube, disrupting communications and inflicting serious damage not only on the Serb communities but on other states upstream dependent upon the river for bulk movements of cargo. The air campaign finally ended on 10 June 1999.

At one stage, plans were prepared for 'an opposed entry', an invasion of Kosovo against Serb resistance, which would have required substantial numbers of troops. At the eleventh hour, the Serb leadership accepted NATO ground forces, avoiding an opposed occupation of Kosovo, provided that Russia could also deploy ground forces. Diplomacy was needed when the Russians were first to gain control of the main airport at Pristina. It was small comfort to find that the Russians were also badly prepared, and initially had to depend on NATO for supplies. The deployment of ground forces was by air and sea, and overland through Montenegro, another former Yugoslav state, but one with a pro-western government.

Throughout the campaign, wide differences had emerged among the NATO countries, whose membership had just been increased by the addition of Poland, Hungary and the Czech Republic. Greece was refusing to allow NATO forces to use the best port in the area, Salonika. By contrast, the United Kingdom and the United States were the most anxious to attack Serbia. The USAF and USN flew more than 80 per cent of the combat missions.

Today, a substantial NATO force has been deployed in Kosovo and has become embroiled in disputes between the opposing factions among the local population. Together, Kosovo and Bosnia account for one-sixth of the British Army's trained manpower, with another sixth deployed in Northern Ireland on internal security duties. The cost of the air campaign and the deployment of troops has led to delays in implementing longer-term defence procurement plans, and has affected participation in NATO exercises and training.

Overall, NATO has 37,000 troops inside Kosovo, but at the time of writing, the commanders on the ground want this number to be increased to 50,000. This would make it the largest peace-keeping commitment anywhere. In addition to securing the return of the Kosovan Albanians to their homes, the NATO troops also have to stop attempts at revenge attacks by the Kosovan Albanians against Serbian civilians also resident in the area. This means that the troops are in the unfortunate position of being caught in the middle between the two opposing factions. Meanwhile, there has been no change in the Serbian regime in Belgrade. The Kosovan operation was unnecessary and, quite probably, illegal. It has produced a major commitment lasting many years. Much smaller forces, under UN auspices, have been on the Green Line separating the Greek and Turkish communities in Cyprus for almost thirty years. Kosovo looks set to keep even larger forces tied down for at least as long.

BIBLIOGRAPHY

Allen, L., *Singapore, 1941–2* (London, Davis & Poynter, 1977).

Beevor, Antony, *Stalingrad* (London, Viking, 1998).

Forty, George, *Tank Action: From the Great War to the Gulf* (Stroud, Sutton, 1995).

Grove, Eric, *Big Fleet Actions: Tsushima, Jutland, Philippine Sea* (London, Arms & Armour Press, 1995).

Halliday, E.M., *The Ignorant Armies* (London, 1961).

Holmes, Richard, *The Western Front* (London, BBC Books, 1999).

Kemp, Paul, *Convoy Protection* (London, Arms & Armour Press, 1993).

Laffin, John, *Damn The Dardanelles! The Story Of Gallipoli* (London, Osprey, 1980).

Lamb, Charles, *War in a Stringbag* (London, Cassell, 1977).

Liddell Archive, University of Leeds.

Liddell Hart, Basil, *The Defence of Britain* (London, Greenwood Press, 1980).

McMurtrie, Francis (ed.), *Jane's Fighting Ships, 1939* (London, Jane's, reprinted 1971).

Micallef, Joseph, *When Malta Stood Alone (1940–43)* (Valletta, self-published, 1981).

Prange, Gordon W., Goldstein, Donald M. and Dillon, Katherine V., *God's Samurai* (Washington DC, Brassey's, 1990).

Price, Alfred, *Blitz on Britain, 1939–45* (London, Ian Allan, 1977).

Saward, Dudley, *Bomber Harris, The Story of Marshal of the Royal Air Force, Sir Arthur Harris* (London, Cassell, Buchan & Enright, 1984).

Swettenham, John, *Allied Intervention in Russia 1918–1919, and the Part Played by Canada* (London, George Allen & Unwin, 1967).

Terraine, John, *The First World War, 1914–1918* (London, Leo Cooper, 1983).

Watts, Anthony J., *Axis Submarines* (London, MacDonald & Jane's, 1977).

Westwood, J.N., *Illustrated History of the Russo-Japanese War* (London, Sidgwick & Jackson, 1973).

Williamson, Murray, *War in the Air, 1914–45* (London, Pimlico, 1994).

Winton, John, *Carrier Glorious* (London, Leo Cooper, 1986).

INDEX